THE CANADIAN PRACTICAL STYLIST

FOURTH EDITION

THE CANADIAN PRACTICAL STYLIST

FOURTH EDITION

Sheridan Baker
University of Michigan, Emeritus

Lawrence B. Gamache
University of Ottawa

 Addison-Wesley

An imprint of Addison Wesley Longman Ltd.

Don Mills, Ontario • Reading, Massachusetts • Harlow, England
Melbourne, Australia • Amsterdam, The Netherlands • Bonn, Germany

PUBLISHER: Brian Henderson
MANAGING EDITOR: Linda Scott
EDITOR: Suzanne Schaan
PERMISSIONS EDITOR: Louise Mackenzie
DESIGN, COVER DESIGN, AND DESKTOPPING: Anthony Leung
PRODUCTION COORDINATOR: Linda Allison
MANUFACTURING COORDINATOR: Sharon Latta Paterson

Canadian Cataloguing in Publication Data

Baker, Sheridan, 1918–
  The Canadian practical stylist

4th ed.
Includes index.
ISBN 0-673-98486-9

1. English language—Rhetoric.   I. Gamache, Lawrence.   II. Title.

PE1408.B26 1998   808'.0427   C97-932546-3

ISBN 0-673-98486-9

Printed and bound in Canada.

A B C D E -WC- 02 01 00 99 98

Contents

Preface

In preparing the previous editions of *The Canadian Practical Stylist*, both Ken Ledbetter, my late collaborator, and I strove to keep the needs and interests of Canadian students as guides in making our version of this text. We chose appropriate Canadian examples to illustrate our points, used traditional Canadian spelling consistently, and selected Canadian research topics and materials. In this newest edition, I have held to that view. As before, references to the history and people of the United States have not been excluded. As part of North America, Canada is necessarily connected to its southern neighbours and ignoring them would misrepresent Canadian reality.

This revision contains much that is new. The original text by Sheridan Baker remains at its heart, but material has been added to the Canadian version. A new opening chapter focuses on the writing process much more directly, and new exercises suggest ways to work on that process. The writing examples are largely Canadian and the selection has been extensively revised to include much more recent material that reflects the diversity of writing in Canada today. Two sample student essays have been included in the research section to illustrate both expository and argumentative approaches to writing research essays, and to exemplify methods other than the pro–con approach emphasized in earlier editions. Newer views of both the writing process and the teaching of composition, including some consideration of the newer electronic and computer technologies, have been influential in the making of this edition, but I feel confident those who are used to the approach of the older editions will find this revision keeps its virtues and adds a freshness they will appreciate.

Finally, I want to express my continuing indebtedness to and appreciation of my late colleague and friend, Ken Ledbetter, whose contribution to this edition comes from an ongoing sense of his vision as a teacher and researcher working in my own thoughts and practices. He is missed.

Acknowledgments

The author and publisher would like to thank the following people for their comments and suggestions on the manuscript of this book: Douglas Babbington, Director, The Writing Centre, Queen's University; Harris Breslow, York University; Elin Edwards, Wilfrid Laurier University; Mike Sider, The Western Effective Writing Program, University of Western Ontario; Anita Hurwitz, University of Windsor; Trish Matson, Douglas College; Hans Allgaier, New Caledonia College. The continuing influence and model of Ken Ledbetter cannot be overstated.

Lawrence B. Gamache

Acknowledgments for
the Seventh U.S. Edition

I again wish to acknowledge my great and unending debt to the teachers who, from the responses of more than three million students, have given me their encouragement and suggestions. I am grateful to the following reviewers for their useful comments and suggestions: William Adair, San Joaquin Delta College; Louis Avery, Houston Community College; Linda Carter, Morgan State University; Robert Dees, Orange Coast College; Kathleen Duguay, North Adams State College; Sarah Harrison, Tyler Junior College; Michael Hogan, University of New Mexico; Ann Johnson, Community College of Denver; George Kennedy, Washington State University; Christopher MacGowan, College of William and Mary; D'Ann Madwell, North Lake College; Mark Miller, North Adams State College; Jim Riser, University of North Alabama; Arthur Wagner, Macomb Community College; Russ Ward, Aims Community College; John White, California State University, Fullerton; Eugene Whitney, Portland Community College; Sue Williams, Olivet Nazarene University; Robert Wiltenburg, Washington University. I continue to be no less grateful to the individual students and private citizens who have written me from as far away as Kenya, Australia, and Japan, and as near home as Ann Arbor, Michigan.

Sheridan Baker

The Writing Process: An Overview

Writing is a process. Studying finished pieces and recognizing the grammatical and rhetorical qualities that make them effective can be useful; however, as a way of learning to write, studying the finished work alone is like trying to become a painter by studying paintings. In focusing on the finished product, you may not discover the subtle manipulations as the artist thoughtfully and imaginatively built layers of paint and worked at the finishing touches. Making the work is the result of crafting materials, and learning the craft enables the apprentice to become an accomplished writer.

Students of writing must learn the process from the beginning. Unfortunately, the focus in classrooms is too often on the final product; sometimes it even excludes the process. *Choosing and properly arranging the most appropriate language to address a clearly defined audience are basic writing tasks.* Language, the writer's material, is comparable to the artist's paint. In each case, the maker shapes the material according to a preconceived design that fulfills the work's purpose; a careful process makes the product a success.

Language is composed of *potentially* meaningful sound units, from morphemes and words to phrases, sentences, and paragraphs, and ultimately to whole compositions. But words *actually* mean something only when shaped by a context. If I use the term "red," you will probably think of a colour, but I could be referring to a Communist. Only when you know my context will you be able to understand my meaning. The shaping of the meaning is totally dependent on the effective development of the context. A writer who fails to control that context through correct usage, grammar, and spelling can misguide readers. Disjointed development of thought or lack of an ordering principle will result in a failure to communicate, as will dullness. A carefully written text that develops an interesting context gives readers the grounds for understanding a writer's meaning.

The Preliminaries

Students of writing must be willing to practise the craft, just as a pianist must practise to become a skilled musician. Before turning to tools like computers or libraries, begin with your own creativity, analytical skills, and imagination. To exercise your mind, talk to instructors and other students, discussing issues that might become the basis of an essay. Read what others have said in books, magazines, and newspapers. Even television programs can offer food for thought; popular entertainment can be provocative if your mind is working while you watch. In your quiet moments, think about potential essay subjects and write journal entries to record your ideas. *Thought that is worthy of another's attention is a prerequisite to having something to write about.* This admonition may seem unnecessary, but you might be amazed to learn how often thoughtless students submit thoughtless papers.

The first step for a thoughtful student should be to analyse the terms of the assignment carefully, determining just how much is required and what the instructor's terms mean, using the textbook and dictionaries to define them clearly. Asking the instructor to clarify any obscurity is not just wise, it is necessary. Keep a record of this preliminary analysis in your journal to prepare yourself to write with intelligence and circumspection.

It is also important to realize that your writing should not be an artificial exercise separate from your daily life. What you say as a writer is a rather permanent record of you and your mind—your character and personality exposed for others to examine. Be judicious; create an impression that is honest and accurate.

The Six Stages of the Writing Process

A builder who started constructing a house without knowing which tools to use, or without having a good set of tools on hand, or without ensuring that the proper materials were available, would not last long on any building site. Furthermore, the builder must have both a carpenter's skills and something of an architect's knowledge. Imagine what would happen if someone lacking the skill to handle the tools or the knowledge to develop a practicable design tried to build a structure. It is the same for writers: thoughtful preparation is essential, and knowing how to use your mind and how to handle language and its structures makes building a good essay possible.

The following explanation introduces and summarizes the six stages of the writing process. The first three focus on the initial process of writer-centred writing, and the last three deal with the process of shaping your writing for an audience. These stages will be developed in detail, with examples and exercises, in the remaining chapters.

Writing for Yourself: Stages 1–3

Writer-centred writing (or *prewriting*) usually occurs when you jot notes to yourself, often recording thoughts somewhat randomly, to develop and clarify your ideas. Such writing may sometimes be more elaborate than a note, but, because it is meant primarily for your own benefit, it is not always written with an audience's needs in mind. This kind of writing does not mean you are unaware of an audience for your ideas. It *does* mean that you need not worry about the effectiveness of your expression at this point.

Before you actually start working on an essay, know the conditions that make you comfortable and your work efficient. There is no single way to work: some might need a quiet room; others might need music or other noise to help concentration. Recognize what distracts you, and eliminate such barriers to effective study.

Learn to "brainstorm" areas of interest; test possible lines of thought by writing your reflections down, even if in a random fashion. Learn how to ask yourself appropriate questions, and how to go about finding and developing possible answers by using appropriate research tools.

If you have access to a computer, it may be helpful to use it in the preliminary stages of essay writing. Some writers make notes on a computer and then write comments in the margins of the printout; this technique can be very helpful during the prewriting stages and in rewriting, revising, and correcting the actual essay later on. You can make notes, develop or eliminate your thoughts, shift the notes around or make copies to be placed in different orders to test their effectiveness, or even carry on a dialogue with yourself. You can create files of the questions you want to ask and print them out to use as questionnaires to fill in as you reflect on the subject and consult primary and secondary sources. By using databases, CD-ROMs, and the Internet, you will be able to search for useful information and other points of view.

All this note taking, however, must not be confused with an essay properly constructed to be addressed to a readership. This stage is primarily you, the writer, talking to yourself, even if what has been written might work well if addressed to an audience. When you are composing the essay, you might include some earlier pieces contained in your notes, but your focus at this point must be on *your own understanding*. Without ideas clearly developed in your own mind, you will have little that is clear to say to an audience.

Stage 1: Selecting an Appropriately Limited Subject

This step starts with a consideration of various topics that might be suitable for the occasion and general purpose of your writing task. Brainstorm for initial ideas and then probe those areas of the most interest to you. You might begin with freewriting—that is, simply putting down in random fashion whatever comes to mind about your writing task, even if it is about not having much to say. This can at least get you started thinking. Random searching through books, magazines, or information sources found on CD-ROMs or the Internet can be helpful at this stage, but remember to keep clear notes and records of sources used. To decide which topic is best, you must consider the following:

Time and Length Constraints   What do you know and what can you learn, given the time available to do the assignment? Never select a topic you have to spend more time on to understand than you can afford. The ramifications of quantum theory in developing a religious explanation of the origins of the universe may interest you and may fit the terms of an assignment in religious studies; if, however, you have never studied physics and have only a vague grasp of quantum theory, then it would seem unwise to try writing an essay about such a topic. Even if you think you know physics well enough, it is unlikely that you can really deal with the topic in a relatively short essay. You, your time constraints, the length of the assignment, and the availability of materials you might need to develop your ideas are important considerations in deciding on a subject.

Occasion   Why do you want or need to write the essay? Who will read it? The *audience* is the reason for your composition, so its needs are paramount. To succeed as a writer, you must not only be understood by your readers, you must also make them willing to consider what you have to say. Show that your paper has value for them. Being interesting is not just a matter of not boring them; it is essential for effective communication.

Purpose   What is your central reason for addressing your audience? Is it to explain something to them you think they should know? Writing for this purpose is usually called *exposition*. Do you want to convince the reader of the truth, or at least the reasonableness, of your point? This kind of writing is usually called *argumentation*. We are most concerned with these two *forms of discourse*, since they are the kind you will use most often in your writing. You should be aware that explaining and convincing are not mutually exclusive, because most expository writing will require some argumentation and argumentation will necessarily entail explanations. The distinction between them as forms of discourse is based on the writer's primary purpose. Is the essay written most basically to prove a point or to explain something? Does the writer want to convince the readers intellectually, or is it enough that they come to know clearly what is explained?

A writer who wants to move an audience to do something, such as vote for a particular candidate or buy a product, will also have to use argument, but should focus on the art of *persuasion*. This kind of writing will require emotional appeal to motivate the audience to act. That readers are convinced intellectually is less important than that they do what the writer wants. So it is that propaganda often ignores the mind and appeals almost entirely to the emotions of the audience.

Another set of purposes, such as to tell a story or describe a scene, as in travel writing, can be included under the general purpose of *entertainment*: writing to divert or amuse or intrigue the audience. Entertainment should not be confused with literary writing of a more serious sort, in which the writer wants to express a human response or deeper perception of some human value, without necessarily considering the needs of the readers. Literature is another way language can be used to make something; it is *expressive* in its purpose, and the writer is usually much more centred on the text itself in deciding what language to use. A literary writer wants the text to work expressively and is guided by its formal structural needs, not by his or her own needs or those of a possible audience. As we will see later, *exposition, argumentation, persuasion,* and *entertainment* can occur as supports within any piece having one or another of these as its main purpose.

Focused Subject   There is a difference between a possible subject for an essay and a reasonable subject. When you have selected an area of interest, be aware that you will have a realistic subject only after you have considered all of the matters noted above, including the amount of time you have and your ability to handle the subject purposefully for a realistic audience. At this point, such activities as freewriting and brainstorming can be particularly helpful. As an exercise, choose a word that relates to a topic; for example, the word *concentration* relates to the topic *good study habits.* If you were to continue following a line of thought extending from the suggestion of *concentration,* randomly developing your ideas, you would eventually see a pattern, a direction in your thinking that could lead to a clear subject to develop into a thesis. Follow this exercise with a series of questions such as *Who? What? When? Where? Why? How?* These questions are discussed in more detail under "Stage 2: Discovering a Thesis." Refer back to this step when you read that section to apply its advice in developing your subject. The stages of the writing process are closely related and interdependent; the process of questioning that can lead to your subject will naturally flow into and be part of your thinking through to a thesis.

The statement of the subject for an essay can usually be best formulated, for an argumentative paper, as a problem to be analysed or as a question to be searched and researched. For example, you might want to examine the role of Louis Riel in the North-West Rebellion; you find that his mental state has been the subject of debate, so you decide to consider the problem of his sanity, or possible lack of sanity. This problem was the original concern of the student who composed the first model essay in Chapter 11 (page 178). As a subject, it was formulated as a question: Was Louis Riel a hero or merely a madman? The question resulted from a *search* of histories of Canada and of articles on the rebellion and Riel's part in it. The next step, finding a position that responded to the question— that is, discovering a thesis—resulted from a carefully developed *research* process, guided and limited all the way by the terms of the question. This procedure for developing a realistic subject can be used to find the subject of any argumentative or expository essay.

So, the steps to follow in selecting a subject are as follows:

1. Search for a reasonable question, problem, or point(s) at issue; to probe your area of interest, use brainstorming, question-and-answer analytic investigation, discussion, and reading. Keep notes to record your reflections.
2. Write out tentative formulations of the problem a number of times until you are satisfied you have discovered a real subject to write about.
3. Assess the subject you chose using the criteria suggested above.

4. Formulate the problem as a statement rather than as a question and write an explanation for yourself of what it means and what research it will require.

Stage 2: Discovering a Thesis

Analysing the subject to discover the point(s) you want to make will result in the discovery of an appropriate, unifying thesis. Clearly you must search out and think sufficiently about relevant ideas and points of view. Library resources, especially books, journals and magazines, and newspapers, can provoke your thoughts at this stage. Taking extensive notes of these ideas is essential. Often these apparently random and disjointed records of your reflections, discussions, and searches can form the basis for important portions of your essay.

The analysis of the subject to discover a thesis is essentially a process of finding the answer to some basic questions: *What? How? Why?* Asking *what* includes finding out *who* is involved in your problem and what elements of time (*when*) and place (*where*) are relevant. Asking *how* involves processes—natural, historical, logical, and psychological. Asking *why* requires the deepest reflection and inquiry into a problem; you are seeking to understand the fundamental conditions, circumstances, influences, and direct or indirect causes relevant to your problem.

What?   This question involves *definition*, that is, identifying what the subject is and setting the limits of its meaning. To extend the process of defining the problem, learn to use *classification* and *division* as logical, analytical tools. *Comparison* and *contrast* can also clarify the subject, as can examining concrete *examples* relevant to your problem. (See pages 87–90 for a more complete explanation of *definition* and its application as an analytic tool; see pages 83–84 regarding *classification*, pages 76–79 for *comparison*, and pages 74–76 for *example*.) *Who? When?* and *Where?* are additional questions that will extend an inquiry and help delimit a subject.

How?   This question involves *process analysis*. The kinds of process that *how* might explore include the following:

- *natural or mechanical:* exploring the operations of a machine or the biological functions of a frog
- *historical:* tracing the development of French–English relations in Quebec or the development of a student's experiences learning mathematics

- *logical:* examining the thought processes involved in an argument defending abortion
- *psychological:* examining the mental and emotional behaviour of Louis Riel to determine his state of mind during the North-West Rebellion

Why? This question is the most complex and is closely related to process analysis. It involves examining causes, effects, and influences working on people, events, and situations, as well as circumstances or conditions that help something happen (see page 80). (It is essential that writers distinguish true causes from conditions and circumstances in order to avoid fallacious reasoning. For example, light to help a person see is a necessary condition for sight to be possible, but light doesn't *cause* the seeing; otherwise, its mere presence would cause the blind to see. Also note that a circumstance like poverty may contribute to delinquency, but it is not the cause, since not all poor people become delinquents.) What differentiates causal analysis (*why*) from process analysis (*how*) is the point of the questioning. In causal analysis, the purpose is to discover the following:

- *the positive:* The proposed cause and the effect must be clearly connected in their natures.
- *the immediate:* Nothing separates the proposed cause from its effect.
- *the remote:* A series of immediately connected forces relate a distant "cause" to a remote "effect" without break.
- *the necessary:* When such forces act, the effect must occur, producing the *cause–effect* relationship.
- *influences and necessary conditions:* These differ from true causes but are often loosely called causal because they are so closely connected to causes and resemble them.

So, the steps to follow in discovering a thesis are as follows:

1. Analyse the problem using a series of well-thought-out questions to guide your research.
2. Make a clear statement of the central point or points you intend to develop as the heart of your thesis. If you can write a single, clear, and unified sentence that states the central, controlling concern of your essay, you have the grounds for ensuring the unity of your essay. Use this statement throughout the rest of the process as a check and guide in the development of your essay.
3. Re-examine the steps of your research to be sure you have not

neglected important matters and that your evidence and arguments are worthwhile.

Stage 3: Organizing Your Thoughts

Establishing a unified, coherent, and emphatic order for the development of the thesis allows you to begin focusing more directly on the needs and interests of the audience. At this stage, the primary concern becomes communicating ideas to a readership. You may discover, as you attempt to organize your thoughts into a unified and coherent development, that your thesis needs to be revised; this is not unusual and should not stop you from completing a good and honestly thought-out work. Your objective is to prepare to write the essay with an audience in mind.

Decide, in light of the audience's needs, what strategies to use to achieve the following purposes of a good *introduction*:

- to stimulate your reader's interest in the problem under consideration and clarify the subject (the usual purpose of the beginning of the introduction)
- to clarify the problem in detail and explain the method you will use to deal with it, to help the reader understand your purpose for writing the essay (what the middle of the introduction should do)
- to make a preliminary statement of the thesis as a transition into the body (the aim of the end of the introduction)

The model essay on Margaret Laurence's stories, in Chapter 11 (page 199), illustrates each of these points as indicated by the marginal notes. Your first plan for the introduction is best used as a guideline for the rest of the essay. It is almost inevitable that you will want to rewrite at least the beginning, to make it more compatible with the final paper; most of the time, the whole introduction will need to be reworked in light of the final development.

Chapters 4 and 5 will examine strategies for building the introduction, body, and conclusion of an essay, focusing in particular on the *pro–con* organization of points and the funnel approach to structuring the whole composition. To develop the *body* of an essay, the qualities you must build through planning are *unity, coherence,* and *emphasis.*

Unity   A clear thesis ensures unity throughout the paper. If you wander off the central focus of your argument, the unity of your essay will be compromised. For example, you could argue—as does the student in the model essay—that in *A Bird in the House*, Margaret Laurence successfully develops both a child's vision of her family and the grown child's mature understanding, without seriously confusing the two points of view. If you spend two pages telling the reader about the author's life, the paper will not be unified, as Laurence's life, while interesting, is irrelevant to the purpose of the essay. *All parts of the paper must relate to the central thesis.*

Coherence   The parts of the paper must not only all relate to the central thesis, but also relate *to each other* through a logically structured chain of connections. This objective is considered in some detail in Chapter 5. Note especially what is said about *transitions*. Before you begin to compose an essay, you must think through, understand, and consciously select a clear principle of organization that suits the purpose of the essay—based on the logic of an argument, or the rules of division, or a structured comparison and contrast, or the development of illustrative and compelling examples that support the thesis, or a combination of these or other strategies. In later chapters, we will use the funnel approach and a pro–con structural technique, especially in building the model essay on Riel, to illustrate the application of a clear strategy to achieve coherence.

Emphasis   In each section of the paper, placing your points in a proper order will give them proper emphasis. Earlier statements tend to impress the reader's mind more strongly than do the middle thoughts in a paragraph or a whole essay. The final comments are also more emphatic than those placed in the middle. Be judicious in arranging your arguments; for example, build toward the more important. Avoid unnecessarily expanding ideas that are unimportant or of lesser significance, especially at the expense of those that should be developed.

Finally, an outline can be helpful if you base it on a clear organizational principle, especially for the body. If you are working with a computer file of brainstormed ideas on your subject, you can create a visual outline by highlighting and arranging in a clear order the essential points (following the principle you chose to organize your ideas after you reviewed them), and then subordinating secondary material below them using levels of indenting to indicate importance. Such an outline can be a useful guide in organizing your essay, but avoid being a slave to it.

When you review your notes to plan your essay's development, ask the following questions and continue to ask them as you prepare to write a first draft. Remember them as you reread the text through each stage of its growth from first to final draft and revision:

1. Am I fulfilling my purpose as stated in the beginning? Do I clearly want to convince? explain? persuade to action? amuse or entertain? Is my thesis consistently developing?
2. Is my audience always clear? Are the tone and language appropriate, and are my examples suitable for my audience?
3. Do my transitions from sentence to sentence and from paragraph to paragraph work?
4. Is my organization clear throughout the development? Could the reader become confused at any point in my development?
5. Have I developed each point to the extent necessary? Have I overstated any points? Are my points treated in an appropriate place to develop my purpose?

Writing for an Audience: Stages 4–6

Once you have selected a subject, defined your thesis, and organized your thoughts and research, you are ready to begin to write in earnest. But before you start, review the occasion and purpose that you first considered in Stage 1, when searching for a subject, and that you reconsidered in Stage 3, when organizing your thoughts. From now on, you must keep your audience and its needs firmly in mind.

Stage 4: Drafting the Essay

Writing a draft means composing an interesting and vigorously expressed appeal to the mind and, if appropriate, emotions of the audience. It should not be confused with the final essay; drafting is an ongoing process, progressing gradually from an initial to a final formulation. Whether you are writing longhand or on a computer, you may include alternative words or phrases in parentheses for later consideration. You should work through your ideas without needlessly interrupting the flow to make stylistic choices that can be dealt with more effectively either in later stages of drafting or during revision of the final draft. If you hit a mental block, mark the spot with an asterisk and come back to it later (the search function on your computer is handy for this). Although formulating your ideas in clear language is the primary concern in drafting the essay, you should, even at this stage, strive for effective expression. As your drafting process progresses, the qualities of good expression—that is, clarity, vigour, and interest—become more important.

As you work, keep in mind the objectives that pertain to each part of the essay. The introduction must arouse interest as well as present the subject of the essay. Although you may not be able to finalize the introduction until you are nearly finished with the final draft, an initial formulation of its essential points will help you move into the body of the essay more readily. The middle should develop what the introduction promised, and the end should conclude the presentation in a logical and satisfying way. Later we will see that these objectives can be achieved using the funnel approach. The introduction, body, and conclusion of the essay each has its beginning, middle, and end; these nine parts require careful planning to achieve your ends and to satisfy the needs of the audience.

If you are working on a computer, open a new file to begin drafting your actual essay, to differentiate clearly between your initial writer-centred notes and the audience-centred focus of the first draft. It is also useful to make a copy and number each draft as you end your work sessions; during revision, you may find an earlier portion you excluded works in the final copy.

The main qualities to aim at in writing the various drafts of an essay are *clarity*, *vigour*, and *interest* in expressing your thoughts.

Clarity   Clarity is achieved by selecting the most economical and exact words that state precisely what you mean. Do not strive to find fancy or fanciful ways of saying what can be made clear using familiar language. A thesaurus can be helpful in searching for exact words, but some students mistakenly use such a tool to find obscure ways of saying things. Style is not something to strive for; the choices you make in how you say something necessarily reflect you, and therefore comprise your style. Many writers develop effective styles using very basic vocabulary and the most common *subject–verb–object* structure of the English sentence.

Vigour   Vigour is achieved by precision and exactness of expression. Clear sentences that move with an appropriate rhythmic arrangement of words, phrases, clauses, and a variety of sentence structures (simple, complex, compound, and complex–compound) best support the flow of your ideas.

Interest   Interest is assured by avoiding monotony, by not being needlessly repetitive, and by not wearying the reader with a tiresome sameness of language and sentence structures. Carefully thought-out and appropriate examples to give your ideas concreteness can add vitality to your writing. Figurative language—metaphorical and logical comparisons and contrasts—will enliven your prose. These devices require much practice to handle well and should be used with great care. They should never become merely decorative embellishments.

While drafting your essay, ask yourself the following questions:

1. Have you achieved unity, coherence, and emphasis? Reconsider the questions listed in Stage 3 to ensure your organization is effective.
2. Is your expression clear and economical? Can you eliminate any unnecessary words, phrases, or sentences? Are the words you use the most precise, not the fanciest?
3. Is there vigour in your expression, enhanced by economy and precision? Do you use clear and effective sentences?
4. Is your essay interesting? Does the beginning engage the reader's attention? Does the body use clear and appropriate examples, and figurative language that is not a distraction? Is the logic clear and consistent? Does the end effectively conclude your paper, making clear the final achievement of your purpose?

Stage 5: Revising the Final Draft

Revising is often the most poorly handled portion of the writing process, yet it probably most ensures a successful composition. As I have said before, rewriting is an ongoing task; editing the language and language structures to make the expression of ideas as economical and precise as possible is a necessity at this stage. Never assume that your first or second draft is adequately written; always edit your text carefully. The final revision stage of composition should be done when you can focus solely on your expression, without much attention needed to organizing or stating your ideas.

To improve your writing at this stage, you may want to substitute one way of saying something for a clearer or more effective expression. You will find yourself deleting wordy or unnecessary statements and reordering elements within sentences, or sentences within paragraphs, or paragraphs within the whole composition. If you have serious doubts about the clarity or the worth of what you have written, you must be willing to eliminate the excess. Economy and precision are absolutely required.

I have found that the use of a computer at this stage has saved me hours of work. Word-processing programs, with their cut, paste, and insert functions, are well suited to the revision process. Be sure to number your drafts to avoid confusion. Save each draft under a new file name, so that you can easily retrieve parts of earlier drafts if you decide they work better than later drafts.

Stage 6: Proofreading

The final step you must take to ensure your paper is acceptable is to correct it. Proofreading to eliminate all errors and infelicities of expression should not be confused with revision; it is a separate and essential stage. You must check the grammar, word usage, punctuation, spelling, and mechanics of your presentation. Restate any awkward portions and eliminate poor usage and weak expressions. To ignore this step, or to do it haphazardly, can mean the difference between a good and an excellent essay.

If you are working on a computer, you can use the spell-check function, but you should always recheck the spelling yourself. A computer program will not tell you when you have used a homonym—*there* for *their*—or made a typing error that results in another word—*shoe* for *show*. Another problem is that the spell-check component of your software may be based on American spelling, so you will have to watch for words such as *centre* and *labour*. Always check the formatting of an essay after printing it out, to ensure that your margins, spacing, and italics are correct.

Breaking down the writing process into the six stages offered here is not the only way it can be explained; most writing textbooks these days will provide a comparable analysis. What is important is that you appreciate that a process is involved, that you grasp its stages in some acceptable and orderly way, and that you attempt to apply that knowledge in all of your writing.

In Chapter 2, we will again consider the preliminaries, but in greater detail. We will examine attitudes toward your audience and the clear expression of your ideas in your own voice and from a firm viewpoint. Finally, we will discuss argumentation and exposition—the forms of discourse you will need to write most in university—and we will consider what style is and what developing your own style really means. Chapters 3–7 will move through the various stages of the process, from the development of a subject and thesis, through strategies for structuring essays, to tactics for writing beginnings, middles, and ends. Suggestions for revising sentences and words (Chapters 8–10) complete our coverage of the process as such. An essential chapter on research methods and the writing of research essays will probably be the section to which you will refer most often after the course is over (Chapter 11). Brief explanations of grammar, punctuation, and other considerations relevant to the final stage—proofreading—are contained in Chapters 12 and 13. Finally, Chapter 14 provides a glossary of commonly misused words and phrases with explanations of proper usage.

Suggested Exercises

1. Begin immediately to keep a daily journal of your thoughts, reflections, and reactions to what you hear, experience, discuss with friends and instructors, and study during the term. Listen to the news, read the paper, watch television programs that provoke thought, and record your thoughts in your journal. Do regular brainstorming and freewriting exercises to sharpen your skills. You can use your journal to suggest ideas for essays.

2. Choose a specific area of interest or possible reflection (such as athletes' attitudes toward their careers, or politicians and moral responsibility) and make notes based only on your random thoughts and analysis. Select a clear example (such as a highly paid athlete); consider any relevance time and place might have (where and when has he played?); examine any processes involved (how has he played, and how has he contributed to the entertainment and financial value of his sport?); and investigate whatever causes (owner's actions), conditions (team's wealth), or circumstances (spectators' attitudes) you think influenced or produced apparent results. Finally, form five possible questions you could explore further.

3. If the editor of the student newspaper asked you to write an editorial reviewing the eating facilities on campus, how would you prepare? Consider various questions:
   a. What do I think a university eating facility should be and do we have such a place?
   b. Who manages it and what is the attitude of its staff? What should be their attitude?
   c. How does it operate? Does it run efficiently and does it produce good food?

   Compose at least five more questions to consider in preparing such a review.

4. Make a full page of notes for each of at least three of the questions developed for a review of your school's eating facilities in Exercise 3. Rewrite each page to reduce the number of words used.

5. If you were asked to address an audience of parents of first-year students, what might you write about and why? What might you not want to write about and why not? Write an explanation for both responses by using brainstorming and freewriting to expand your thoughts. Rewrite your explanation using half the number of words.

The Point of It All: The Preliminaries

Write for Your Share

Writing is one of the most important things we do. Writing helps us capture our ideas, realize our thoughts, and stand out as fluent, persuasive people, both on paper and on our feet in a meeting or with the boss. Reading and writing enlarge our education and our speech. Even television, through its written scripts, reinforces the words and habits that literacy has built into our speech and thinking.

The language we share is Standard English—somewhere between what is customary in Britain and what is sometimes called "edited Standard American English." But actually we "edit" almost everything we say. We instinctively select one word or another when we talk to our friends or our friends' parents, to dignitaries or children, to the boss or the new assistant. Whatever our backgrounds in different parts of the country, rural or urban, in different ethnic and linguistic surroundings, we come together in this common language as our minds spontaneously edit the choices. We intuitively fill in the grammar, expanding, rephrasing, just as if we were writing and rewriting: ". . . er . . . I mean . . . but really. . . ."

So writing is an extension of the way we naturally handle language. Writing simply straightens out and clarifies our intuitive editing, and in turn makes the editing itself more fluent. Writing perfects thought and speech. Indeed, over the millions of years from our ancestors' first emotive screams and gurgles to the bright dawn of literacy, writing—thinking well dressed for its purpose—seems to be where speech has been going all the time.

Your composition course will prepare you for the challenges not only of university but also of life, whatever your career choice may be. You must write in almost every course. You must write for admission to postgraduate studies. You must write proposals for grants and programs. You must write to convince people of your worth—demonstrated in your literacy—and of the worth of your ideas. You must write to develop and advance those ideas—and yourself. You must write for your share of life. Thinking and arguing rationally are your business, and the business of your course in composition. All communication is, at least in part, largely argumentation and persuasion. Even your most factual survey as engineer or educator must convince its audience, win approval by its perception and clarity and organization—in short, by its writing.

Attitude

Writing well is a matter of conviction. You learn in school by exercises, of course; and exercises are best when taken as such, as body-builders, flexions and extensions for the real contests ahead. But when you are convinced that what you write has meaning, that it has meaning for you— and not in a lukewarm, hypothetical way, but truly—then your writing will stretch its wings. For writing is simply a graceful and articulate extension of the best that is in you. Writing well is not easy. As it extends the natural way we express ourselves, it nevertheless takes unending practice. Each essay is a polished exercise for the next to come, each new trial, as T.S. Eliot says, a new "raid on the inarticulate" ("East Coker").

In writing, as we discussed in the writer-centred stages in Chapter 1, you clarify your own thoughts and strengthen your convictions. Indeed, you probably grasp your thoughts for the first time. Writing is a way of thinking. Writing actually creates thought and generates your ability to think: you discover thoughts you hardly knew you had and come to know what you know. You learn as you write. In the end, after you have rewritten and rearranged for the best rhetorical effectiveness, your words will carry readers with you to see as you see, to believe as you believe, to understand the subject as you now understand it.

Don't Take Yourself Too Seriously

Take your subject seriously—if it is a serious subject—but take yourself with a grain of salt. Your attitude is the very centre of your prose. If you are too self-important, your tone will go hollow, your sentences will go mouldy, your page will go fuzzy with *ofs* and *whiches* and nouns clustered in passive constructions. In your academic career, the worst dangers are immediately ahead. First-year students usually learn to write tolerably well, but from the second year on the academic mildew often sets in.

You must constantly guard against acquiring the heavy, sobersided attitude that makes for wordiness along with obscurity, dullness, and anonymity. Do not lose your personality and your voice in monotonous official prose. You should work like a scholar and scientist, but you should write like a writer, one who cares about the economy and beauty of language and has some individual personality. Your attitude, then, should form somewhere between a confidence in your own convictions and a humorous distrust of your own rhetoric, which can so easily carry you away. You should bear yourself as a member of humankind, knowing that we are all sinners, all redundant, and all too fond of big words. Here is an example from—I blush to admit—the pen of a professor:

> The general problem is perhaps correctly
> stated as inadequacy of nursing personnel
> to meet demands for nursing care and ser-
> vices. Inadequacy, it should be noted, is
> both a quantitative and qualitative term
> and thus it can be assumed that the problem
> as stated could indicate insufficient num-
> bers of nursing personnel to meet existing
> demands for their services; deficiencies in
> the competencies of those who engage in the
> various fields of nursing; or both.

Too few good nurses and a badly swollen author—that is the problem. "Nursing personnel" may mean nurses, but it also may mean "the nursing of employees," so that the author seems to say, for a wildly illogical moment, that someone is not properly pampering or suckling people. Notice the misfiring *it* (fourth line), which seems to refer to *term* but actually refers to nothing. And the ponderous jingle of "deficiencies in the competencies" would do for a musical comedy. The author has used the wrong model, is taking herself too seriously, and is leading her readers almost nowhere.

Consider Your Readers

If you are to take your subject with all the seriousness it deserves and yourself with as much sceptical humour as you can bear, how are you to take your readers? Who are they, anyway? Some instructors suggest using your classmates as your audience. This is a good beginning. But the problem remains with all those other classes, with those papers in history or social science, with the reports, the applications for jobs and grants, the letters to the editor. At some point, you must become a writer facing the invisible public, the so-called "universal audience." Such an abstraction is misleading, however, since you could never be writing for everybody—Chinese peasants, Arab oil executives, graduate students, and fifth graders. You should be aware of the limits of your potential audience.

To some extent, therefore, your audiences will necessarily vary. You imagine yourself addressing slightly different personalities when you write about snorkelling and when you write about nuclear reactors. If you write about baseball in North America, you make certain assumptions about your audience. But if you write about baseball for a British newspaper, you assume a different audience. Your language will vary as you reach out to their needs; for example, if you know something about cricket, you could explain baseball even more effectively for your British readers. Whatever you write, you must sense your audience's capacity, its susceptibilities, and its prejudices.

But even as you adjust your language to different audiences, you are working within a comfortable range. You are *writing*, thereby eliminating the lower range of speech. The written word presupposes a literate norm that frees you from worry about the fringes of your personal or ethnic vocabulary. Your only adjustment is generally upward toward a kind of verbal worldliness, a grammatical tightening and rhetorical heightening to make your thoughts clear, emphatic, and attractive.

Consider your audience a mixed group of intelligent and reasonable adults. You want them to think of you as well informed and well educated. You wish to explain what you know and what you believe. You wish to persuade them pleasantly that what you know is important and what you believe is right. Try to imagine what they might ask you, what they might object to, what they might know already, what they might find interesting. Be simple and clear, amusing and profound, using plenty of illustration to show what you mean. *But do not talk down to them.* That is the great danger in adjusting to your audience. Bowing to your readers' supposed level, you insult them by assuming their inferiority. Thinking yourself humble, you are actually haughty. The best solution is simply to assume that your readers are as intelligent as you. Even if they are not, they will be flattered by the assumption. Your written language, in short, will be respectful toward your subject, considerate toward your readers, and somehow amiable toward human failings.

The Written Voice
Make Your Writing Talk

That the silent page should seem to speak with the writer's voice is remarkable. With all gestures gone, no eyes to twinkle, no notation at all for the rise and fall of utterance, and only a handful of punctuation marks, the level line of type can yet convey the writer's voice, the tone of his or her personality.

To achieve this tone, to find your own voice and style, simply try to write in the language of intelligent conversation, cleared of all the stumbles and weavings of talk. Indeed, our speech, like thought, is amazingly circular. We can hardly think in a straight line if we try. We think by questions and answers, repetitions and failures; our speech, full of *you know*s and *I mean*s, follows the erratic ways of the mind, circling around and around as we stitch the simplest of logical sequences. Your writing will carry the stitches, not those loopings and pauses and rethreadings. It will, on its own, carry some attractive colour and rhythm from your personal background, but it should be literate. It should be broad enough of vocabulary and rich enough of sentence to show that you have read a book. It should not be altogether unworthy to place you in the company of those who have written well in your native tongue. But it should nevertheless retain the tone of intelligent and agreeable conversation. It should be alive with a human personality—yours—which is probably the most persuasive rhetorical force on earth. Good writing should have a voice, and the voice should be unmistakably your own.

Suppose your spoken voice sounded something like this in one of your classes:

> Well, I think what Davis says about Freud is, I don't know, prejudiced, or biased. He, or maybe Freud, well they think sex is the only thing. I guess the Oedipus and Electra bit is true all right. But what about friendship, I mean, what about the kind of friends, your friendship with another girl, or another boy, that has nothing to do with whether you want to marry your mother or kill your father and all that. It's finding someone like yourself, or maybe just a little different, someone to share your feelings with and laugh at the same things, like that. That hasn't anything to do with sex.

Your written voice might then emerge from this with something of the same tone, but with everything straightened out, filled in, and polished up:

> Davis's Freudian psychology omits at least one essential human experience: friendship. Davis seems to connect all human relationships to the sexual drives that begin with the infant's sensual relationship with its mother. But the famous Oedipus complex has nothing to do with the friendship between people of the same sex in which the individual psyche discovers that it is not alone, that another one shares the same fears and pleasures. Friendship is a bond somewhat different from the basic sexual drives.

You might wish to polish that some more. You might indeed have said it another way, one more truly your own. The point, however, is to write in a tidy, economical way that wipes up the lapses of talk and fills in the gaps of thought, and yet keeps the tone and movement of good conversation, in your own voice.

Establish a Firm Viewpoint

"In my opinion," the beginner will write repeatedly, until he seems to be saying, "It is only *my* opinion, after all, so it can't be worth much." He has failed to realize that his whole essay represents his opinion of the truth of the matter. Don't make your essay a personal letter to Diary, or to Mother, or to Instructor, a confidential report of what happened to you last night as you agonized over a certain question. Recognize the difference between writing for your audience and writing for yourself. Your audience will not really be interested in your personal commentaries said in a way only suitable for your own records. "*To me*, Irving Layton is a great poet"—this is really writing about yourself. You are only confessing private convictions. To find the public reasons often requires no more than a trick of grammar: a shift from "*To me*, Irving Layton is . . ." to "Irving Layton is . . . ," from "*I thought* the book was good" to "The book is good," from you and your room last night to your subject and what it is. Eliminate merely subjective statements. Change "I cried" to "The scene is very moving." The grammatical shift represents a whole change of viewpoint, a shift from self to subject. You become the informed adult, showing the reader around firmly, politely, and persuasively.

Once you have effaced yourself and addressed your assertions to a reader, once you have erased *to me* and *in my opinion* and all such signs of amateur terror, you may later let yourself back into the essay for emphasis or graciousness: "Mr. Watson errs, I think, precisely at this point." You can thus ease your most tentative or violent assertions, and show that you are polite and sensible, reasonably sure of your position but aware of the possibility of error. Again: the reasonable adult.

You go easy on the *I*, in short, to keep your reader focused on your subject. But you can use the *I* as much as you like to *illustrate* your point, once established, using a personal experience among several other pieces of evidence, or even all by itself. Of course, your instructors will sometimes ask for a wholly autobiographical theme. Indeed, some courses focus altogether on the *I* of personal experience. And your autobiographical résumé in applying for graduate school, grants, and jobs will of course require the *I*. But for the usual essay, use the personal anecdote and the *I* to illustrate a point or to interject a tactful remark.

Effacing the *I*, then letting it back in on occasion, fixes your point of view. But what about the other pronouns, *we, you, one*? *One* objectifies the personal *I*, properly generalizing the private into the public. But it can seem too formal, and get too thick:

> FAULTY: One finds one's opinion changing as one grows
> older.
> REVISED: Opinions change with age.
> REVISED: Our opinions change as we grow older.

We is sometimes a useful generalizer, a convenient haven between the isolating *I* and the impersonal *one*. *We* can seem pompous, but not if it honestly handles those experiences we know we share, or can share. Suppose we wrote:

> As I watched program after program, I got bored and began
> to wonder what values, if any, they represented.

We can easily transpose this:

> As we watch program after program, we are progressively
> bored, and we begin to wonder what values, if any, they rep-
> resent.

(Notice that shifting to the present tense is also part of the generalizing process.) Thus, *we* can generalize without going all the way to *one*, or to the fully objective:

> Program after program, television bores its audiences and
> leaves its sense of values questionable.

We also quite naturally refers to earlier parts of your demonstration, through which you have led your reader: *as we have already seen*. But you will have noticed from the preceding examples that *we* tends slightly toward wordiness. Used sparingly, then, *we* can ease your formality and draw your reader in. Overused, it can seem too presumptuous or chummy. Try it out. See how it feels, and use it where it seems comfortable and right.

You raises similar problems. The first is the one we have been discussing: how to extend that *I* effectively into something else, either *one* or *we* or full objectivity. The indefinite *you*, like the indefinite *they*, is usually too vague, and too adolescent:

> FAULTY: You have your own opinion.
> FAULTY: They have their own opinion.
> REVISED: Everyone has his or her own opinion.
> REVISED: We all have our own opinions.

You, like *we*, can also seem patronizing, attributing to you things not like you at all:

> FAULTY: Like most people, you probably learned to hate
> grammar because your instructor also hated it.
> REVISED: Many people dislike grammar because their instruc-
> tors also disliked it.

I have consistently addressed this book to *you*, the reader. But this is a special case, the relationship of tutor to student projected onto the page. None of my own essays, I think, contains any *you* at all. Our stance in an essay is a little more formal, a little more public. We are better holding our pronouns to *one* or *we*, an occasional *I*, or none at all, as we find a comfortable stance between our subject and audience and find our written voice.

The Point: Argumentation and Exposition

In argumentation, the point is to convince your readers through rational argument or to move them to action through emotional persuasion. In exposition, the point is to explain as clearly, thoroughly, and economically as possible the relevant details that will clarify your subject and your thoughts about it. Your written voice, remember, is one of the keys to your effectiveness. But having a point to make or clarify is the real centre of both exposition and argumentation, the likely goals of most of your writing and public speaking in university and in contemporary life. Hence, the focus of your composition course is indeed argumentation and exposition. Argumentation is perhaps the more appealing, since most topics will lend themselves to debate. Even explaining the Battle of Batoche or the Oedipus complex invites an argumentative thrust as you convince your readers of the most significant causes and crucial events. Argumentation thus ranges through the coolest explanation, or exposition, up to the burning issues you support. Argumentation and exposition, as we will see, absorb every kind of writing you can think of. Narration, dialogue, anecdotes, persuasion, description, newspaper headlines, statistical tables, and chemical formulas may all illustrate your point and may all be given life by your own written personality.

Plan to Rewrite

As you write your weekly assignments and find your voice, you will also be learning to groom your thoughts, to present them clearly and fully, to make sure you have said what you thought you said. This is the process of composition, of putting your thoughts together, beginning with jotted questions and tentative ideas, all to be mulled over, selected, rejected, expanded as you discover your ideas and write them into full expression. Ultimately, good writing comes only from *re*writing. Even your happy thoughts will need resetting, as you join them to the frequently happier ones that a second look seems to call up. Whether you write longhand or on the computer, even an apparently letter-perfect paper will improve almost of itself if you simply run through it again. You will find, almost unbidden, sharper words, better phrases, new figures of speech, and new illustrations and ideas to replace the weedy patches not noticed before. Indeed, this process of rewriting is what strengthens that instinctive editing you do as you speak extemporaneously or write impromptu essays and exams when revision is out of the question. Rewriting improves your fluency, making each rewrite less demanding.

Allow time for revision. After you have settled on something to write about, have written down your ideas, have found a central idea, and feel ready to write the whole thing out, plan for at least three drafts—and try to manage four. Thinking of things to say is the hardest part at first. Even a short assignment of 500 words seems to stretch ahead like a Sahara. You have asserted your central idea in a sentence, and that leaves 490 words to go. But if you step off boldly, one foot after the other, you will make progress, find an oasis or two, and perhaps end at a run in green pastures. With longer papers, some kind of outline will keep you from straying, and even for short ones you will have your prewriting notes, but the principle is the same: step ahead and keep moving until you've arrived. That is the first draft.

The second draft is a pencilled correction of the first. Here you refine and polish, checking your dubious spellings in the dictionary, sharpening your punctuation, clarifying your meaning, pruning away the deadwood, adding a thought here, extending an illustration there—running in a whole new paragraph. You will also be tuning your sentences, carefully adjusting your tone until it is clearly that of an intelligent, reasonable person at ease with the topic and the audience. Your third draft, a run-through and smoothing of your pencilled revision, will generate further improvements.

Your computer revises in a wink—so easily, in fact, that successive local revisions may stall your flow of ideas. As with any first draft, revise here and there as you go, as we do spontaneously in speech and in any writing, but push on to the end. Your computer can help you with quick checks for spelling and typos, and you can even have it list out your favourite bad habits. But, finally, print out your draft and revise it in pencil for better control over words and the whole. Then make your corrections on the screen where it is easy to revise wording, recast paragraphing, and shift whole sections.

Here is an assignment that has gone the full course. To get the class underway, the instructor asked for a paragraph on a pet gripe, something close to home, written to persuade others.

First Printout with Pencilled Corrections

~~German is probably the hardest language to~~
~~learn. It is rigid routine learning with~~
~~nothing creative asked for~~. University
chokes off creativity with too many
requirements. In a university education,
students should be allowed to ~~make~~ _choose_ their
own course. ~~Too many~~ _All the_ requirements ʌ_they must_ ~~are dis-~~
~~couraging to~~ _take discourage_ people's creativity, and they
cannot learn anything which is not motivat-
ed ~~for him~~ to learn. ~~With~~ _R_ requirements
restrict
ʌtheir freedom to choose ~~what he is inter-~~ _and their eagerness to learn._
~~ested in is taken~~ _They are only discouraged_ away by having to study
dull subjects like German, ʌ~~which he is not~~ _in which they can see_
no relevance to their interests.
~~interested in.~~

Though he starts with his gripe about German, the student discovers, as he writes, a wider interest in freedom of choice. He recognizes this when he reads the printout, and cuts his first two sentences as he also tightens up his phrasing. Below you see what he handed in after a second run (and some further changes) with the instructor's marks on it. Then you see the final product, with the whole idea of creativity dropped to strengthen the point about freedom and make it more coherent.

The Paper, with Instructor's Markings

University chokes off creativity with too many requirements. In a university educa- *can you get rid of the passive?*
tion, students <u>should be allowed</u> to choose their own curricula and select their own courses. *redundant?* <u>All the requirements they must take</u> stifle their <u>creativity</u>. Moreover, *true?* <u>they cannot</u> learn anything they are not *relevant?* motivated to learn. Requirements restrict their freedom to choose and their eagerness to explore the subjects they are interested in. <u>They are only discouraged</u> by having *activate* to study dull subjects like German, in which they can see no relevance.

Revised Paper

Students should choose their own education, their own curricula, their own courses. Their education is really theirs alone. Every university requirement threatens to stifle the very enthusiasms upon which true education depends. Students learn best when motivated by their own interests, but, in the midst of a dozen complicated requirements, they can hardly find time for the courses they long to take. Requirements therefore not only restrict their freedom to choose but also destroy their eagerness to explore. Dull subjects like German, in which they can see no relevance anyway, take all their time and discourage them completely.

Aiming for a Style of Your Own

By writing frequently, you will create a style of your own—and with it, a good bit of your future. But what is style? At its best, it is much like style in a car, a gown, a Greek temple—the ordinary materials of this world so poised and perfected as to stand out from the landscape and compel a second look, something that hangs in the reader's mind, like a vision. It is a writer's own voice, with the hems and haws chipped out, speaking the common language uncommonly well. It comes from an artisan who has discovered the gnarls and potentials in the material, one who has learned to enjoy phrasing, syntax, and the very punctuation that keeps them straight. It is the labour of love, and like love it can bring pleasure and satisfaction.

But style is not for the gifted only. Quite the contrary. Indeed, as I have been suggesting, everyone already has a style, and a personality, and can develop both. The stylistic side of writing is, in fact, the only side that can be analysed and learned. The stylistic approach is the practical approach: you learn some things to do and not to do, as you would learn strokes in tennis. Your ultimate game is up to you, but you can at least begin in good form. Naturally, it takes practice. You have to keep at it. Like the doctor and the lawyer and the golfer and the tennis player, you just keep practising—even to write a nearly perfect letter. But if you like the game, you can probably learn to play it well. You will at least be able to write a respectable sentence and to express your thoughts clearly, without puffing and flailing.

In the essay, as in business, trying to get started and getting off on the wrong foot account for most of our lost motion. So we will next consider how to find a thesis, which will virtually organize your essay for you. Then we will study the relatively simple structure of the essay and the structure of the paragraph—the architecture of spatial styling. Then we will experiment with various styles of sentences, playing with length and complexity to help you find the right mix to convey your personal rhythm. And finally we will get down to words themselves. Here again you will experiment to find those personal ranges of vocabulary, those blends of the breezy and the formal, that will empower your personal style. But again, there are things to do and things not to do, and these can be learned. So, to begin.

Suggested Exercises

1. Compose an occasion and purpose for yourself as a writer, but not one related to a class assignment. For example, you might want to address a political organization on campus, or write a movie review for the student newspaper, or a letter to the editor of the local city newspaper. Explain how you would prepare to deal with a topic of interest or relevance to your audience, record your reflections on the topic, and explain your choice of a subject, to show you have made a realistic choice.

2. If you have a short essay done for another class or that you wrote last year, redo it by putting it through each of the stages in the process once again. Keep your notes, drafts, revisions, and proofreading work to submit with the final, *rewritten* version.

3. Take the notes from one of your classes that have a unifying focus. Comment on their meaning and expand them for your own better understanding, and then arrange them in an order based on a principle of order you can state in one clear sentence.

4. Give at least five points of significance about each of the following topics:
   a. Canadian identity
   b. athletic programs in university
   c. the military in the 1990s
   d. high school as a preparation for university
   e. the value of intelligent discussion

5. Suggest possible ways to introduce a paper based on one of the topics in Exercise 4.

6. Select one of your textbooks and explain its audience appeal, the impression you have of its author(s), and its organization of the material it deals with. Write a 500–750 word review of the text. Submit your notes, revisions, and the final review.

7. Write an essay about a pet peeve, something that really irritates you, like junk mail, television advertising, Don Cherry, or gossips. Put the topic through each of the stages of the process, keeping careful notes, and develop a short essay.

Making a Beginning: From Subject to Thesis

Getting Set

Get set! Writing an essay isn't exactly a hundred-metre dash, but you do need to get ready and get set before you can go to it. Writing requires a time and place, an habitual environment to coax and support those inspired moments that seem to flow spontaneously into language. Your best scheme is to plan two or three sittings for each assignment. Your place should be fixed. It should be comfortable and convenient. Your times should be regular, varied in length from short to long, and set to fit your schedule and your personal rhythm, as morning person or night owl, sprinter or long-distance runner. Arrange your first period for a time as soon as possible after assignments, perhaps only half an hour for thinking and making preliminary notes. Your next two sessions should be longer, the last with expandable time to get the job done.

What Should I Write?

First you need a subject (Stage 1), and then you need a thesis (Stage 2). Yes, but *what should I write?* Here you are, an assignment before you and the screen as blank as your mind, especially if your instructor has left the subject up to you. Consider carefully, however, all the directions given for the assignment to discover elements of occasion and general purpose implicit in the terms. Look for something that interests you, something you know about, some hobby—something that shook you up, left you perplexed, started you thinking. Perhaps something you have written about in your journal would be suitable.

Writing will help you discover that something. Don't stare at the void. Set yourself the task of writing for ten minutes no matter what. Start moving and keep going, even beginning with *Oh no, what should I write? Write on anything, the assignment said. OK, but what what what what what? Fishing? Baby-sitting? Crime? Nuclear power? Oh no. Crime? Rape? How about the time I ripped off a chocolate bar and got caught? The shock of recognition. Everyone's done it at some time or other. Everyone's guilty. Everyone's tempted. Something for nothing. The universal temptation of crime*. . . . Keep going until your watch tells you to stop. That's a good start. A subject is rising from that chocolate bar. Take a break and let your thoughts sink in and accumulate.

Probe your own experiences and feelings for answers as to why people behave as they do, especially in times of crisis. Prestige? The admiration of peers? Fear of not going with the gang? Now have another bout, perhaps just jotting the questions down, perhaps discovering some answers as you go. You have found your subject—and indeed have already moved a good way toward a thesis. The more your subject matters to you, the more you can make it matter to your readers. It might be skiing. It might be dress. It might be roommates, the Somalia affair, a political protest, a personal discovery of racial tensions, an experience in a summer job. But do not tackle a big philosophical abstraction, like Freedom, or a big subject, like the Supreme Court. They are too vast, your time and space and knowledge all too small. You would probably manage no more than a collection of platitudes. Start rather with something specific, like a personal experience, and let the ideas of freedom and justice and responsibility arise from there. An abstract idea is a poor beginning. As you move ahead through your course in writing, you will work more directly with ideas, with problems posed by literature, with questions in the great civilizing debate about what we are doing in this strange world and universe. But again, look for something within your concern. The best subjects lie nearest at hand, and nearest the heart.

You can personalize almost any subject and cut it down to size, getting a manageable angle on it. Forming it as a question that is very exact in its limits can be useful. Stating your point of concern as a problem to be studied is another way of testing the precision of your formulation of the subject. On an assigned subject, particularly in courses like political science, anthropology, or sociology, look for something that connects you with it. Suppose your instructor assigns a paper on social assistance. Think of a grandparent, a parent, a neighbour, a friend—or perhaps yourself as a student—receiving (or not receiving) benefits, and how reductions would or would not affect your life. You will have a vivid illustration as well as one corner of the huge problem to illuminate. Nuclear energy? Perhaps you have seen on television the appalling space suits and mechanical arms required to handle and get rid of the radioactive waste. Perhaps you remember an article or a sentence that started you thinking. With subjects to find, keep an eye and an ear open as you read the newspaper or *Maclean's*, watch television, or talk with your friends. Your classes and textbooks will inevitably turn up subjects for your composition course, if you watch for them, that you can bring into your personal range. Pollution? All of us have seen a local swamp or dump, or have choked on fumes in traffic jams. You need to find a personal interest in your subject to have something to say and to interest others. Form clear questions or statements of problems to provide a realistic subject as a starting point for preparing an essay, and remember that having a subject means you are ready to start, to begin moving *toward* an essay; you are not ready to write for your audience yet.

From Subject to Thesis

Suppose, for the present, we start simply with "Drugs." Certainly most of us have been tempted, or had to resist, or to go along, have experimented, or gotten hooked, or have known someone who has—especially if we include cigarettes and alcohol. "Drugs" is a subject easily personalized. Taking a subject like this will also show how to generalize from your own experience and how to cut your subject down to manageable size. Your first impulse will probably be to write in the first person, but your experience may remain merely personal and may not point your subject into a thesis. As I have said, a personal anecdote makes a lively *illustration*, but first you need to generate your thesis and establish it for your reader— that is, you need to formulate your response to the question or problem you developed. You need to move out of that bright, self-centred spotlight of consciousness in which we live before we really grow up, in which the child assumes that all his or her experiences are unique. If you shift from "me" to "the beginner" or "the young adult," however, you will be stepping into maturity: acknowledging that others have gone through exactly the same thing, that your experiences have illustrated once again the general dynamics of the individual and the group. So instead of writing "I was afraid to refuse," you write:

> The beginner is afraid to refuse and soon discovers the
> tremendous pressure of the group.

By extending your private feelings, you change your subject into a thesis—your expository focus or argumentative proposition. You simply assume you are normal and fairly representative, and you then generalize with confidence, transposing your particular experiences, your particular thoughts and reactions, your individual response to an issue, into statements about the ways of the larger world. Put your proposition, your thesis, into one sentence. This will get you focused. And now you are ready to begin.

Where Essays Fail

You can usually blame a bad essay on a bad beginning. If your essay falls apart, it probably has no primary idea, no thesis, to hold it together. "What's the big idea?" we used to ask. The phrase will serve as a reminder that you must find the "big idea" behind your several smaller thoughts and musings and drafts before you can start to shape your final essay. In the beginning was the *logos*, says the Bible—the idea, the plan, caught in a flash as if in a single word. Find your *logos*, and you are ready to round out your essay and set it spinning.

Suppose you had decided to write about a high-speed ride—another case of group dynamics. If you have not focused your big idea in a thesis, you might begin something like this:

> All people think they are good drivers. There are more accidents caused by young drivers than any other group. Driver education is a good beginning, but further practice is very necessary. People who object to driver education do not realize that modern society, with its suburban pattern of growth, is built around the automobile. The car becomes a way of life and a status symbol. When teenagers go too fast they are probably only copying their own parents.

A little reconsideration, aimed at a good thesis sentence, could turn this into a reasonably good opening paragraph, with your thesis, your big idea, asserted at the end to focus your reader's attention:

> Modern society is built on the automobile. Children play with tiny cars; teenagers long to take the car out alone. Soon they are testing their skills at higher and higher speeds, especially with a group of friends along. One final test at extreme speeds usually suffices. It is usually a sobering experience, if survived, and can open one's eyes to the deadly dynamics of the group.

Thus your thesis is your essay's life and spirit. If it is sufficiently firm, it may tell you immediately how to organize your supporting material. But if you do not find a thesis, your essay will be a tour through the miscellaneous—"We have just seen this; now let us turn to this"—an essay with no vital idea. A purely factual essay, one simply on "Cats," for instance, will have to rely on outer scaffolding alone (some orderly progression from Persia to Siam), since it really has no idea at all. It is all subject, all cats, instead of being based on an idea *about* cats, with a thesis *about* cats.

The Argumentative Edge
Find Your Thesis

Finding the argumentative thrust implicit in any potential subject makes it easier for the writer to interest a reader. The *about*ness puts an argumentative edge on the subject; even expository papers gain interest by having an argumentative edge. When you have something to say *about* cats, you have found your underlying idea. You have something to defend, something to fight about: not just "Cats" but "The cat is really our best friend." Now the hackles on all dog people are rising, and you have an argument on your hands. You have something to prove. You have a thesis.

The most dynamic thesis is a kind of affront to somebody. No one will be very much interested in listening to you discuss the thesis "The dog is our best friend." Everyone knows that already. Even the dog lovers will be uninterested, convinced they know better than you. But the cat. . . .

So it is with any unpopular idea. The more unpopular the viewpoint and the stronger the push against convention, the stronger the thesis and the more energetic the essay. Compare the energy in "Democracy is good" with that in "Separatism is good," for instance. The first is filled with platitudes, the second with plutonium. By the same token, if you can find the real energy in "Democracy is good," if you can get down through the sand to where the roots and water are, you will have a real essay, because the opposition against which you generate your energy is the heaviest in the world: boredom. Probably the most energetic thesis of all, the greatest inner organizer, is some tired old truth that you dig up to spurt with new life.

Remember, to find a thesis and to put it into one sentence is to narrow and define your subject to workable size. Under "Cats" you must deal with all felinity from the jungle up, carefully partitioning the eons and areas, the tigers and tabbies. But proclaim the cat the friend of humanity, and you have pared away whole categories and chapters; you need only think up the arguments sufficient to overwhelm the opposition. So put an argumentative edge on your subject—and you will have found your thesis.

Neutral exposition, to be sure, has its uses. You may want to tell someone how to build a doghouse, how to can asparagus, how to follow the outlines of relativity, or even how to write an essay. Performing a few exercises in simple exposition will no doubt sharpen your insight into the problems of finding orderly sequences, of considering how best to lead your readers through the hoops of writing clearly and accurately. It will also illustrate how much more engaging an argument is.

You will see that picking an argument immediately simplifies the problems so troublesome in straight exposition: the defining, the partitioning, the narrowing of the subject. Not that you must be constantly pugnacious or aggressive. I have overstated my point to make it stick. Actually, you can put an argumentative edge on the flattest of expository subjects. "How to build a doghouse" might become "Building a doghouse is a thorough introduction to the building trades, including architecture and civil engineering." "Canning asparagus" might become "An asparagus patch is a course in economics." "Relativity" might become "Relativity is not so inscrutable as many suppose." Literary subjects take an argumentative edge almost by nature. You simply assert what the essential point of a poem or play seems to be: "*Hamlet* is essentially about a world that has lost its values." You assume that your readers are in search of clarity, that you have a loyal opposition consisting of the interested but uninformed. You have given your subject its edge; you have limited and organized it at a single stroke. Pick a point to *argue*, and you will automatically be defining and narrowing your subject, and all the partitions that you don't need will fold up. Instead of dealing with things, subjects, and pieces of subjects, you will be dealing with an idea and its consequences.

Sharpen Your Thesis

Come out with your subject pointed. You have chosen an issue that interests you, a problem you have thought about, read about, something preferably of which you have also had some experience—perhaps, let us say, seeing a friend loafing while cashing welfare cheques. So take a stand. Make a judgment of value, make a *thesis*. Be reasonable, but don't be timid. It is helpful to think of your subject-to-thesis development, the forming of your main point at issue, as a *debating question*—"Resolved: Welfare payments must go"—taking out the "Resolved" when you actually write your thesis down. But your resolution will be even stronger, your essay clearer and tighter, if you can sharpen your thesis even farther—"Resolved: Welfare payments must go because _____." Fill in that blank, and your worries are practically over. The main idea is to put your whole argument into one sentence.

Try, for instance, "Welfare payments must go because they are making people irresponsible." I don't know if that is true, and neither will you until you write your way into it, asking *how* and *why*, considering probabilities, alternatives, objections, and especially the underlying assumptions. In fact, no one, no master sociologist or future historian, can tell absolutely if it is true, so multiplex are the causes in human affairs, so endless and tangled the consequences. The basic assumption—that irresponsibility is growing—may be entirely false. No one, I repeat, can tell absolutely. But likewise, your educated guess may be as good as another's. At any rate, you are now ready to write. You have found your *logos*.

Now you can put your well-pointed thesis sentence on a card on the wall in front of you to keep from drifting off target. But you will now want to dress it for the public, to polish it and make it attractive. Suppose you try

> Welfare payments, perhaps more than anything else, are eroding personal initiative.

But is this fully true? Perhaps you had better try something like

> Despite their immediate benefits, welfare payments may actually be eroding personal initiative and depriving society of needed workers.

This is your full thesis. You have acknowledged the opposition ("immediate benefits"); you have spelled out your *because* (erosion, deprivation). This is your opinion, stated as certainty. But how do you know, without all the facts? Well, no one knows everything. People would never write anything if they waited until they did. To a great extent, the writing of a thing is the learning of it—the discovery of truth. So make a bold thesis and get into the arena. If it becomes increasingly clear that your thesis is untrue, turn it around and use the other end. If your convictions have begun to falter with

> Despite their immediate benefits, welfare payments undermine initiative. . . .

try it the other way around, with something like this:

> Although welfare payments may offend the rugged individualist, they relieve much want and anxiety, and they enable many a family to maintain its integrity.

You will now have a beautiful command of the major objections to your new position. And you will have learned something about human fallibility and the nature of truth. You simply add enough evidence to persuade your reader that what you say is probably true, finding arguments that will stand up in the marketplace—public reasons for your private convictions.

Look for the Fallacies

We saw the fallacies fade as we worked with "Welfare." Here are some further samples from students' papers that may help you improve your uncertain starts:

> The answer to crime is longer sentences and more prisons.

Discussion soon showed that "crime" was too sweeping—everything from shoplifting to atrocious murder. The thesis also assumes that the debate about the death penalty in Canada will not be revived. It needs more specifics:

> Since the death penalty has proved both ineffective and, to
> many, repugnant, the only remaining answer to serious crimes
> is longer sentences and more prisons.

Your thesis, of course, may not always find its cure in covering neglected alternatives with a *since, although, despite,* or the like. One student's thesis started:

> Registration of guns will lead to confiscation of guns.

Classmates pointed out that registration merely validates ownership. Confiscation would ensue only from illegal ownership. In the end, the simplest way to revise this thesis was to reverse it and qualify *confiscation*:

> Claims that registration of guns will lead to some universal
> confiscation are illogical and unfounded.

Here are some theses, too narrow and too wide, and some suggested revisions.

> NARROW: The tourist trade only brings financial gain to a few
> lucky landlords.
> REVISED: The tourist trade contributes significantly to the
> economy as it meets an essential need for recreation and
> natural beauty.

> WIDE: This campus is unique in many ways.
> REVISED: This campus is atrocious because economy has over-
> ruled beauty in several major decisions.

WIDE: Abortion is a controversial problem that many people disagree on.

REVISED: Laws prohibiting abortion to avoid unwanted births help to keep people from trying to play God for selfish reasons.

REVISED: Laws prohibiting abortion to avoid unwanted births inhibit freedom of choice and endanger physical and mental health.

The process of writing will usually discover the holes in a weak thesis and show the way to its, and the paper's, redrafting. But, however it may work out in the end, get your thesis down, in one sentence, for a good beginning.

Use Your Title

After your thesis, think of a title. A good title focuses your thinking even more sharply and catches your reader's thoughts on your finished paper. Your title is your opening opportunity. It is an integral part of your paper. Don't forget it.

Work up something from your thesis. It will be tentative, of course. Your thinking and your paper may change in the writing, and you will want to change your title to match. But a good title, like a good thesis, has a double advantage: (1) it helps you keep on track as you write; (2) it attracts and helps keep your readers on track as they read. It is the first step in your persuasion. So try something attractive:

Farewell to Welfare
The Sentence of Prisons
Check Your Guns
The Trade in Tourism
Ugly Building
Who's Right in Abortion?

You can probably do better. You will do better when you finish your paper. But don't make it sound like a newspaper headline, and don't make it a complete statement. Don't forget your title is a starter, both for your writing and for your written paper. Capitalize all significant words (see page 261 for details). Titles do not take periods, but do take question and exclamation marks if you need them. Your title and your opening sentence should be independent of each other. With a title like "Polluted Streams," for instance, don't begin with "*This* is a serious problem."

Sample: From Subject to Thesis

Now with the concepts in hand, we need a framework, a structure, to put them in. We will look at this structure in the next chapter. But let us close with a student's paper to illustrate the points of this chapter as it looks ahead to the structural points of the next one. The author's writing is a little wordy and awkward. She is a little uncertain of her language. Her *ones*, for instance, seem far too stiff and insistent. This is her first paper, and she has not yet fully discovered her own written voice. But it is an excellent beginning. It shows well how a personal experience produces a publicly valid thesis, then turns around to give that thesis its most lively and specific illustration. The assignment had asked for a paper of about 500 words on a book (or movie, or television program) that had proved personally meaningful. Even a memorable experience would do—fixing a car, or building a boat, or being arrested. The aim of the assignment was to generalize from a personally valuable experience and to explain to others how such an experience can be valuable to them.

On Finding Oneself in New Guinea

Reading for pleasure is not considered to be popular. Young adults prefer the television with which they have spent so many childhood hours. Too many attractions beckon them away from the books that the teacher recommended to the class for summer reading. One's friends come by to listen to the latest music. The kids go to the movies or to the beach, and the book one had intended to read remains on the shelf, or probably the library, where one has not yet been able to find the time to go. Nevertheless, *a book can furnish real enjoyment.* [Opposing View] [Thesis]

The reader enjoys the experience of being in another world. While one reads, one forgets that one is in one's own room. The book has served as a magic carpet to take one to India, or Africa, or Sweden, or even to the cities and areas of one's own country where one has never been. It has also transported one into the lives of people with different experiences and problems, from which one can learn to solve one's own problems of the future. The young [Generalized Support] person, in particular, can learn by the experience of reading what it is like to be a complete adult.

A book is able to help the young person to mature even further, and change one's whole point of view. *Growing up in New Guinea* by Margaret Mead is a valuable experience for this reason. *I found my mother's old paperback on our shelf, after having seen a TV program on the pioneering achievement of Margaret Mead.* I was interested in her because the teacher had referred to her book entitled *Coming of Age in Samoa*. I was surprised to find this one about New Guinea. I thought it was a mistake. I opened it and read the first sentence:

> The way in which each human infant is transformed into the finished adult, into the complicated individual version of his city and his century, is one of the most fascinating studies open to the curious minded.

The idea that the individual is a version of his city and his century was fascinating. I started reading and was surprised when I was called to dinner to learn that two hours had passed. I could hardly eat my dinner fast enough so that I could get back to New Guinea.

From this book I learned that different cultures have very different conceptions about what is right and wrong, in particular about the sex relations and the marriage ceremony, but that people have the same problems all over the world, namely the problem of finding one's place in society. *I also learned that books can be more enjoyable than any other form of pleasure.* Books fascinate the reader because while one is learning about other people and their problems, particularly about the problem of becoming a full member of society, one is also learning about one's own problems.

Using the Thesis in Other Ways

Formulating a thesis can also help in your reading, in any of your courses. At the end of each chapter or section, try to put down in one sentence that chapter's point—not "This chapter discusses racial discrimination," but "Racial discrimination arises from powerful biological drives to seek one's own kind and to shun aliens." This practice strengthens your knowledge, aids your analysis—has your author said it anywhere as well as you have?—and develops your ability to generate theses for your own thoughts. It works equally well for poems, stories, and plays.

You can also cash in your thesis making on your essay exams in any course. Here's the trick: *make yourself answer the question in one sentence,* and then just keep writing. This single opening sentence forces all you know on the question into its widest dimension. Everything you throw in after that will seem to illustrate your opening declaration, and your instructor will say, "Now *this* one is really organized—a real grasp of the subject."

Be sure, first, to glance through the whole exam to get it and your time in perspective. Next, attend to your question's directive words like *summarize, consider, discuss, justify, enumerate, compare.* Then use the question's language in your thesis sentence. This strategy works even with the broadest kind of question:

1. Discuss the fall of the Roman Empire.
2. What is the most valuable thing you have learned in this course?
3. Demonstrate your knowledge of the materials of this course.

Your one-sentence openers might go like this:

1. The Roman Empire fell because of decay from within and attack from without.
2. The most valuable thing I have learned this semester is that people usually conceal their true motivations from themselves.
3. The materials of this course illustrate biological evolution, particularly the role of mutation in the survival of the fittest.

If you have time to jot down some points and quickly arrange them to save best for last, you are really off and running.

Suggested Exercises

1. *(Best done in class, with comparisons and discussion.)* Try a thesis off the top of your head. Put down quickly the first three or four subjects you can think of—like *golf, art, nail polish, tomatoes.* These topics must have interested you sometime, somewhere. Now take each one and say something about it, making a one-sentence argumentative thesis, filling it out, if appropriate, with reasons, as in "Although tennis _____, golf accomplishes more because _____."

2. Write a thesis statement and a title for each of the following subjects:
   a. gun control
   b. jogging (or some similar activity)
   c. the appearance of your campus
   d. a book you have read
   e. Canada–United States relations

3. Now take one of these thesis statements and write a paper about the length of the one on reading and New Guinea. First, introduce your thesis with a few remarks to get your reader acquainted with your subject, then write your paper straight through to illustrate your thesis as fully as you can. Then go back over this draft and make it publicly presentable. Think of yourself as a reader to be attracted and persuaded. Are your phrases really clear to someone else? Are your thoughts really explained? Let it rest awhile, and then revise it up to its full potential.

Your Paper's Basic Structure

Beginning, Middle, End

As Aristotle long ago pointed out, works that spin their way through time need a beginning, a middle, and an end to be complete. You need a clear beginning to give your essay character and direction so the readers can tell where they are going and can look forward with expectation. Your beginning, of course, will set forth your thesis. You need a middle to amplify and fulfil. This will be the body of your argument, the bulk of your essay. You need an end to let readers know that they have arrived, a summation and reassertion of your theme in the final paragraph. So give your essay the three-part *feel* of completion, of beginning, middle, and end, a unified and coherent whole. Many a beginner's essay has no structure and leaves no impression. It is all chaotic middle. It has no beginning, it just starts; it has no end, it just stops, burned out at two in the morning.

The beginning must feel like a beginning, not like an accident. It should be at least a full paragraph that leads your readers into the subject and culminates with your thesis. The end, likewise, should be a full paragraph, one that drives the point home, pushes the implications wide, and brings the readers to rest, back at the fundamental thesis with a sense of completion. When we consider paragraphing in the next chapter, we will look more closely at beginning paragraphs and end paragraphs. But first let us look at the basic structural tactics that carry your readers from beginning to end (Stage 3), concentrating at this point on the argumentative essay using the *pro–con* structure.

Argumentative Tactics
Arrange Your Points in Order of Increasing Interest

Once your thesis has sounded the challenge, your readers' interest is probably at its highest pitch. Readers want to see how you can prove so outrageous a thing, or what the arguments are for this thing they have always believed but never tested. Each step of the way into your demonstration, they are learning more of what you have to say. But, unfortunately, their interest may be relaxing as it becomes satisfied: a reader's normal line of attention progressively declines. Against this decline you must oppose your forces, making each successive point more interesting and emphatic. And save your best till last. It is as simple as that.

Here, for example, is the middle of a short, three-paragraph essay on the thesis that "Working your way through university is valuable." The student's three points ascend in interest:

> The student who works finds that the experience is worth more than the money. He learns to budget his time. He now supports himself by using time he would otherwise waste, and he studies harder in the time he has left because he knows it is limited. He also makes real and lasting friends on the job, as compared to the other casual acquaintances around the campus. He has shared rush hours, nighttime clean-ups with the dishes piled high, and conversation and jokes when business is slow. Finally, he gains confidence in his ability to get along with all kinds of people and to make his own way. He sees how businesses operate and gains an insight into the real world, which is a good contrast to the more intellectual and idealistic world of the university student.

Again, make each successive item more interesting than the last, or you will suddenly seem anticlimactic. Actually, minor regressions of interest make no difference so long as the whole tendency is uphill and your last item clearly the best. Suppose, for example, you were to try a thesis about cats. You decide that four points would make up the case, and that you might arrange them in the following order of increasing interest: (1) cats are affectionate but make few demands; (2) cats actually look out for themselves;

(3) cats have, in fact, proved extremely useful to society throughout history in controlling mice and other plaguey rodents; (4) cats satisfy some human need for a touch of the jungle and have been worshipped for the exotic power they still seem to represent. It may be, as you write, that you will find number 1 developing attractive or amusing instances and perhaps even virtually usurping the whole essay. Numbers 2, 3, and 4 should then be moved ahead as interesting but brief preliminaries.

Interests vary, of course, and various subjects will suggest different kinds of importance: from small physical details to large, from incidental thought to basic principles. Sometimes chronology will supply a naturally ascending order of interest, as in a tennis match or hockey game, or in any contest against natural hazards and time itself, like crossing a glacier with supplies and endurance dwindling. Space, too, may offer natural progressions of interest, as you move from exterior to interior or from place to place. But usually interest is drawn by ideas, and these quite naturally come from your own interest in your subject; with a little thought, you can tell which points to handle first and which to arrange in increasing importance, saving the best until last. In short, your structure should range from least important to most important, from simple to complex, from narrow to broad, from pleasant to hilarious, from mundane to metaphysical—whatever "leasts" and "mosts" your subject suggests.

Acknowledge and Dispose of the Opposition

Your cat essay, because it is moderately playful, can proceed rather directly, throwing only an occasional bone of concession to the dogs, and perhaps most of your essays, as you discuss Confederation or explain a poem, will have no opposition to worry about. But a serious controversial argument demands one organizational consideration beyond the simple structure of ascending interest. Although you have taken your stand firmly as a *pro*, you will have to allow scope to the *cons*, or you will seem not to have thought much about your subject. The more opposition you can manage as you carry your point, the more triumphant you will seem, like a high-wire artist daring the impossible.

This balancing of pros against cons is one of the most fundamental orders of thought: the dialectic order, which is the order of argument, one side pitted against the other. Our minds naturally swing from side to side as we think. In dialectics, we simply give one side an argumentative edge, producing a thesis that cuts a clear line through any subject: "This is better than that." The basic organizing principle is to get rid of the opposition first and to end on your own side. Probably you will have already organized your thesis sentence in a perfect pattern for your con–pro argument:

Despite their many advantages, welfare payments. . . .
Although dogs are fine pets, cats. . . .

The subordinate clause (see pages 112–13) states the subordinate part of your argument, which is your concession to the *con* viewpoint; your main clause states your main argument. As the subordinate clause comes first in your thesis sentence, so does the subordinate argument in your essay. Sentence and essay both reflect a natural psychological principle. You want, and your readers want, to get the opposition out of the way. And you want to end on your best foot. (You might try putting the opposition last, just to see how peculiarly the last word insists on seeming best, and how, when stated last by you, the opposition's case seems to be your own.)

Your opposition, of course, will vary. Some of your audience will agree with you but for different reasons. Others may disagree hotly. You need, then, to imagine what these varying objections might be, as if you were before a meeting in open discussion, giving the hottest as fair a hearing as possible. You probably would not persuade them, but you would ease the pressure and probably persuade the undecided by your reasonable stance. Asking what objections might arise will give you the opposing points that your essay must meet—and overcome.

Get rid of the opposition first. This is the essential tactic of argumentation. You have introduced and stated your thesis in your beginning paragraph. Now start the middle with a paragraph of concession to the *cons*:

Dog-lovers, of course, have tradition on their side. Dogs are indeed affectionate and faithful. . . .

And with that paragraph out of the way, go to bat for the cats, showing their superiority to dogs in every point.

Sometimes, as we have seen with the New Guinea essay, you can use the opposition itself to introduce your thesis in your first paragraph, getting some of it out of the way at the same time:

Shakespeare begins *Romeo and Juliet* with ominous warnings about fate. His lovers are "star-crossed," he says: they are doomed from the first by their contrary stars, by the universe itself. They have sprung from "fatal loins." Fate has already determined their tragic end. The play then unfolds a succession of unlucky and presumably fated accidents. Nevertheless, we soon discover that Shakespeare really blames the tragedy not on fate but on human stupidity and error.

But usually your beginning paragraph will lead down to your thesis somewhat neutrally, and you will attack your opposition head-on in paragraph two, as you launch into your argument.

If the opposing arguments seem relatively slight and brief, you can get rid of them neatly all together in one paragraph before you get down to your case. Immediately after your beginning, which has stated your thesis, you write a paragraph of concession: "Of course, security is a good thing. No one wants people begging." And so on to the end of the paragraph, deflating every conceivable objection. Then back to the main line: "But the price in moral decay is too great." The structure of the essay, paragraph by paragraph, might be diagrammed something like the scheme shown in Diagram I:

DIAGRAM I

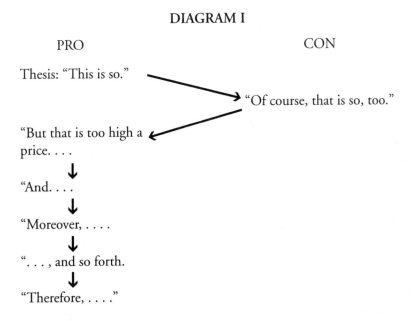

PRO

CON

Thesis: "This is so."

"Of course, that is so, too."

"But that is too high a price. . . ."

↓

"And. . . ."

↓

"Moreover, ..."

↓

". . . , and so forth.

↓

"Therefore, ..."

If the opposition is more considerable, demolish it point by point, using a series of cons and pros, in two or three paragraphs, before you steady down to your own side. Each paragraph can be a small argument that presents the opposition, then knocks it flat—a kind of Punch-and-Judy show: "We must admit that . . . But . . . ." And down goes the poor old opposition again. Or you can swing your argument through a number of alternating paragraphs: first your beginning, the thesis, then a paragraph to the opposition (con), then one for your side (pro), then another paragraph of con, and so on. The main point, again, is this: *get rid of the opposition first.* One paragraph of concession right after your thesis will probably handle most of your adversaries, and the more complicated argumentative swingers, like the one shown in Diagram II below, will develop naturally as you need them.

DIAGRAM II: Controlling Handguns–Pro and Con

PRO   CON

Thesis: Possession of handguns in Canada should be controlled.

To be sure, self-protection is a natural right. . . .

But pistols in homes kill many more relatives than intruders. . . .

Of course, ownership by sportsmen and collectors is justified. . . .

Large numbers of weapons in homes, however, give easy access to theft. . . .

I concede that any restrictions invade privacy and freedom. . . .

Nevertheless, the intrusion is no more restrictive than registering an automobile. . . .

↓

Indeed, all arguments about individual rights pale before the crime rate and the annual slaughter of individuals. . . .

↓

Handguns in the United States kill more people than elsewhere, yet it is there that their control is most resisted. . . .

↓

Therefore, controlling handguns in Canada is reasonable and necessary.

You will notice that *but* and *however* are always guides for the pros, serving as switches back to the main line. Indeed, *but, however,* and *nevertheless* are the basic pros. *But* always heads its turning sentence (not followed by a comma); *nevertheless* usually does (followed by a comma). I am sure, however, that *however* is always better buried in the sentence between commas. *However* at a sentence's beginning is the habit of heavy prose. *But* is for the quick turn, the inlaid *however* for the more elegant sweep.

Run Comparisons Point by Point

After blasting the opposition first, only one argumentative principle remains: *run your comparisons point by point.* This principle holds in any kind of comparison. Simply comparing and contrasting two poems, two stories, two ball players, brings insight. It can illuminate the unfamiliar through the familiar, or help you discover and convey to your readers new perspectives on things well known—two popular singers, two automobiles, two nursery rhymes. But the principle is the same.

Compare point for point. Don't write all about sheep for three pages, then all about goats. Every time you say something about a sheep, say something about a goat, pelt for pelt, horn for horn, beard for beard. Otherwise your essay will fall in two, and you will need to repeat all your sheep points when you get down to goats and at last begin the comparison. The tendency to organize comparisons by halves is so strong that you will probably find that you have fallen into it unawares, and in revising you will have to reorganize everything point for point—still arranging your pairs of points from least important to most. Finally, the most effective comparison is one that aims to demonstrate a superiority, that is, one with an argumentative thesis—"Resolved: Sheep are more useful than goats."

———

Now you have almost finished your essay. You have found a thesis. You have worked it into a decent beginning. You have then worked out a convincing middle, with your arguments presented in a sequence of ascending interest. You have used up all your points and said your say. You and your argument are both exhausted. But don't stop. You need an end, or the whole thing will unravel in your readers' minds. You need to buttonhole them in a final paragraph, to imply "I told you so" without saying it, to hint at the whole round of experience and leave them convinced, satisfied, and admiring. One more paragraph will do it: beginning, middle, *and* end.

Developing an Expository Essay

The tactics suggested for presenting an argumentative paper are not essentially different from those used in expository writing. It is the fundamental purpose you have in using them that will make the difference. Exposition is aimed at clarifying what you have determined is necessary for your audience to understand in the light of your occasion and general purpose. The logic of your organization should be rooted in a method suited to the nature of the thesis you will develop. A process, whether natural (how ice fog develops) or historical (how Canada's prime ministers have affected the nature of their office), easily lends itself to a step-by-step presentation. If the point or points you want to make are based on a comparison or contrast, then developing point by point, with concrete illustrations, will probably work. An order based on a rising degree of importance of the central ideas is usually appropriate. The second model research essay in Chapter 11 illustrates one way to develop an expository paper.

Suggested Exercises

1. Warm up with two or three pro-and-con thesis sentences beginning "Although. . . ."

2. For the following assertions, write one argument against and one argument for. Then combine your statements into one thesis sentence.

   Example
   ASSERTION: Movies should not be censored.
   CON: Children should not be exposed to obscene and explicitly sexual images on the screen.
   PRO: Obscenity is far too subjective a thing for any person to define for anyone else.
   THESIS STATEMENT: Although young people probably should not be exposed to explicit sex in films, movies still should not be censored because obscenity is so subjective that no one can legitimately serve as censor for the rest of us.

   a. ASSERTION: Discussion classes are superior to lectures.
   b. ASSERTION: Rapid and convenient transit systems must be built in our cities.
   c. ASSERTION: The federal government should continue to subsidize large companies in danger of bankruptcy.
   d. ASSERTION: Medical schools should reduce the time required for a degree in general medicine from four years to two.
   e. ASSERTION: University degrees should require an apprenticeship away from the campus.

3. Here is a short sample of a first draft of a pro–con paper. See what you can do to rewrite it persuasively, rearranging the points, filling in with points and examples of your own, dropping what doesn't work, and supplying the missing pro and con switches: *but, however, nevertheless, of course, I admit,* and the like. Find a more persuasive title.

Public Transportation

To anyone who has spent a few hours in traffic jams, the need for public transportation is obvious. We waste hours stalled in one place. The pollution and smog are obvious. Public transportation has gone bankrupt because of the automobile. We must revive our systems of public transportation.

Public transportation is obsolescent because of the automobile. Rebuilding public transportation would be very expensive. It would save fuel and cut down pollution. Our economy depends on the automobile. People need cars to get to work. The automobile industry generates a great many jobs and millions of dollars. Cars were once built to last. Now built-in obsolescence generates these jobs and dollars. For shopping and work, the car is a necessity. The freedom to go when and where one wants is part of the Canadian way.

4. Write your own pro–con dialectical swinger, following Diagram I or II on pages 47 and 48.

5. Write an expository essay that explains how to do something you have learned either through work experience or through study. Be sure to make clear to your reader your reason for explaining the process you will write about.

Paragraphs: Beginning, Middle, End

The Standard Paragraph

A paragraph is a structural convenience—a building block to get firmly in mind. I mean the standard, central paragraph, setting aside for the moment the climactic beginning and ending paragraphs. You build the bulk of your essay with blocks of concrete ideas, and they must fit smoothly. But they must also remain as perceptible parts, to rest your readers' eyes and minds. Indeed, the paragraph originated, among the Greeks, as a resting place and place-finder, being first a mere mark (*graphos*) in the margin alongside (*para*) an unbroken sheet of handwriting—the proofreader's familiar ¶. You have heard that a paragraph is a single idea, and this is true. But so is a word, usually, and so is a sentence, sometimes. It seems best, after all, to think of a paragraph as something you use for your readers' convenience, rather than as a form written in stone.

The medium determines the size of the paragraph. Your average longhand paragraph may look the same size as a typed one, much like a paragraph in a book. But the printed page would show your handwritten paragraph a short embarrassment, and your typed one barely long enough for decency. The beginner's insecurity produces inadequate paragraphs, often only a sentence each. Journalists, of course, are one-sentence paragraphers. The narrow newspaper column makes a sentence look like a paragraph, and narrow columns and short paragraphs serve the newspaper's rapid transit. A paragraph from a book might fill a whole newspaper column with solid lead. It would have to be broken—paragraphed— for the readers' convenience. A news story on the page of a book would look like a gap-toothed comb, and would have to be consolidated for the readers' comfort. So make your paragraphs ample.

Plan for the Big Paragraph

When drafting your essay (Stage 4), imagine yourself writing for a book. Force yourself to write four or five sentences at least, visualizing your paragraphs as identical rectangular frames to be filled. This practice will allow you to build with orderly blocks, to strengthen your feel for structure. Since the beginner's problem is usually thinking of things to say rather than trimming the overgrowth, you can do your filling out a unit at a time, always thinking up one or two sentences more to fill the customary space. You will probably be repetitive and wordy at first—this is our universal failing—but you will soon learn to fill your paragraph with interesting details. You will develop a structural rhythm, coming to rest at the end of each paragraphic frame.

Once accustomed to a five-sentence frame, say, you can then begin to vary the length for emphasis, letting a good idea swell out beyond the norm, or bringing a particular point home in a short and sharp paragraph—even in one sentence, like this.

The paragraph's structure, then, has its own rhetorical message. It tells the reader visually whether or not you are in charge of your subject. Tiny, ragged paragraphs display your hidden uncertainty, unless clearly placed among big ones for emphasis. Brief opening and closing paragraphs sometimes can emphasize your thesis effectively, but usually they make your beginning seem hasty and your ending perfunctory. So aim for the big paragraph all the way, and vary it only occasionally and knowingly, for rhetorical emphasis.

Find a Topic Sentence

Looked at as a convenient structural frame, the paragraph reveals a further advantage. Like the essay itself, it has a beginning, a middle, and an end. The beginning and the end are usually each one sentence long, and the middle gets you smoothly from one to the other. Since, like the essay, the paragraph flows through time, its last sentence is the most emphatic, your home punch. The first sentence holds the next most emphatic place. It will normally be your *topic sentence*, stating the paragraph's point like a small thesis of a miniature essay, something like this:

The Attitude [toward Toronto] of the outsider is compounded of envy, malice and pity in about equal quantities. It is admitted that Torontonians make large sums of money but not much else; certainly they never have any fun. There is none of the leisurely Gracious Living that is to be found in Montreal, say, or Halifax or Okotoks, Alberta. When a young man sets out for Toronto (and, sooner or later, all young men set out for Toronto) he is surrounded by a covey of friends—all loudly commiserating with him and whispering to him to look about for a job for them in the big city. It is generally acknowledged that the bereaved young man will return, but he rarely does. If he sees his friends again, he sees them in Toronto where they all have a good cry, and talk over the grand old days when they were poor in Pelvis or West Webfoot.[1]

If, like a good map, your topic sentence covers everything within your paragraph, your paragraph will be coherent and will lead your readers into your community block by block. If your end sentence brings them briefly to rest, they will know where they are and appreciate it.

This is the basic frame. As you write, you will discover your own variations: an occasional paragraph that illustrates its topic sentence with parallel items and no home punch at the end at all, or one beginning with a hint and ending with its topical idea in the most emphatic place, like the best beginning paragraphs.

Beginning Paragraphs: The Funnel

State Your Thesis at the *End* of Your First Paragraph

Your beginning paragraph should contain your main idea and present it to best advantage. Its topic sentence is also the *thesis sentence* of your entire essay. The clearest and most emphatic place for your thesis sentence is at the *end*—not at the beginning—of the first paragraph. Of course, many an essay begins with a subject statement, a kind of open topic sentence for the whole essay, and unfolds amiably from there. But these are usually the more personal meditations of seasoned writers and established authorities.

---

[1] Pierre Berton, *The New City: A Prejudiced View of Toronto*, photographs by Henri Rossier (Toronto: Macmillan, 1961), 18.

Francis Bacon, for instance, usually steps off from a topical first sentence: "Studies serve for delight, for ornament, and for ability." Similarly, A.A. Milne begins with "Of the fruits of the earth, I give my vote to the orange"—and just keeps going.

But for the less assured and the more structurally minded, the funnel is the reliable form, as the thesis sentence brings readers to rest for a moment at the end of the opening paragraph, with their bearings established. If you put your thesis sentence first, you may have to repeat some version of it as you bring your beginning paragraph to a close. If you put it in the middle, readers will very likely take something else as your main point, probably whatever the last sentence contains. The inevitable psychology of interest, as you move your readers through your first paragraph and into your essay, urges you to put your thesis last—in the last sentence of your beginning paragraph.

Think of your beginning paragraph, then, not as a frame to be filled, but as a funnel. Start wide and end narrow:

OPENING INVITATION

THESIS

If, for instance, you wished to show that "Learning to play the guitar pays off in friendship"—your thesis—you would start somewhere back from that thesis idea with something more general—about music, about learning, about the pleasures of achievement, about guitars: "Playing the guitar looks easy"; "Music can speak more directly than words"; "Learning anything is a course in frustration." You can even open with something quite specific, *as long as it is more general than your thesis:* "Pick up a guitar, and you bump into people." A handy way to find an opener is to take one word from your thesis—*learning, play,* or *guitar,* for instance—and make a sentence out of it. Say something about it, and you are well on your way to your thesis, three or four sentences later.[2] Your opening line, in other words, should look forward to your thesis, should be something to engage interest easily, something to which most readers would assent without a rise in blood pressure. (Antagonize and startle if you wish, but beware of having the door slammed before you have a chance to make your point and of making your thesis an anticlimax.) Therefore: broad and genial. From your opening geniality, you move progressively down to smaller particulars. You narrow down: from learning the guitar, to its musical and social complications, to its rewards in friendship (your thesis). Your paragraph might run, from broad to narrow, like this:

> Learning anything has unexpected rocks in its path, but the guitar seems particularly rocky. Playing it looks so simple. A few chords, you think, and you are on your way. Then you discover not only the musical and technical difficulties, but also a whole unexpected crowd of human complications. Your friends think you are showing off; the people you meet think you are a fake. Then the frustrations drive you to achievement. You learn to face the music and the people honestly. You finally learn to play a little, but you also discover something better. You have learned to make and keep some real friends, because you have discovered a kind of ultimate friendship with yourself.

Now, that paragraph turned out a little different from what I anticipated. I used the informal *you*, and it seemed to suit the subject. I also overshot my original thesis, discovering, as I wrote, a thesis one step farther—an underlying cause—about coming to friendly terms with oneself. But it illustrates the funnel, from the broad and general to the one particular point that will be your essay's main idea, your thesis. Here is another example:

> The environment is the world around us, and everyone agrees it needs a cleaning. Big corporations gobble up the countryside and disgorge what's left into the breeze and streams. Big trucks rumble by, trailing their fumes. A jet roars into the air, and its soot drifts over the trees. Everyone calls for massive action, and then tosses away a cigarette butt or gum wrapper. The world around us is also a sidewalk, a lawn, a lounge, a hallway, a room right here. Cleaning the environment can begin by reaching for the scrap of paper at your feet.

In a more argumentative paper, you can sometimes set up your thesis effectively by opening with the opposition, as we have already noted (page 46):

---

[2] I am grateful to James C. Raymond, of the University of Alabama, for this helpful idea.

Science is the twentieth century's answer to everything. We want the facts. We conduct statistical polls to measure the prime minister's monthly popularity. We send spaceships to bring back pieces of the moon and send back data from the planets. We make babies in test tubes. We believe that eventually we will discover the chemical formula for life itself, creating a human being from the basic elements. Nevertheless, some vital element may be beyond the grasp of science and all human planning, as Michael Crichton's novel *The Lost World* suggests.

Middle Paragraphs
Write Full Middle Paragraphs with Transitions

The middle paragraph is the standard paragraph, the little essay in itself, with its own little beginning and little end. But it must also declare its allegiance to the paragraphs immediately before and after it. Each topic sentence must somehow hook onto the paragraph above it, must include some word or phrase to ease the reader's path, a transition to ensure coherence.

There are various ways to create a transition from one paragraph to the next:

1. You may simply repeat a word from the sentence that ended the paragraph just above.
2. You may bring down a thought generally developed or left slightly hanging in the air: "Smith's idea is different" might be an economical topic sentence with automatic transition.
3. You may get from one paragraph to the next by the usual stepping-stones, like *but, however* (within the sentence), *nevertheless, therefore, indeed, of course.*

One brief transitional touch in your topic sentence is usually sufficient.

The topic sentences in each of the following three paragraphs by Rudy Wiebe contain clear transitions. I have just used an old standby myself: repeating the words *topic sentence* from the close of my preceding paragraph. Wiebe begins his second paragraph with a transitional sentence, using the phrase "this linguistic structural understanding" to refer back to the topic of the first paragraph and the phrase "further explain what I mean" to move into the second paragraph. At the beginning of the next paragraph, he uses the transitional phrase "of course" to mark the opposition between the topic of this paragraph (*areal dimension*) and that of the previous one (*linear dimension*). The paragraphs are all similar in length, all cogent, clear, and full. Notice how Wiebe develops his thought with smooth transitions from sentence to sentence. No one-sentence paragraphing here, no gaps, but all a vivid, orderly progression:

> The Inuit understanding of visible phenomena is expressed by their language as two dimensional: the very grammar of Inuktitut requires that you express all the phenomena as either roughly equal in size—things are as broad as they are long, that is, *areal*, or as unequal—they are longer than they are broad, that is, *linear*. This understanding explains why it is really impossible for a living being to be ultimately lost on the vast expanses of the arctic landscape, whether tundra or ice.
>
> Two corollaries expand this linguistic structural understanding and further explain what I mean: first, an areal thing changes dimension and becomes linear when it moves; second, any area without easily observable limits (a field of ice, the sea, an expanse of tundra) is automatically classified as long and narrow, that is, as linear also. In order to live a human being must move; to live in the Arctic a human being must, generally speaking, move quite a lot to acquire enough food. Therefore in order to live he/she must become a linear dimension in a linear space. That means that another moving person (also linear) will certainly find them because even in the largest space their moving lines must at some point intersect, and the very rarity of those lines in the "empty" Arctic makes them all the more conspicuous.
>
> All this changes radically of course when the human being's dimension changes back to areal, that is, the person becomes motionless. To locate a body may take very long; to find even a few of Franklin's 130 dead sailors took thirteen years, and Andrée, the Swedish lighter-than-air balloonist and his two assistants who began their misconceived drift for the North Pole on July 11, 1897, were not found until July 9, 1930, and that by accident. A body may truly be lost forever, even if it quickly freezes and lasts for years. But on the so-called empty barrens of the Arctic it is actually impossible for a living person to stay lost; or by the same token, it is impossible to hide.[3]

---

[3] Rudy Wiebe, "On Being Motionless," in *Playing Dead* (Edmonton: NeWest, 1989), 50–51.

Check Your Paragraphs for Clarity and Coherence

Wiebe's paragraphs run smoothly from first sentence to last. They are coherent. The *topic sentence* is the key. It assures that the subsequent sentences will fall into line, and it is the first point to check when you look back to see if they really do. Many a jumbled paragraph can be unified by writing a broader topic sentence. Consider this disjointed specimen:

```
Swimming is healthful. The first dive into
the pool is always cold. Tennis takes a
great deal of energy, especially under a
hot sun. Team sports, like hockey, base-
ball, and volleyball, always make the awk-
ward player miserable. Character and health
go hand in hand.
```

What is all that about? From the last sentence, we can surmise what the writer intended. But the first sentence about swimming in no way covers the paragraph, which treats several sports not in the least like swimming and seems to be driving at something other than health. The primary remedy is to find the paragraph's thesis and to devise a topic sentence that will state it, thus covering everything in the paragraph. Think of your topic sentence as a roof—covering your paragraph and pulling its contents together.

POOR COVERAGE   GOOD COVERAGE

The first dive. Tennis.   *Swimming. The first dive.*
Hockey, baseball, volleyball.   *Tennis. Hockey, baseball, volleyball.*
Character and health.   *Character and health.*

Suppose we add only a topic sentence, suggested by our right-hand diagram. It will indeed pull things together:

```
Sports demand an effort of will and muscle
that is healthful for the soul as well as
the body. Swimming is healthful. The first
dive into the pool is always cold. Tennis
```

> takes a great deal of energy, especially
> under a hot sun. Team sports, like hockey,
> baseball, and volleyball, always make the
> awkward player miserable. Character and
> health go hand in hand.

But the paragraph is still far from an agreeable coherence. The islands of thought still need some bridges. Gaining coherence is primarily a filling in, or a spelling out, of submerged connections. You may fill in with thought and specific illustrative detail; you may spell out by tying your sentences together with transitional tags and repeated words or syntactical patterns. Let us see what we can do with our sample paragraph.

From the first, you probably noticed that the writer was thinking in pairs: the pleasure of sports is balanced off against their difficulty; the difficulty is physical as well as moral; character and health go hand in hand. We have already indicated this doubleness of idea in our topic sentence. Now to fill out the thought, we need merely expand each sentence so as to give each half of the double idea its due expression. We need also to qualify the thought here and there with *perhaps, often, some, sometimes, frequently, all in all,* and the like. As we work through the possibilities, more specific detail will come to mind. We have already made the general ideas of *character* and *health* more specific with *will, muscle, soul,* and *body* in our topic sentence, and we will add a touch or two more of illustration, almost automatically, as our imagination becomes more stimulated by the subject. We will add a number of transitional ties like *but, and, of course, nevertheless,* and *similarly.* We will look for chances to repeat key words, like *will,* if we can do so gracefully, and to repeat syntactical patterns, if we can emphasize similar thoughts by doing so, as with *no matter how patient their teammates . . . no matter how heavy their hearts,* toward the end of our revision below. The original phrases are in italics:

> *Sports demand an effort of will and muscle*   Topic Sentence
> *that is healthful for the soul as well as*
> *the body. Swimming is* physically *healthful,*   Illustrative
> of course, although it may seem undemanding   Sentences
> and highly conducive to lying for hours   with
> inert on a deck chair in the sun. But *the*   Transitions
> *first dive into the pool is always cold:*
> taking the plunge always requires some
> effort of will. And swimmers soon summon
> the will to compete for greater distances
> and greater speed, doing twenty laps where
> they used to do one. Similarly, *tennis*
> *takes* quantities of *energy,* physical and
> moral, *especially* when the competition

stiffens *under a hot sun. Team sports, like hockey, baseball, and volleyball,* perhaps demand even more of the amateur. *Awkward players* are *miserable* when they strike out, or miss an easy fly, or lose the puck, no matter how patient their teammates. They must drive themselves to keep on trying, no matter how heavy their hearts. Whatever the sport, a little determination can eventually conquer awkwardness and timidity, and the reward will be more than physical. *Character and health* frequently *go hand in hand.*

End Sentence: The Point

Here we can see the essence of coherence: repetition. In this case, repetition works through repeating parallel examples, like *swimming, tennis, team sports,* as if stacking them up to support the topic sentence. Transitions *within* a paragraph also contribute to its coherence. Since beginners usually do not think of transitions, try to include a helpful *of course, but, and, similarly, perhaps, consequently, still,* and the like.

Here are the five points to remember about middle paragraphs:

1. Think of the middle paragraph as a *miniature essay,* with a beginning, a middle, and an end. Its beginning will normally be its topic sentence, the thesis of the miniature essay. Its middle will develop, explain, and illustrate your topic sentence. Its last sentence will drive home the idea.

2. You may instinctively vary the standard paragraph when the topic sentence suggests *repetition.* This could involve repeating the same or similar words or ideas, or using a series of parallel illustrations (*swimming, tennis, hockey, baseball, volleyball*), or opening your paragraph with some hint to be fulfilled in a topical conclusive sentence (*Sports build body and soul*).

3. See that your paragraph is *coherent,* not only flowing smoothly but with nothing in it not covered by the topic sentence.

4. Make your paragraphs *full* and *well developed,* with plenty of details, examples, and full explanations, or you will end up with a skeletal paper with very little meat on its bones.

5. Remember *transitions.* Though each paragraph is a kind of miniature essay, it is also a part of a larger essay. Therefore, hook each paragraph smoothly to the paragraph preceding it, with some transitional touch in each opening sentence.

End Paragraphs: The Inverted Funnel
Reassert Your Thesis

If the beginning paragraph is a funnel, the end paragraph is a funnel upside down: the thought starts moderately narrow—it is more or less the thesis you have had all the time—and then pours out broader and broader implications and finer emphases. The end paragraph reiterates, summarizes, and emphasizes with decorous fervour. This is your last chance. This is what your readers will carry away—and if you can carry *them* away, so much the better. All within decent intellectual bounds, of course. You are the person of reason still, but the person of reason supercharged with conviction, sure of your idea and sure of its importance.

If your essay is anecdotal, however, largely narrative and descriptive, your ending may be no more than a sentence, or it may be a ruminative paragraph generalizing outward from the particulars to mirror your beginning paragraph, as in a more argumentative essay. The dramatic curve of your illustrative incident will tell you what to do. An essay illustrating how folly may lead to catastrophe—a friend dead from an overdose, or drowned by daring too far on thin ice—might end when a story has told itself out and made its point starkly: "The three of us walked numbly up the street toward home."

But the usual final paragraph conveys a sense of assurance and repose, of business completed. Its topic sentence is usually some version of the original thesis sentence, since the end paragraph is the exact structural opposite and complement of the beginning one. Its transitional word or phrase is often one of finality or summary—*then*, *finally*, *thus*, and *so*:

> So, the guitar is a means to a finer end.
> The environment, then, is in our lungs and at our fingertips.

The paragraph would then proceed to expand and elaborate this revived thesis. We would get a confident assertion that both the music and the friendships are really by-products of an inner alliance; we would get an urgent plea to clean up our personal environs and strengthen our convictions. One rule of thumb: the longer the paper, the more specific the summary of the points you have made. A short paper will need no specific summary of your points at all; the renewed thesis and its widening of implications are sufficient.

Here is an end paragraph by Sir James Jeans. His transitional phrase is *for a similar reason*. His thesis was that previous concepts of physical reality had mistaken surfaces for depths:

> The purely mechanical picture of visible nature fails for a similar reason. It proclaims that the ripples themselves direct the workings of the universe instead of being mere symptoms of occurrences below; in brief, it makes the mistake of thinking that the weather-vane determines the direction from which the wind shall blow, or that the thermometer keeps the room hot.[4]

Here is an end paragraph by Marie-Claire Blais. The list of authors provides a transition from the preceding paragraphs. Her thesis is that, even in a "privileged" society, the creative freedom of writers and other artists can be threatened by intolerance for their ideas:

> Gide, Proust, Wilde, and Radclyffe Hall fought to give us the relative freedom we have now. They fought against the slavery imposed by prejudice, just as Dostoevsky, Dickens, and Zola fought against wage slavery and the reduction of women, men, and children to slavery in factories, in mines, in domestic service. We can write more freely now because of them, but the struggle against every aspect of oppression must go on in every part of the world. For some writers are less free today than writers were fifty or one hundred years ago, and even in the Western world, our liberty is threatened by a reactionary tide. All those writers who are part of the resistance in totalitarian countries are fighting for an ideal of liberty which they think we have here, but we cannot be wholly free until we have helped them attain it.[5]

Remember to write a conclusion when you have used up all your points and had your say. One more paragraph will do it: beginning, middle, *and* end.

The Whole Essay

You have now discovered the main ingredients of a good essay. You have learned to find and to sharpen your thesis in one sentence, to give your essay that all-important argumentative edge. You have learned to arrange

---

[4] Sir James Jeans, *The New Background of Science* (Cambridge: Cambridge University Press, 1933), 261.

[5] Marie-Claire Blais, "The Unending Struggle," in *The Writer and Human Rights*, ed. The Toronto Arts Group for Human Rights (Toronto: Lester & Orpen Dennys, 1983), 136–37.

your points in order of increasing interest, and you have practised disposing of the opposition in a pro–con structure. You have seen that your beginning paragraph should seem like a funnel, working from broad generalization to thesis. You have tried your hand at middle paragraphs, which are almost like little essays with their own beginnings and ends. And finally, you have learned that your last paragraph should work like an inverted funnel, broadening and embellishing your thesis.

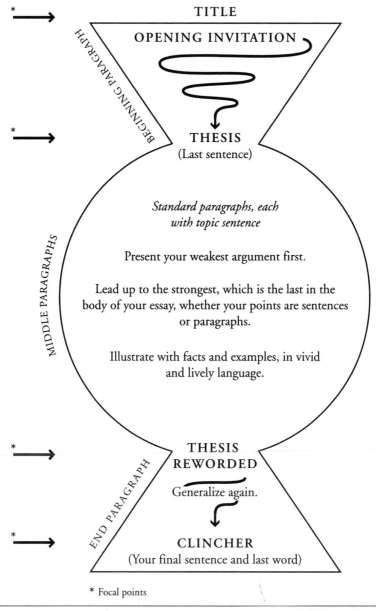

TITLE

OPENING INVITATION

BEGINNING PARAGRAPH

THESIS
(Last sentence)

MIDDLE PARAGRAPHS

Standard paragraphs, each with topic sentence

Present your weakest argument first.

Lead up to the strongest, which is the last in the body of your essay, whether your points are sentences or paragraphs.

Illustrate with facts and examples, in vivid and lively language.

THESIS
REWORDED

Generalize again.

END PARAGRAPH

CLINCHER
(Your final sentence and last word)

* Focal points

Some students have pictured the essay as a Greek column, with a narrowing beginning paragraph as its top, or capital, and a broadening end paragraph as its base. Others have seen it as a keyhole, as suggested by the diagram on the previous page. Picturing your structure like this is very handy. This is the basic pattern; keep it in mind as you write. Check your drafts against it to see where you might amplify or rearrange. The keyhole pattern works out in convenient detail the inevitability of Aristotle's beginning, middle, and end.

The student's essay that follows illustrates this basic structure fairly well. He has picked from his own experience a topic meaningful to anyone.

A Year to Learn

Broad Subject

Learning takes time. A year from first to second grade adds only the rudiments of reading. But after a few years of high school, I thought I knew it all. Diving, with a great coach, took over my interest, and I got into university with a sports scholarship. Then my classes caught fire. I

Narrowing

learned that I wanted to know something, but I needed time to find out what. I took

Thesis

a year off and learned again. *I learned that many students need more of this kind of time off, time to discover who they really want to be.*

Opposition

Of course, *the one who gets through university early gets the preliminary interviews.* You now know your field, as you hope. You now can write those applications for jobs. The competition is stiff, and you are in it from the first, meeting the people from the big companies, getting your name on their lists, hoping you have worn the right things, and said the right things.

Counter-Argument

But a year off takes off the pressure of time. Most of those first interviewees won't land in the land of dreams. They will face the inevitable rejections, the re-applications, the doubts, the changes of goal. A year away from the campus is a valuable step away from all this and into the real world, into learning about yourself and what you really want to know.

Learning takes time. I took that year off from financial necessity. I grew, physically, in fact, and learned. That early pressurized competition had evaporated. I discovered what I really wanted to know. Aside from meeting people and making yourself known to them, and others, a required year off, in a job or social service, *would mature every student for the courses and challenges ahead.*

Thesis Restated

The Clincher

With careful revision, this essay in the keyhole pattern could be effective, because its structure is clear.

Suggested Exercises

1. Below is a list of thesis sentences. Choose one (or its opposite), or make one of your own on the same pattern. Then back off from it at least four or five sentences, and write a funnel-like beginning paragraph leading your readers down to your thesis, the last sentence of your beginning funnel.

   Example (thesis italicized)

   The coal operators will tell you that stripping is cheaper and more efficient than conventional mining. Their 250-cubic-metre draglines, their 200-cubic-metre shovels, their 30-tonne trucks, can rip the top off a mountain and expose a whole seam of coal in a fraction of the time it takes to sink a shaft. "It is cheaper," they will say, "to bring the surface to the coal than to bring the coal to the surface." And of course they are right; in a sense it is cheaper. But visit a mine site and look at the real price we pay for stripped coal. Visit a stripped area and you will see that, no matter how low the price for a truckload of stripped coal, *the real price for strip-mining has to be reckoned in terms of blighted land, poisoned streams, and stunted human lives.*

   a. Television should be cleaned up.
   b. The computer has contributed to the modern sense of alienation.
   c. If Parliament's question period is supposed to guarantee respect for minority opinion, it usually turns out to be a flagrant waste of time.
   d. The evident strength of French-Canadian pride is rooted in an awareness of Quebec's rich cultural heritage.
   e. If girls score lower than boys on math tests, having them compete with boys for scholarships is unfair.

2. Now try the inverted funnel for an end paragraph in which your topic sentence is some version of the thesis you used in Exercise 1, broadening its implications outward to leave the readers fully convinced and satisfied.

   Example (rephrased thesis, or topic sentence, italicized, and some evidence from the paper's middle summarized for emphasis)

   So, at last, we should add up the real costs of strip-mining; we should admit that the ultimate price of coal is far too high if we must rape the land, poison the streams, and wreck human lives to mine it. For after the draglines have gone, even after the coal itself has been burned, the bills for strip-mining will keep coming in. So far, following the expedient path, we have laid bare more than 5,000 square kilometres of our land, and we show no signs of stopping. Every year we strip an additional 20,000 hectares. Just as we cut down our forests in the nineteenth century and fouled our air in the twentieth, we still blunder along toward ecological and social disaster. Isn't it time to stop?

3. Staying with the same topic sentence, develop a full middle paragraph, remembering the five points: (1) the miniature essay, with beginning, middle, and end; (2) repetition; (3) coherence; (4) fullness; (5) transition.

Example (transitional touches italicized)

The streams tell the story *as drearily as* the *eroded land.* In winter, *they* are red with running silt, and sometimes black with *coal* dust. *In summer, many* are no *streams* at all, merely gullies through which the *winter* rains have rushed. Before *the draglines stripped* the earth of its skin, the massed roots of grasses, shrubs, and trees held the soil in place and soaked up the *water,* easing it into the *streams* for a full year's run. Fish fed in pools below *grassy* banks and among the weeds that slowed the *water* to a leisurely pace. Now the *water* is soon gone, if not *poisoned* with *industrial waste,* and the *land* is *gone* with it.

Now you will have a three-paragraph essay that should convey a thorough sense of beginning, middle, end. You might like to add another good middle paragraph or two of illustration, with transitions, for a richer essay, giving a stronger impetus to your end paragraph.

4. To strengthen your feel for coherence and transitional tags, take another look at pages 60–62 and see what you can do with this skeleton:

Forest fires burn thousands of hectares each year. Lodgepole pines release their seeds only when fire sears their cones. Aging and dead trees provide fuel for the fires. Most large animals, like elk and grizzly bears, reach unburned areas. Ashes fertilize seeds of grasses, wild flowers, and shrubs. Some seeds have lain dormant for a hundred years. Aspens spring up again from their roots.

Middle Tactics: Description and Narration; Modes of Exposition

With the whole essay in mind, we will now look more closely at the possibilities in arranging those middle points, the descriptive, narrative, and expository orders that illustrate your argument and carry your ideas. Description talks about what we see; narration, about what we do. Exposition, which often includes both, essentially follows modes of thought—definition, classification and division, comparison and contrast, and cause and effect. All are tactics for the development and arrangement of ideas, and should be kept in mind as you draft your essay (Stage 4). We will consider in particular their relevance to argument and persuasion.

Description

All of your essays partake of description as you bring some point before your readers' eyes: "Children play with tiny cars." Many will need whole paragraphs of description, and some may be purely descriptive as you engage your readers, revealing that *This is beautiful.* Description tells your readers what you see, as in Dionne Brand's description of a leatherback turtle laying her eggs on a beach:

> When my eyes became accustomed to the dark I saw her. She was ancient, her head larger than a human's but somehow human-like and her eyes full of silver tears, her skin, black with tiny white spots, wrinkled. She dug a nest in the sand behind her, measuring, measuring the length of her fin. . . .

She was seventy by her size, broad as the span of my arm and as tall as I am laying down and when she was done and sighed again she covered the hole in the sand and began circling, camouflaging the place she had laid her eggs, making other places looking the same until I could not tell where she had laid them. A leatherback turtle cries on a night like this, her tears are silver and when she is done circling, doing all that she can do she heads laboriously for the sea.[1]

Description is essentially *spatial*. Arranging details in some kind of tour through space is as natural as walking. You can frequently underline your argument with a brief visual tour. When your subject is physical space—the layout of a campus, for instance—you literally take your readers with you. You can sometimes organize by paragraphs as units of space, one for the gate, one for the first building, conducting your readers in an orderly progress down the street or around the quadrangle. Or you show them a rooming house floor by floor, from the apartment by the entry to the garret four flights up, where the graduate student lives on books and cheese. Within the paragraph, you similarly take your readers from one detail to the next in spatial order. Your topic sentence summarizes the total effect: "The Whistler Building was once elegant, three classic stories of brick with carved stoned pediments." Then your paragraph proceeds with noteworthy details in any convenient spatial order: first the sagging front door, then the windows to the left, then those to the right, then the second-floor windows, with their suggestion of dingy apartments, then those of the third, which suggest only emptiness.

You describe what you see, but the other senses may aid your vision, as when Alberto Manguel enters a square in Kairouan, Tunisia:

Kairouan belongs, at least its central core, to the Middle Ages. We arrive in a white public square with squalid palm trees and slowly moving crowds. Ali parks the car outside the butter-yellow wall encircling Old Kairouan and we walk in. There is a scent of tamarind and nutmeg in the air, and of wet wool, the former rising from the spice stalls huddled against the wall, the latter from the many carpet shops displaying their wares on the sidewalks. A bearded man with a black turban growls something at us as we pass. "Crazy," says Ali by way of explanation. "A fundamentalist," he adds. "Crazy with God."[2]

---

[1] Dionne Brand, "Just Rain, Bacolet," in *Writing Away* (Toronto: McClelland and Stewart, 1994), 26–27.

[2] Alberto Manguel, "After Carthage," in *Writing Away*, 166–67.

A city's slum or its crowded parking, a river's pollution, a mountain's trees from valley to timberline—any spatial subject will offer a convenient illustration of your argument, from bottom to top, or top to bottom, left to right, east to west, centre to periphery. You will instinctively use a series of spatial signals: *on the right, above, next, across, down the slope*. Your concern is to keep your progress orderly, to help your reader see what you are talking about, as in Timothy Findley's description of St. Lawrence Gap in Barbados:

> At the southern tip of Barbados, in the parish of Christ Church, there is a stretch of coral sand that is known as St. Lawrence Gap. To the east—with its historic churches, chattel houses, and fish market—the town of Oistins lies in the curve of a wide, green bay. This is where you go when you want to buy fish taken from the sea that morning—or fresh shrimp. Away to the west, beyond the Needham Point Lighthouse, the old city of Bridgetown spreads its narrow streets and alleyways in a maze of charming chaos. Along the roads that run between these towns, there are dozens of hotels and restaurants offering a choice of food and lodging for every taste and pocketbook.[3]

As you can *see*, literally, the best spatial description follows the perceptions of a person looking at or entering the space described, reporting the impressions, the colours, textures, sights, or sounds as they come, as with Jane Urquhart's return to a house in France where she had once lived for a year:

> Because I chose late November to make this pilgrimage, it was already dark when I arrived in the village on a Thursday afternoon. I collected the key and six brown eggs from the farming family across the street, and opened the familiar oak door. The interior of the house was just as I remembered it; the tiles in the kitchen, the cream-coloured walls, the old stone sink, the crack in the bedroom ceiling. I lit room after room, expecting to be confronted with some evidence of change. There was none. Spoons in drawers, goblets in cabinets, the grain on the oak stairs, the pattern on the salon rug, mirrors and pictures on walls, the figures of birds worked into lace curtains were just as they had been.[4]

Some novels proceed like this paragraph after paragraph, as in the beginning of Thomas Hardy's *The Return of the Native*, in which we are moved

---

[3] Timothy Findley, "Barbados: The Very Pineapple of Perfection," in *Writing Away*, 63. Copyright © Pebble Productions Inc.

[4] Jane Urquhart, "Returning to the Village," in *Writing Away*, 318.

into the setting from a great distance, as if, years before moving pictures, we are riding a cinematographer's dolly.

Description frequently blends time and space, picking out striking features then moving along. This is the usual way of describing people, as in this paragraph about a Barbadian woman who sells pineapples on the beach:

> The Pineapple Woman must be in her seventies. Her grey hair is cropped short, most of it hidden beneath a soft wool hat. Her legs are bare and bowed. She wears a cotton dress, one day of white and blue, another day of red and yellow. Sandals on her feet, a crucifix at her throat, and several beaten silver bracelets on her arms. As she walks away along the beach, she hoists the multi-coloured satchel onto her head and, counting her take, moves on to her next encounter.[5]

Narration

In contrast with description, narration is essentially *temporal*. Like space, time is a natural organizer. Hour follows hour, day follows day, year follows year, life follows life. Again, you illustrate your argument by taking your readers along the natural sequence of what happens—to us, or to nations, or to any items in experience or experiment. We understand processes most clearly by tracking the way they move through time, even processes complicated by other, simultaneous events:

> And when this wheel turns, that lever tips the food into the trough.
> While this conveyor moves into the oven, the other one is bringing the chassis to point B.
> And all the time he talked, his hands were moving the shells and flicking the invisible pea.

Any event, whether a football game or the swearing in of a prime minister, can be best perceived as you have perceived it—through time—and you can bring your reader to perceive it by following the sequence of things as they happened, stepping aside as necessary to explain background and simultaneous events, guiding your reader along with temporal sign-posts: *at the same time, now, when, while, then, before, after, next, all the time.*

---

[5] Timothy Findley, "Barbados: The Very Pineapple of Perfection," in *Writing Away*, 62. Copyright © Pebble Productions Inc.

As Audubon, the nineteenth-century naturalist, describes the passenger pigeon and its astounding flights in masses 2 kilometres wide and 300 kilometres long, he naturally gives us his observations through the order of time. I have italicized the temporal words in one of his paragraphs:

> *As soon as* the pigeons discover a sufficiency of food to entice them to alight, they fly round in circles, reviewing the country below. *During* their evolutions, *on such occasions*, the dense mass which they form exhibits a beautiful appearance, *as* it changes direction, *now* displaying a glistening sheet of azure, *when* the backs of the birds come *simultaneously* into view, *and anon*, *suddenly* presenting a mass of rich deep purple. They *then* pass lower, over the woods, and *for a moment* are lost among the foliage, *but again* emerge, and are seen gliding aloft. They *now* alight, but *the next moment*, as if *suddenly* alarmed, they take to wing, producing by the flappings of their wings a noise like the roar of distant thunder, and sweep through the forests to see if danger is near. Hunger, however, *soon* brings them to the ground. *When* alighted, they are seen industriously throwing up the withered leaves. . . .[6]

Sometimes an argumentative essay will give over its entire middle to a narrative of some event that illustrates its thesis, as in George Orwell's great "Shooting an Elephant." Orwell's thesis is that imperialism tyrannizes over the rulers as well as the ruled. To illustrate it, he tells of an incident during his career as a young police officer in Burma, when he was compelled, by the expectations of the crowd, to shoot a renegade elephant. Here is a narrative paragraph in which Orwell reports a crucial moment; notice how he mixes external events and snippets of conversation with his inner thoughts, pegging all perfectly with a topic sentence:

> But I did not want to shoot the elephant. I watched him beating his bunch of grass against his knees, with that preoccupied grandmotherly air that elephants have. It seemed to me that it would be murder to shoot him. At that age I was not squeamish about killing animals, but I had never shot an elephant and never wanted to. (Somehow it always seems worse to kill a large animal.) Besides, there was the beast's owner to be considered. Alive, the elephant was worth at least a hundred pounds; dead, he would only be worth the value of his tusks, five pounds, possibly. But I had got to act quickly. I turned to some experienced-looking Burmans who had been there when we arrived,

---

[6] John James Audubon, *Ornithological Biography* (Edinburgh: Black, 1831–49).

and asked them how the elephant had been behaving. They all said the same thing: he took no notice of you if you left him alone, but he might charge if you went too close to him.[7]

Orwell is simply recounting events and his thoughts, as they happened, one after the other. Almost any kind of essay could use a similar paragraph of narrative to illustrate a point.

Modes of Exposition

Exposition is a setting forth, an explaining, that naturally may include both description and narration. But it also includes some essential modes of thought: comparison and contrast, cause and effect, classification, definition. Good exposition depends on specific details and examples to illustrate its general point.

Loren Eiseley, for instance, illustrates his generalization "These apes are not all similar" not only with comparative contrasts but also with particularized specifics, as he upholds Alfred Russel Wallace's view against Charles Darwin's as to the evolution of the human brain from that of the humanoid ape:

> These apes are not all similar in type or appearance. They are men and yet not men. Some are frailer-bodied, some have great, bone-cracking jaws and massive gorilloid crests atop their skulls. This fact leads us to another of Wallace's remarkable perceptions of long ago. With the rise of the truly human brain, Wallace saw that man had transferred to his machines and tools many of the alterations of parts that in animals take place through evolution of the body. Unwittingly, man had assigned to his machines the selective evolution which in the animal changes the nature of its bodily structure through the ages. Man of today, the atomic manipulator, the aeronaut who flies faster than sound, has precisely the same brain and body as his ancestors of twenty thousand years ago who painted the last Ice Age mammoths on the walls of caves in France.[8]

Notice how he spells out the specifics of bodies, jaws, and skulls. He does not say "aeronauts," plural, but *the* single and specific *aeronaut*, adding

---

[7] George Orwell, "Shooting an Elephant," in *Shooting an Elephant and Other Essays.* Copyright © Mark Hamilton as the Literary Executor of the Estate of the Late Sonia Brownell Orwell. Reprinted by permission of Martin Secker & Warburg Limited and A. M. Heath & Co. Ltd.

[8] Loren Eiseley, "The Real Secret of Piltdown," in *The Immense Journey* (New York: Random House, 1955). Copyright © 1955 by Loren C. Eiseley.

the further specific *who flies faster than sound*, letting that single specific person illustrate the whole general range of what man can do with machines. He does not say merely "ancestors," but *ancestors of* specifically *twenty thousand years ago*; not merely "lived," but *who painted*, and not merely "pictures," but *the last Ice Age mammoths*, and specifically on *walls* in specific *caves* in one specific country, *France*. The point is to try to extend each of your generalizations by adding some specific detail to illustrate it. Don't stop with *awkward players are miserable*: go on to *when they strike out, miss an easy fly, or lose the puck*.

Your illustration may also be hypothetical, as it frequently is in scientific explanation. With a thesis like *Relativity is not so inscrutable as many think*, you might illustrate with a paragraph something like this:

> Suppose someone riding in a car drops a ball. We see it fall straight down to the floor. But the ball also traces a long line slanting downward relative to the rapidly receding highway beneath the car. If the highway curves, the ball also traces an invisible curve. Adding the ball's drop relative to the earth's movement around the sun may be hard to imagine, but calculations of such relative motion are what send our rockets to their meetings with the moon or Mars.

Comparison and Contrast: Run Contrasts Side by Side

Comparison and contrast is a natural mode of thought, a natural organizer of exposition, making two specifics vivid by bringing them side by side. It may be the very basis of thought itself, as it certainly is of dialectic persuasion. All knowledge involves comparing things for their similarities and noticing their contrasting differences. We group all people as people and then tell them apart as individuals.

We instinctively know our friends in this way, for instance. Two of them drift side by side in our thoughts. We are comparing them. They are both men; they are the same age and stature; we like them both. But one bubbles up like a mountain spring, and the other runs deep. Their appearances, mannerisms, and tastes match their contrasting personalities. One's room is messy; the other's is neat. One races his car; the other reads the Romantic poets. We compare the similar categories—looks, habits, hobbies, goals—and contrast the difference. Your thesis might be something neutrally expository like "Differences make life interesting," or it may affirm what makes a better person.

Your topic sentence sets the comparison and makes the contrast:

> Opposites seem to attract. *My father, a lawyer, is quiet and studious, a music lover. My mother, a clinical psychologist, is vivacious and gregarious.* She loves a party, a play, a crowd of friends, being in the social whirl. Dad, though good with people, would probably just as soon stay home with a book and a symphony on the stereo. He builds model airplanes. Mom plays bridge almost at the master's level. But when they come in from their different days, they grin and compare notes, she taking in some calm, he some zest for human involvements. They obviously still find each other attractive.

Contrast

Comparison and Contrast: Illustrate by Analogy

An analogy emphasizes similarities between things otherwise dissimilar. With an analogy, you help your reader grasp your subject by showing how it is like something familiar. Your topic sentence asserts the comparison, and then your paragraph unfolds the comparison in detail:

> School spirit is like patriotism. Students take their school's fortunes as their own, defending and promoting them against those of another school, as citizens champion their country, right or wrong. Their school is not only their alma mater but their fatherland as well. Like soldiers, they will give their utmost strength in sports and intellectual contests for both personal glory and the greater glory of the domain they represent. And, in defeat, they will mourn as if dragged in chains through the streets of Rome.

Here is Farley Mowat describing how an Inuit's deerskin clothing acts as a "house." His comparison shows that analogy is really a form of extended metaphor:

> The tent and the igloo are really only auxiliary shelters. The real home of the Ihalmio is much like that of the turtle, for it is what he carries about on his back. In truth it is the only house that can enable men to survive on the merciless plains of the Barrens. It has central heating from the fat furnace of the body, its walls are insulated to a degree of perfection that we white men have not been able to surpass, or even to emulate. It is complete, light in weight, easy to make and easy to keep in repair. It costs nothing, for it is a gift of the land,

Topic Sentence with Analogy

through the deer. When I consider that house, my opinion of the astuteness of the Ihalmiut is no longer clouded.[9]

That is probably as long as an analogy can run effectively. One paragraph is about the limit. Beyond that, the reader may tire of it.

Comparison Versus Contrast

Comparison illuminates the unknown with the known, emphasizing similarities:

> This year's team has all the makings of last year's champions.
> Throstle is a twentieth-century Wordsworth.

The essays under these theses would then favour these unknowns, point by point, with their similarities to the paragons.

Contrast, on the other hand, compares similar things to emphasize their differences—formal gardens as against natural gardens, for example—usually to persuade the readers that one is in some or most ways better than the other.

Remember to keep both sides before the readers. You may do this in one of two ways: (1) by making a topic sentence to cover one point—gardens—and then continuing your paragraph in paired sentences, one for the formal, one for the natural, another for the formal, and so on; or (2) by writing your paragraphs in pairs, one paragraph for the formal, one for the natural, using the topic sentence of the first paragraph to govern the second, something like this:

Topic Sentence *The formal garden still holds a certain edge over the natural garden that overtook it in the eighteenth century.* Small box hedges, cut squarely and sharply in geometrical lines and orderly arabesques, contain glories of bright begonias, sweet williams, and violas. Sharp cones of yews punctuate the expanding order of smooth lawns. . . .

Contrast *In the natural garden, on the other hand, unkempt hedges wander off.* Flowering trees bloom wildly for a week. Yews sprawl along extending meadows. . . .

In an extended contrast, you will probably want to contrast some things sentence against sentence, within single paragraphs, and to contrast others by giving a paragraph to each. But remember to keep your readers sufficiently in touch with both sides.

---

[9] Farley Mowat, *People of the Deer* (Toronto: McClelland and Stewart, 1975), 127. Used by permission of McClelland and Stewart, Inc., *The Canadian Publishers*.

Here are two paragraphs from a student's paper neatly contrasted without losing touch:

In fact, *in some respects the commercials are* Topic Sentence
really better than the shows they sponsor. The
commercials are carefully rehearsed, expertly First Subject
photographed, highly edited and pol-
ished. They are made with absolute attention
to detail and to the clock. One split-second
over time, one bad note, one slightly wrinkled dress, and they are done over again.
Weeks, even months, go into the production of
a single sixty-second commercial.

The shows, on the other hand, are slapped Contrast
together hastily by writers and performers who
have less than a week to put together an hour
show. Actors have little time to rehearse, and
often the pieces of a show are put together
for the first time in front of the camera.
Lighting, sound reproduction, and editing are
workmanlike, but unpolished; a shadow from an
overhead microphone on an actor's face causes
no real concern in the control room. In all,
it often takes less time and money to do an
hour show than to do the commercials that
sponsor it.

Contrasts done sentence by sentence, or by clauses hinged on a semi-colon, are also effective:

The most essential distinction between athletics and education lies in the institution's own interest in the athlete as distinguished from its interest in its other students. Universities
attract students in order to teach them what they do not
already know; they recruit athletes only when they are already
proficient. Students are educated for something which will be
useful to them and to society after graduation; athletes are
required to spend their time on activities the usefulness of
which disappears upon graduation or soon thereafter.
Universities exist to do what they can for students; athletes are
recruited for what they can do for the universities. This makes
the operation of the athletic program in which recruited players are used basically different from any educational interest of
colleges and universities.[10]

---

[10] Harold W. Stoke, "College Athletics: Education or Show Business?" *Atlantic Monthly* (March 1954): 46–50. Copyright © 1954 by Harold W. Stoke.

Cause and Effect: Trace Back or Look Ahead

Because is the impulse here: "Such and such is so *because*. . . ." You think back through a train of causes, each one the effect of something prior; or you think your way into the future, speculating about the possible effects of some present cause. In other words, you organize your paragraph in one of two ways:

1. You state a general effect, then deal with its several causes.
2. You state a general cause, then deal with its possible effects.

In Arrangement 1, you know the effect (a lost football game, or the solar system, let us say), and you speculate as to causes. In Arrangement 2, you know the cause (a new restriction, or abolishing nuclear weapons, let us say), and you speculate as to the effects.

Arrangement 1: Effect Followed by Causes

> An unusual cluster of bad luck lost the game. Many blamed Fraser's failure to block the tackler who caused the fumble that produced the winning touchdown. But even here, bad weather and bad luck shared the blame. Both teams faced a slippery field, of course. But Fraser was standing in a virtual bog when he lunged for the block and slipped. Moreover, the storm had delayed the bus for hours, tiring and frustrating the team, leaving them short of sleep and with no chance to practise. Furthermore, Hunter's throwing arm was still not back in shape from his early injury. Finally, one must admit, the Ravens were simply heavier and stronger, which is the real luck of the game.

You will probably notice, as you try to explain causes and effects, that they do not always run in a simple linear sequence, one thing following another, like a row of falling dominoes. Indeed, mere sequence is so famously untrustworthy in tracing causes that one of the classical errors of thought is named *post hoc, ergo propter hoc* ("after this, therefore because of this"). In other words, we cannot reasonably suppose that A caused B simply because A preceded B. The two may have been entirely unrelated. But the greatest danger in identifying causes is to fasten upon a single cause while ignoring others of equal significance. Both your paragraph and your persuasiveness will be better if you do not insist, as some did, that only Fraser's failure to block the tackler lost the game.

In the lost ball game, you were interested in explaining causes, but sometimes your interest will lie with effects. When describing a slum problem, for instance, your topic sentence might be "The downtown slum is a screaming disgrace" (the effect), and you might then in a single sentence set aside the causes as irrelevant, as water over the dam, as so much spilt milk: "perhaps caused by inefficiency, perhaps by avarice, perhaps by the indifference of Mayor Richman." Your interests will dictate your proportions of cause and effect. You might well write an entire essay that balances the slum's causes and effects in equal proportions: a paragraph each on inefficiency, avarice, and the mayor's indifference, then a paragraph each on ill health, poor education, and hopelessness.

Here is how a brief essay, in three paragraphs, can deal with cause and effect alone. I begin and end with the *effect* (the peculiar layout of a town). First, I locate the *immediate cause* (cattle) as my thesis, and then, in the middle paragraph, I move through the cause and its *conditions* up to the *effect* again—the town as it stands today:

North of the Tracks

If you drive out west from Chicago, you will notice something happening to the towns. *After the country levels into Nebraska, the smaller towns are built only on one side of the road.* When you stop for a rest, and look south across the broad main street, you will see the railroad immediately beyond. *All of these towns spread northward from the tracks. Why?* As you munch your hamburger and look at the restaurant's murals, *you will realize that the answer is cattle.* [Effect / Effect / Thesis]

These towns were the destinations of the great cattle drives from Texas. They probably had begun at the scattered watering places in the dry land. Then *the wagon trails and,* finally, *the transcontinental railroad had strung them together.* Once the railroad came, the whole Southwest could raise cattle for the slaughterhouses of Chicago. The droves of cattle came up from the south, and *all of these towns reflect the traffic:* corrals beside the tracks to the south, the road for passengers and wagons parallelling the tracks on the northern side, then, along the road, the row of hotels, saloons, and businesses, with the town spreading northward behind the businesses. [Cause Conditions / Causes / Effect]

The cattle business itself shaped these one-sided Nebraska towns. The conditions in which this immediate cause took root were the growing population in the East and the railroad that connected the plains of the West, and Southwest, with the tables of New York. The towns took their hopeful being north of the rails, on the leeward side of the vast cattle drives [Causes] from the south. The trade in cattle has now changed, all the way from Miami to Sacramento. But *the great herds of the old Southwest, together with the transcontinental railroad and man's need to make a living, plotted these Western towns north of the tracks.*

Arrangement 2: Cause Followed by Probable Effects

Arrangement 2 is the staple of deliberative rhetoric, of all political and economic forecasting, for instance. Your order of presenting cause and effect is reversed. You are looking to the future. You state a known cause (a new ban on smoking in restaurants) or a hypothetical cause ("If this ban is passed"), and then you speculate about the possible, or probable, effects. Your procedure will then be much the same as before. But, for maximum persuasiveness, try to keep your supposed effects, which no one can really foresee, as nearly probable as you can.

Lending Students Debt

With costs for education rising annually, more students must supplement their family's funds or miss university completely. Many work during summers and find part-time jobs for the academic year. Many also still need loans, particularly for advanced degrees. But an expanded system of government-guaranteed loans to students carries more burdens than benefits.

On the surface, such loans promise entrance to university to many students otherwise unable to attend. Some regions have few local funds available for loans, and taxpayers are against more help for students that would add to the local government's debt. A program of federal loans would seem to promise equal opportunity for all qualified students.

Actually, most universities do offer financial aid to needy and worthy students. Many fellowships go unclaimed because no one applies for them. The temptation of an easy loan against paying as you go with extra work is the essential defect of governmental assistance.

To be sure, concentrating on one's studies without the drain on time and energy from a job would seem a distinct advantage. But if we honestly look at our schedules, we have more free time

Margin labels: Thesis: Cause with Effects · Effects: Con · Pro, Factual · Effects: Pro · Effects: Con

than we admit, a lot of it spent in nonacademic
activities. A few hours of work actually budgets Effects: Pro
one's time and concentrates the hours of study.

If more governmental aid for students would Effects: Con
spread opportunity for all, it would also spread Effects: Pro
bureaucracy, with new agencies to set up loans
and track them down. Local loans to students, on
the other hand, are now managed by local staff
already in place and effectively doing other
things too.

But the cost to individual students is prob- Effects: Pro
ably the biggest burden. Instead of paying as
they go, perhaps with some short-term local help
or even by working for a year, they would be
tempted to borrow more than they can afford and
would then have to face monthly payments for
years to come.

This student's projected effects hold fairly well to the probable.
Occasionally, of course, you may put an improbable hypothetical cause to
good use in a satiric essay, reducing some proposal to absurdity: "If all
restrictions were abolished. . . ." "If no one wore clothes. . . ." Or the
improbable *if* may even help clarify a straightforward explanation of real
relationships, as in the following explanation of a scientific idea for the
layperson. The paragraph states the general condition, proposes a hypothetical cause with an *if,* then moves to the effects:

> Fred Hoyle, the British astronomer and mathematician, mod-
> ified the theories of Newton and Einstein. He began with the
> idea that the mass and gravity of the sun and Earth are influ-
> enced both by each other and by other stars and galaxies. Then
> he hypothesized that, if the universe were cut in half, gravity
> within the solar system would double, and Earth would move
> closer to the sun. As a result, the weight of people on Earth
> would also double. The increased gravity would increase the
> pressure within the sun, which would therefore burn hotter
> and brighter and create more energy, and living beings on
> Earth would be burnt to a crisp.

Classification: Use the Natural Divisions

Many subjects fall into natural or customary classifications, contrasting
one category with the next: Reform, Conservative, Liberal, NDP; right,
middle, left; municipal, provincial, federal. You can easily follow these

divisions in organizing a paragraph, or you can write one paragraph for each division, and attain a nicely coherent essay. Similarly, any manufacturing process, or any machine, will already have distinct steps and parts. These customary divisions will help your readers, since they know something of them already. Describe the Liberal position on inflation, and they will naturally expect your description of the Reform or Conservative position to follow. If no other divisions suggest themselves, you can often organize your paragraph—or your essay—into a consistent series of parallel answers, or "reasons for," or "reasons against," something like this:

> A broad liberal education is best:
> 1. It prepares you for a world of changing employment.
> 2. It enables you to function well as a citizen.
> 3. It enables you to make the most of your life.

Many problems present natural classifications. Take the Panama Canal, for instance. Its construction divides into three neat problems—political, geological, and biological—each with its solutions, as the following paragraph shows:

> Building the Panama Canal posed problems of politics, geology, and human survival from the beginning. *A French company, organized in 1880 to dig the canal, repeatedly had to extend its treaties at higher and higher prices as the work dragged on.* Uneasy about the French, *the United States made treaties with Nicaragua and Costa Rica* to dig along the other most feasible route. *This political threat,* together with the failure of the French and the revolt of Panama from Colombia, *finally enabled the United States to buy the French rights and negotiate new treaties,* which, nevertheless, continued to cause political trouble until the 1980s. *Geology also posed its ancient problems:* how to manage torrential rivers and inland lakes; whether to build a longer but more enduring canal at sea level, or *a shorter, cheaper, and safer canal with locks.* Economy eventually won, but the problem of *yellow fever and malaria,* which had plagued the French, remained. *By detecting and combatting the fever-carrying mosquito, William Gorgas solved these ancient tropical problems.* Without him, the political and geological solutions would have come to nothing.

Labels in margin: Problem 1, Solution 1, Problem 2, Solution 2, Problem 3, Solution 3

You could easily organize this into three paragraphs of problem and solution, with topic sentences like these:

> The Panama Canal posed three major problems, the first of which was political.
> The second problem was geological, a massive problem of engineering.

The third problem, that of human survival, proved the most
stubborn of all.

Any problem and its solution can produce a neatly ordered paragraph—
or essay, for that matter: choosing a university, or something to wear (if
you want to be lighthearted), making an apartment or a commune work,
building the Eiffel Tower or the pyramids. You can often similarly classify sets of comparisons and contrasts, causes and effects, combining your
tactics with magnified force.

In the following paper, a student has nicely amalgamated description,
narration, and the classification implied in a problem and its solution to
analyse a fascinating process.

Nothing Primitive About It

Stonehenge, the gigantic prehistoric construction on the Salisbury Plain in
England, cannot fail to fascinate us with a
number of nearly unanswerable questions.
How long has it been there? Who built it?
Why? But of all the questions Stonehenge
raises, none is more intriguing than *"How*   Thesis
was it built?" How did these primitive peo-   Problem 1
ple, whose only tools were rock, bone, or   Description
crudely fashioned sticks, who had not yet   and Narration
even discovered the wheel, *manage to trans-*
port the huge rocks, most of them more than
six metres in length and weighing over
thirty tonnes, *more than thirty kilometres*
and overland? And by what ingenuity did   Problem 2
they manage, having transported the rocks,
to stand them on end and support them so
that now, thousands of years later, most of
them still stand? What primitive engineering geniuses were these?

Transporting the stones from their orig-   Narrating the
inal site at Marlborough Downs, some thir-   Process
ty kilometres to the north of Stonehenge,
must have been, by any of the possible
means, a very slow process. One possibili-
ty is that *hundreds of people*, some pulling   Solutions to 1
on the rock, some cutting down trees and   First
filling in holes as they went, *simply*   Classification
dragged the stones over the bare ground. Or
perhaps they used snow or mud to "grease"
the path. Metre by metre, and day by day,

they may have dragged the rocks all the way from Marlborough Downs to Stonehenge. *Another guess is that these primitive people*, even though they had not yet invented the wheel, *knew about using logs as rollers*. If so, perhaps they mounted each stone on a sledge, and rolled the sledge slowly forward, workers placing logs in its path as it moved. Such a method, while a good deal easier than dragging the rock along the ground, would still have required as many as seven or eight hundred people, and perhaps as much as a decade to move all the stones. *A third possibility is that the stones were moved along riverbeds*, the shallow water helping to buoy the weight, and the muddy banks helping to slide the weight along. Though much less direct than the overland route, the riverbed route would have provided these primitive people with a relatively clear path that ran approximately halfway from the stones' point of origin to their final location. Of course, the point is that any of these three means of transporting the stones must have been an incredibly laborious task, occupying as many as a thousand people, year after year after year.

Lifting the stones into an upright position, once they had been transported, was another triumph of ingenuity and brute strength. Apparently, the workers dug closely fitted holes where they wanted the stones eventually to stand. Probably they cut away one side of the hole, the side nearest the stone, to form a ramp. Perhaps they also lined the hole with wooden skids. Then gradually they eased the stone down the ramp until it rested in a tilted position at the bottom of the hole. Next, they used brute strength, some people pushing, some pulling on primitive ropes, to raise the rock into a vertical position. If we suppose each person lifted 75 kilograms, it might have taken as many as 400 workers to

stand the stones upright. Finally, while
some workers held the rock in position,
others quickly filled in the excavation
left by the ramp. For many months afterward
they probably refilled and pounded the dirt
until it was completely firm. They probably
placed the huge transverse pieces across
the tops of columns by similarly dragging
them up long earthen ramps. The fact that
most of the rocks are still standing after
thousands of years is testimony of their
planning and work.

We may never know quite why these primitive people chose to build Stonehenge, or
who they were. We may never know where they
came from, or where they went. *In
Stonehenge, however, they have left a testament to their perseverance and their
ingenuity. Clearly, they rivalled any of
the builders of the ancient world.*

Thesis
Restated

Definition: Clear Up Your Terms

Definition is another mode of classification, in which we clear away hidden
assumptions along with unwanted categories. What the Cubans and Chinese call
a People's Democracy is the very opposite of what Canadians call democracy,
assumed also to be of and for and by the people. Ideally, your running prose
should make your terms clear to your reader, avoiding those definitions that seem
too stiff and stuffy, and should especially avoid quoting the dictionary: "As
Webster's says. . . ." Nevertheless, what we mean by *egotism, superiority, education,*
or *character* may need laying on the table.

Richard Hofstadter, for instance, found it necessary in his essay
"Democracy and Anti-Intellectualism in America" to devote a number of
paragraphs to defining both *democracy* and *intellectual,* each paragraph
examining the evidence and clarifying one aspect of his term. Coming
early in his essay, after he has set his thesis and surveyed his subject, his
section of definition begins with the following paragraph:

> *But what is an intellectual, really?* This is a problem of definition
> that I found, when I came to it, far more elusive than I had antic-
> ipated. *A great deal of what might be called the journeyman's work
> of our culture*—the work of engineers, physicians, newspaper-
> men, and indeed of most professors—*does not strike me as dis-*

Topic Sentence
as Question

What It Is *Not*

tinctively intellectual, although it is certainly work based in an

What It *Is*

important sense on ideas. *The distinction that we must recognize, then, is one* originally made by Max Weber *between living **for** ideas and living **off** ideas. The intellectual lives for ideas;* the jour-

Con: Examples

neyman lives off them. *The engineer or the physician*—I don't mean here to be invidious—*needs to have a pretty considerable capital stock in frozen ideas* to do his work; but they *serve for him a purely instrumental purpose: he lives off them, not for them.* Of

Pro: Examples

course *he may also be, in his private role and his personal ways of thought, an intellectual,* but it is not necessary for him to be in order to work at his profession. There is in fact no profession

Con: Detailed Opposition

which demands that one be an intellectual. *There do seem to be vocations, however, which almost demand that one be an anti-intellectual,* in which those who live off ideas seem to have implacable hatred for those who live for them. The marginal intellectual workers and the unfrocked intellectuals who work in journalism, advertising, and mass communication are the bitterest and most powerful among those who work at such vocations.[11]

Your subject will prompt you in one of two ways, toward inclusiveness or toward exclusiveness. Hofstadter found that he needed to be inclusive about the several essentials in *democracy* and *intellectual*—terms used commonly, and often loosely. Inclusiveness is the usual need, as you will find in trying to define *love* or *loyalty* or *education.* But you may sometimes need to move in the opposite direction, toward exclusiveness, as in sociological, philosophical, or scientific discussion, when you need to nail your terms firmly to single meanings: "By *reality,* I mean only that which exists in the physical world, excluding our ideas about it."

Such exclusive defining is called *stipulative,* since you stipulate the precise meaning you want. But you should avoid the danger of trying to exclude more than the word will allow. If you try to limit the meaning of the term *course* to "three hours a week a semester," your discussion will soon encounter courses with different hours; or you may find yourself inadvertently drifting to another meaning, as you mention something about graduating from an "engineering course." At any rate, if you can avoid the sound of dogmatism in your stipulation, so much the better. You may well practise some disguise, as with *properly speaking* and *only* in the following stipulative definition: "Properly speaking, the *structure* of any literary work is only that framelike quality we can picture in two, or three, dimensions."

---

[11] Richard Hofstadter, "Democracy and Anti-Intellectualism in America," *The Michigan Alumnus Quarterly Review* 59 (1953): 282. Copyright © 1953 by the University of Michigan.

Definitions frequently seem to develop into paragraphs, almost by second nature. A sentence of definition is usually short and crisp, seeming to demand some explanation, some illustration and sociability. The definition, in other words, is a natural topic sentence. Here are three classic single-sentence kinds of definition that will serve well as topics for your paragraphs:

1. *Definition by synonym.* A quick way to stipulate the single meaning you want: "Virtue means moral rectitude."
2. *Definition by function.* "A barometer measures atmospheric pressure"—"A social barometer measures human pressures"—"A good quarterback calls the signals and sparks the whole team's spirits."
3. *Definition by synthesis.* A placement of your term in striking (and not necessarily logical) relationship to its whole class, usually for the purpose of wit: "The fox is the craftiest of beasts"—"A sheep is a friendlier form of goat"—"A lexicographer is a harmless drudge"—"A sophomore is a sophisticated moron."

Three more classic kinds of definition follow, of broader dimensions than the single-sentence kinds above, but also ready-made for a paragraph apiece, or for several. Actually, in making paragraphs from your single-sentence definitions, you have undoubtedly used at least one of these three kinds, or a mixture of them all. They are no more than the natural ways we define our meanings.

4. *Definition by example.* The opposite of *definition by synthesis.* You start with the class ("crafty beasts") and then name a member or two ("fox—plus monkey and raccoon"). But of course you would go on to give further examples or illustrations—accounts of how the bacon was snitched through the screen—that broaden your definition beyond the mere naming of class and members.
5. *Definition by comparison.* You just use a paragraph of comparison to expand and explain your definition. Begin with a topic sentence something like "Love is like the sun." Then extend your comparison on to the end of the paragraph (or even separate it, if your cup runneth over, into several paragraphs), as you develop the idea: "Love is like the sun because it too gives out warmth, makes everything bright, shines even when it is not seen, and is indeed the centre of our lives."
6. *Definition by analysis.* This is Hofstadter's way, a searching out and explaining of the essentials in terms used generally, loosely, and often in ways that emphasize incidentals for biased reasons, as when it is said that an *intellectual* is a manipulator of ideas.

Here are four good steps to take in reaching a thorough definition of something, assuring that you have covered all the angles. Consider:

1. What it *is not like.*
2. What it *is like.*
3. What it *is not.*
4. What it *is.*

This program can produce a good paragraph of definition:

> Love may be many things to many people, but, all in all, we
> agree on its essentials. *Love is not like a rummage sale,* in which   1
> people try to grab what they want. *It is more like a Christmas,*   2
> in which gifts and thoughtfulness come just a little unexpect-
> edly, even from routine directions. *Love, in short, is not a mat-*   3
> *ter of seeking self-satisfaction; it is first a matter of giving and*   4
> *then discovering,* as an unexpected gift, *the deepest satisfaction*
> *one can know.*

The four steps above can also furnish four effective paragraphs, which you would present in the same order of ascending interest and climax. But, finally, the point is simply to consider the advantage of the dialectic *is not* in highlighting the *is* in your definitions.

Definition: Avoid the Pitfalls

1. Avoid echoing the term you are defining. Do not write "Courtesy is being courteous" or "Freedom is feeling free." Look around for synonyms: "Courtesy is being polite, being attentive to others' needs, making them feel at ease, using what society accepts as good manners." You can go against this rule to great advantage, however, if you repeat the *root* of the word meaningfully: "Courtesy is treating your girlfriend like a princess in her *court.*"
2. Don't make your definitions too narrow—except for humour ("Professors are only disappointed students"). Do not write: "Communism is subversive totalitarianism." Obviously, your definition needs more breadth, something about sharing property, and so forth.
3. Don't make your definition too broad. Do not go uphill in your terms, as in "Vanity is pride" or "Affection is love." Bring the definers down to the same level: "Vanity is a kind of frivolous personal pride"—"Affection is a mild and chronic case of love."

Suggested Exercises

1. Write a paragraph describing a unit of space, taking your readers from the outside to the inside of your own home, for instance, or dealing with some interesting spatial unit, as in the following paragraph from a student's paper.

    Example

    > The courtyard of the hotel at Uxmal was a wonderfully cool and welcome surprise after the sweaty bus trip out from Mérida. Surrounding the whole yard was a large *galería,* its ceiling blocking out the few rays of the sun that managed to filter through the heavy plantings that filled the yard. Overhead, along the *galería,* ceiling fans quietly turned, and underfoot the glazed tile floors felt smooth and delightfully cool even though the temperature on the road had pushed up past 32 degrees. Airy wicker chairs lined the railing, and just a few feet away, flowering jungle plants rose almost to the top of the stone arches on the second floor. Under the branches of a tall tree in the middle of the courtyard, out beyond the rail and the thick plantings, raised tile walkways crisscrossed the yard, bordered all along by neatly cultivated jungle flowers. And right in the middle of the yard, at the base of the big tree, a small waterfall splashed down over mossy rocks into a tiny bathing pool. The splashing water, the shade, the cool tile—all made the road outside seem very far off indeed.

2. Write a narrative paragraph in which you blend the incidents and thoughts of a crucial moment, as in Orwell's paragraph on page 74.

3. Write a paragraph comparing two people—like the one on page 77.

4. **a.** Write a paragraph developed by contrasts, running them point by point, as in the paragraph contrasting "students" and "athletes" on page 79.
    b. Write two paragraphs contrasting something like high school and university, small town and city, football and baseball, men and women—the first paragraph describing one, the second the other, and the two using parallel contrasting terms, as in the example contrasting the kinds of garden (page 78) or the television commercials and shows (page 79).

5. Write a paragraph of *effect* followed by *causes,* like that on page 80 (Arrangement 1).

6. Write a paragraph about some *cause* followed by its probable *effects,* like that on page 83 (Arrangement 2). Work in a hypothetical effect if you can.

7. Here are some topics that fall conveniently into natural divisions. For each topic, list the divisions that occur to you.
    a. causes affecting the rate at which a population grows
    b. levels of government
    c. undersea exploration
    d. geological eras
    e. mathematics in public school

8. Write a paragraph using one of the topics and the divisions you have worked out in Exercise 7.

9. Using the classifications of problem and solution, write a three- or four-paragraph paper in which you describe the process behind some particularly interesting architectural or engineering accomplishment. Choose any topic you wish. For example, how do architects design high-rise buildings to withstand the shock of severe earthquakes? Or how did medieval man make a suit of armour? Or how do you plan to convert your VW bus into a camper that will sleep four people? In the first paragraph, state the problem as your thesis sentence. Then go on to describe how the problem could be, or was, solved.

10. Work out a paragraph defining some term like *barometer, computer, class, humanities, intelligence.* Avoid sounding like a dictionary. Consider, and use if possible: (1) what it is not like, (2) what it is like, (3) what it is not, and, finally, (4) what it is. See page 90.

Straight and Crooked Thinking: Working with Evidence

All along, through the process of organizing your thoughts (Stage 3) and beginning to draft your essay (Stage 4), you have been working to support your thesis and persuade your readers with evidence. Evidence is an example, or several examples. Your thesis has, in fact, emerged from the evidence, from thinking about the specific things you have experienced, seen, or heard, in person, in reading, or on television. To support that thesis, you have simply turned the process around, bringing in those same specific things, and others, as evidence—descriptive, narrative, and expository. You have been deciding logically on the weight and shape of that evidence, comparing, working out causes and effects, classifying, defining. But your evidence and its connections are always exposed to certain logical fallacies that may defeat its persuasiveness.

Degrees of Evidence
Write as Close to the Facts as Possible

The nature of *fact*, and of *belief, opinion*, and *preference*, poses some problems for the writer. You cannot really present the "hard facts" themselves. You cannot reach through the page to hand out actual lumps of coal and bags of wheat. You can only tell *about* these things, and then persuade your readers to see them as you believe they should be seen. Facts are the firmest kind of thought, but they are *thoughts* nevertheless—verifiable thoughts about the coal and wheat and other entities of our experience.

The whole question of fact comes down to verification: things not susceptible to verification leave the realm of fact. Fact is limited, therefore, to the kinds of things that can be tested by the senses (verified empirically, as the philosophers say) or by inferences from physical data so strong as to allow no other explanation. *Statements of fact* are assertions of a kind provable by referring to experience. The simplest physical facts—that a stone is a stone and that it exists—are so bound into our elementary perceptions of the world that we never think to verify them, and indeed could not verify them beyond gathering testimonials from the group. With less tangible facts, verification is simply doing enough to persuade any reasonable person that the assertion of fact is true, beginning with what our senses can in some way check.

Measuring, weighing, and counting are the strongest empirical verifiers; assertions capable of such verification are the most firmly and quickly demonstrated as factual:

> Smith is 150 centimetres high and 120 centimetres wide.
> The car weighs 1100 kilograms.
> Three members voted for beer.

In the last assertion, we have moved from what we call physical fact to historical fact—that which can be verified by its signs: we have the ballots. Events in history are verified the same way, although the evidence is scarcer the farther back we go.

So facts are those things, states, or events of a kind susceptible to verification. Notice: *of a kind* susceptible to verification. Some perfectly solid facts we may never verify. The place, date, and manner of Catullus's death; whether a person is guilty as accused or innocent as claimed—these we may never know, may never establish as facts, because we lack the evidence to verify them. But we would not want to remove them from the realm of fact: they are the *kind* of thing that *could* be verified, if only we could get at the evidence. They are valid grounds for speculation from the facts we have. Book after book has speculated about who Jack the Ripper was, or how the universe began.

Believe What You Write—But Belief Needs Argument

Facts, then, are things susceptible to verification. Belief presents an entirely different kind of knowledge: things believed true but yet beyond the reach of sensory verification—a belief in God, for instance. We may infer a Creator from the creation, a Beginning from the beginnings we see around us. But a doubting Thomas will have nothing to touch or see; judging our inferences wrongly drawn, he may prefer to believe in a physical accident, or in a flux with neither beginning nor end. The point is that although beliefs are unprovable, they are not necessarily untrue, and they are not unusable as you discourse with your readers. Many beliefs, of course, have proved false as new evidence turns up—new sensory verification like sailing around the world believed flat. And many beliefs have proved true, like Galileo's belief that the earth moved.

But empirical verification is surprisingly far from reach. We take almost all our knowledge, even factual knowledge, from the reports of others, who have it from others. Even pictures give us, secondhand, only one partial view. Karl Popper suggests persuasively that the only way toward truth and our belief in it is through *Conjectures and Refutations*, as his title says. We can come no closer to truth than conjectures as to probability established by argument, over time, against the widest range of refutations. We conjecture our beliefs and hold them more firmly, or revise them as we must, under the battering of refutations, as the pre-Socratic philosophers and Plato demonstrated and Popper has shown.

So the dialectic process of argument serves our highest quest for knowledge and our firmest beliefs, both in the laboratory and out in the realms of value. Assert your belief. This is your thesis, your *pro* conjecture about the truth. Then look around for the evidence and the reasons to support it against the refuting *cons* as they rise. Make your belief stick. But, for politeness and persuasion, you may wish to qualify your least demonstrable convictions with a judicious "I believe," "we may reasonably suppose," "perhaps," "from one point of view," and the like—unless the power of your conviction moves you beyond the gentilities, and you are writing heart to heart.

Handle Your Opinions with Care

Opinion is a kind of lesser—or more immediate—belief, another candidate for truth, to be verified by the outcome or left to haunt the probabilities. One horse, one team, one candidate will win; the social impact of working mothers will await the verdict of centuries. Opinions are the daily bread of our editorial pages, our sports sections, our books of ideas, our reviews of novels, films, concerts, exhibits, fashions, diets, and social habits.

As with belief, the testing of opinions to discover the truth is the central business of argumentation. When you assert something as fact, you indicate (1) that you assume it true and easily verified, and (2) that its truth is generally acknowledged. When you assert something as opinion, you imply some uncertainty about both these things. Here are two opinions that seem to persist in spite of social change and that will probably remain opinions exactly because of fervid disagreement:

> Girls are brighter than boys.
> Men are superior to women.

We know that the terms *brighter* and *superior* have a range of meaning hard to pin down. Superior in what way? Even when agreeing upon the tests for numerical and verbal abilities, for memory and ingenuity, for health and strength of character, we cannot be sure that we will not miss other kinds of brightness and superiority, or that our tests will measure these things in any thorough way. The range of meaning in our four other terms, moreover, is so wide as virtually to defy verification. We need only ask "At what age?" to illustrate how broad they are. So in these slippery regions of opinion, keep your assertions tentative with *may* and *might* and *perhaps*.

Be Even More Careful with Preferences

Preferences are something else again. They are farther from proof than opinions—indeed, beyond the pale of proof. And yet they are more firmly held than opinions, because they are primarily subjective, sweetening our palates and warming our hearts. *De gustibus non est disputandum*: tastes are not to be disputed. So goes the medieval epigram, from the age that refined the arts of logic. You can't argue successfully about tastes, empirical though they be, the logicians say, because they are beyond empirical demonstration. Are peaches better than pears? Whichever you choose, your choice is probably neither logically defensible nor logically vulnerable. The writer's responsibility is to recognize the logical immunity of preferences, and to qualify them politely with "I think," "many believe," "some may prefer," and so forth.

So go ahead, dispute over tastes, and you may find some solid grounds for them. Shakespeare is greater than Ben Jonson. Subjective tastes have moved all the way up beside fact: the grounds for Shakespeare's margin of greatness have been exhibited, argued, and explored over the centuries, until we accept his superiority, as if empirically verified. Actually, the questions that most commonly concern us are beyond scientific verification. But you can frequently establish your preferences as testable opinions by asserting them reasonably and without unwholesome prejudice, and by using the secondary evidence that other reasonable people agree with you in persuasive strength and number.

Assessing the Evidence
Logical Fallacies

From the first, in talking about a valid thesis, about proof, about assumptions and implications and definition, we have been facing logical fallacies—that is, flaws in thought, things that do not add up. Evidence itself raises the biggest question of logic. Presenting any evidence at all faces a logical fallacy that can never be surmounted: no amount of evidence can *logically* prove an assertion because *one* and *some* can never equal *all*. The fact that the sun has got up on time every morning so far is—the logicians tell us—no logical assurance that it will do so tomorrow. Actually, we can take comfort in that fallacy. Since we can never *logically* produce enough evidence for certitude, we can settle for a reasonable amount and call it quits. One piece of evidence all by itself tempts us to cry, "Fallacy! *One* isn't *all* or *every*." But three or four pieces will probably suit our common sense and calm us into agreement.

Cite Authorities Reasonably

An appeal to some authority to prove your point is really an appeal beyond logic, but not necessarily beyond reason. We naturally turn to authorities to confirm our ideas. "Einstein said" can silence many an objection. But appeals to authority risk four common fallacies. The first is in appealing to the authority outside of his field, even if his field is the universe. After all, the good doctor, of the wispy hair and frayed sweater, was little known for understanding money too.

The second fallacy is in misunderstanding or misrepresenting what the authority really says. Sir Arthur Eddington, if I may appeal to an authority myself, puts the case: "It is a common mistake to suppose that Einstein's theory of relativity asserts that everything is relative. Actually it says, 'There are absolute things in the world but you must look deeply for them. The things that first present themselves to your notice are for the most part relative.'"[1] If you appeal loosely to Einstein to authenticate an assertion that everything is "relative," you may appeal in vain—since *relative* means relative to something else, eventually to some absolute.

---

[1] Sir Arthur Eddington, *The Nature of the Physical World* (Ann Arbor: University of Michigan Press, 1958), 23.

The third fallacy is in assuming that one instance from an authority represents him or her accurately. Arguments for admitting the split infinitive (see page 291) to equal status with the unsplit, for instance, often present split constructions from prominent writers. But they do not tell us how many splits the writers avoided, or how they themselves feel about the construction. A friend once showed me a split infinitive in the late Walter Lippmann's column after I had boldly asserted that careful writers like Lippmann never split them. Out of curiosity, I wrote Mr. Lippmann; after all, he might have changed his tune. He wrote back that he had slipped, that he disliked the thing and tried to revise it out whenever it crept in.

The fourth fallacy is deepest: the authority may have faded. New facts have generated new ideas. Einstein has limited Newton's authority. Geology and radioactive carbon have challenged the literal authority of Genesis. Jung has challenged Freud; and Keynes, Marx.

The more eminent the authority, the easier the fallacy. Ask these four questions:

1. Am I citing the authority outside his or her field?
2. Am I presenting the authority accurately?
3. Is this instance really representative?
4. Is he or she still fully authoritative?

Do not claim too much for your authority, and add other kinds of proof or other authorities. In short, don't put all your eggs in one basket.

Handle Persistent Beliefs as You Would Authorities

That an idea's persistence constitutes a kind of unwritten or cumulative authority is also open to logical challenge. Because a belief has persisted, the appeal goes, it must be true. Since earliest times, for example, man has believed in some kind of supernatural being or beings. "Something must be there," the persistence seems to suggest. But the appeal is not logical; the belief could have persisted from causes other than the actuality of divine existence, perhaps only from man's psychological need. As with authority, new facts may vanquish persistent beliefs. The belief that the world was a pancake, persistent though it had been, simply had to give way to Columbus and Magellan. For all this, however, persistence does have considerable strength as an *indication* of validity, to be supported by other reasons.

Inspect Your Documentary Evidence

Documents are both authoritative and persistent. They provide the only evidence, aside from oral testimony, for all that we know beyond the immediate presence of our physical universe, with its physical remains of the past. Documents point to what has happened, as long ago as Nineveh and Egypt and as recently as the tracings on last hour's blackboard. But documents vary in reliability. You must consider a document's historical context, since factuality may have been of little concern, as with stories of heroes and saints, or with propaganda. You must allow, as with newspapers, for the effects of haste and limited facts. You should consider a document's author, his or her background, range of knowledge and belief, assumptions, prejudices, probable motives, possible tendencies to suppress or slant the facts.

Finally, you should consider the document's data. Are the facts of a kind easily verifiable or easily collected? Indeed, can you present other verification? For example, numerical reports of population can be no more than approximations, and they are hazier the farther back you go in history, as statistical methods slacken. Since the data must have been selected from almost infinite possibilities, does the selection seem reasonably representative? Are your source's conclusions right for the data? Might not the data produce other conclusions? Your own data and conclusions, of course, must also face questioning.

Statistics are particularly persuasive evidence, and because of their psychological appeal, they can be devilishly misleading. To reduce things to numbers seems scientific, incontrovertible, final. But each "1" represents a slightly different quantity, as a glance around a class of 20 students will make clear. Each student is the same, yet entirely different. The "20" is a broad generalization convenient for certain kinds of information: how many seats the instructor will need, how many people are absent, how much the instruction costs per head, and so forth. But clearly the "20" will tell nothing about the varying characteristics of the students or the education. Therefore, present your statistics with some caution so that they will honestly show what you want them to show and will not mislead your readers. Averages and percentages can be especially misleading, carrying the numerical generalization one step farther from the physical facts. The truth behind a statement that the average student earns $10 a week could be that nine students earn nothing and one earns $100.

Some Inductive Traps
Keep Your Hypothesis Hypothetical

Induction and deduction are the two paths of reasoning. Induction is "leading into" (*inducere*, "to lead in"), thinking through the evidence to some general conclusion. Deduction is "leading away from" some general precept to its particular parts and consequences. All along, you have been *thinking inductively* to find your thesis, and then you have turned the process around, *writing deductively* when you present your thesis and support it with your evidence. Both modes have their uses, and their fallacies.

Induction is the way of science: one collects the facts and sees what they come to. Sir Francis Bacon laid down the inductive program in 1620 in his famous *Novum Organum, sive indicia vera de interpretatione naturae* ("The New Instrument, or true evidence concerning the interpretation of nature"). Bacon was at war with reasoning based on the syllogism; its abstract deductions seemed too rigid to measure nature's subtlety. His new instrument greatly influenced the course of thought. Before Bacon, thinkers usually deduced the consequences of general ideas; after Bacon, they looked around and induced new generalizations from what they saw. Observed facts called the old ideas into question, and theories replaced "truths." As you may know, Bacon died from a cold caught while stuffing a chicken's carcass with snow for an inductive test of refrigeration.

Induction has great strength, but it also has a basic fallacy. The strength is in taking nothing on faith, in having no ideas at all until the facts have suggested them. The fallacy is in assuming that the mind can start blank. Theoretically, Bacon had no previous ideas about refrigeration. Theoretically, he would experiment aimlessly until he noticed consistencies that would lead to the icebox. Actually, from experience, one would already have a hunch, a half-formed theory, that would suggest the experimental tests. Induction, in other words, is always well mixed with deduction. The major difference is in the tentative frame of mind: in making an hypothesis instead of merely borrowing an honoured assumption, and in keeping the hypothesis hypothetical, even after the facts seem to have supported it.

Use Analogies to Clarify, Not to Prove

In logic, the simplest kind of induction is analogy: because this tree is much like that oak, it too must be some kind of oak. Figurative analogies couple dissimilar things in metaphors on the strength of a striking similarity—death and a shadow, the heart and a pump. But logically, you identify the unknown by its likeness to the known. Inductively, you look over the similarities until you conclude that the trees are very similar, and therefore of the same kind. You see that a large number of details agree, that they are salient and typical, and that the exceptions are unimportant.

Analogies are tremendously useful indications of likeness. They are virtually our only means of classifying things, putting things into groups and handling them by naming them. Analogy also illustrates the logical weakness of induction: assuming that *all* characteristics are analogous after finding one or two analogous. We check a few symptoms against what we know of colds and flu, and conclude that we have a cold and flu; but the doctor will add to these a few more symptoms and conclude that we have a virulent pneumonia.

Similarity does not mean total identity, and analogies must always make that shaky assumption. In your writing, you may use analogy with great effect, as we saw when Farley Mowat compares deerskin clothing to a house. But again, watch out for the logical gap between *some* and *all*. If the brain seems in some ways like a computer, be careful not to assume it is in all ways like a computer. Keep the analogy figurative: as a metaphor, it can serve you well, illustrating the unknown with the known. It is helpful evidence but not conclusive proof.

Look Before You Leap

The hypothetical frame of mind is the essence of the inductive method, because it acknowledges the logical flaw of induction, namely, the *inductive leap*. No matter how many the facts, or how carefully weighed, a time comes when thought must abandon the details and leap to the conclusion. We leap from the knowledge that *some* apples are good to the conclusion: "[All] apples are good." This leap, say the logicians, crosses an abyss no logic can bridge, because *some* can never guarantee *all*, or even *most*, except as a general *probability*. The major lesson of induction is that *nothing* can be proved, except as a probability. The best we can manage is an *hypothesis*, while maintaining a perpetual hospitality to new facts. This is the scientific frame of mind; it gets as close to substantive truth as we can come, and it keeps us healthily humble about our theories.

Probability underscores the generalizations to which we must eventually leap. You know that bad apples are neither so numerous nor so strongly typical that you must conclude: "Apples are unfit for human consumption." You also know what causes the bad ones. Therefore, to justify your leap and strengthen your generalization, make sure that you fulfil these conditions:

1. Your samples are reasonably numerous.
2. Your samples are truly typical.
3. You can explain the atypical exceptions.

The inductive leap might also be in the wrong direction: the same evidence may prompt more than one conclusion. Here again, the inductive frame of mind can help. It can teach you always to check your conclusions by asking if another answer might not do just as well. Some linguists have concluded that speech is superior to writing because speech has many more "signals" than writing. But from the same facts one might declare writing superior: it conveys the same message more economically.

The lesson of induction is the lesson of caution. Logically, induction is shot full of holes and human error. But it makes as firm a statement as we can expect about the physical universe and our experience in it. It keeps our feet on the ground while we make sense of our evidence. It keeps the mind open for new hypotheses, reminding us that no explanation is absolute.

The Common Logical Fallacies: Trust Your Common Sense

All in all, we can uncover most fallacies in writing—our own and others'—simply by knowing they lurk and by using our heads. We must constantly ask if our words are meaning what they say, and saying what we mean. We must check our assumptions. Then we must ask if we are inadvertently taking *some* for *all*, or making that inductive leap too soon or in an errant direction. Common sense will tell you that something is wrong.

But here is a list of the classic common fallacies. Being wary of them will help protect your flanks as you advance your ideas. Recognizing them in your opponents, and naming them, will give you a nice argumentative edge.

1. *Either–or.* You assume only two opposing possibilities: "Either we abolish requirements or education is finished." Education will probably amble on, somewhere in between. Similarly, *if–then*: "If I work harder on the next paper, then I'll get a better grade." You have overlooked differences in subject, knowledge, involvement, inspiration. A recent Quebec premier argued that he would be put in the position of having to resist court decisions affecting any referendum on separation if the federal government became directly involved in a pending court case. The premier was simply putting the ball in the federal government's court with the old *either–or* twist. Actually, he could, and did, continue to compromise and angle for cooperation.

2. *Oversimplification.* As with *either–or,* you ignore alternatives. "A student learns only what he wants to learn" ignores all the pressures from parents and society, which in fact account for a good deal of learning. Like most mass demonstrations, both "Pro Life" and "Pro Choice" rallies vastly oversimplify a complex social and moral issue and its many varied consequences.

3. *Begging the question.* An unhandy term, arising in Shakespeare's day, perhaps as a poor translation of the medieval Latin *petitio principii* ("the claim of the beginning"), since *petere* also means "to request, to beg." At any rate, the Latin phrase and our "begging the question" both mean taking for granted something that really needs proving. "Free all political prisoners" begs the question whether some of those concerned have committed an actual crime, like blowing up the chemistry building in a political protest.

   Edmund Wilson, in "The Ambiguity of Henry James," asserted of "The Turn of the Screw" that "the whole story has been primarily intended as a characterization of the governess"—who tells the story and whom he considers one of James's sexually repressed spinsters, so haunted that she sees nonexistent ghosts. Wilson has begged the question of James's intention, assuming it without proving it. An author's intention is notoriously elusive, even if he states it, as many have pointed out.

4. *Ignoring the question.* The question of whether it is right for a neighbourhood to organize against a newcomer shifts to prices of property and taxes. Someone is convicted of murder: the question of innocence or guilt shifts to the numbers who escape conviction or get lighter sentences.

5. *Non sequitur* ("it does not follow"). "He's certainly sincere; he must be right." "He's the most popular; he should be president." The conclusions do not reasonably follow from sincerity and popularity.

Aristotle cites the conclusion that Prince Paris had a lofty soul because he shunned society and lived "loftily" on Mount Ida. Or someone says, "He planned carefully; it's not his fault the meeting failed." That may be true, of course, but it is a non sequitur if his plans overlooked some crucial possibilities.

6. *Post hoc, ergo propter hoc* ("after this, therefore because of this"). The non sequitur of events: "He stayed up late and therefore won the race." He probably won in spite of late hours, and for other reasons. This is the politician's favourite fallacy. "Liberal prime ministers believe in war"—because Canada had Liberal prime ministers during the First and Second World Wars, and Korea. But many forces, both prior and contemporary, have involved us in wars.

Conversely, prime ministers and presidents invariably claim the prosperity already in motion before their election and blame setbacks on their predecessors. Most fallacies, like this one, are also oversimplifications.

7. *Argumentum ad hominem* ("argument toward the man"). Using unfavourable personal traits to attack a work of art, an accomplishment, an ability, a precept—this is also a species of ignoring the question. "He walked out on his wife and children: his sculpture is terrible." His sculpture is what it is, apart from his personal conduct. Political campaigning is frequently *ad hominem*. In 64 B.C., when Cicero was running for the Roman consulate against Catiline, his brother Quintus advised: "Contrive to get some new scandal aired against your rivals for crime, corruption, or immorality." Although Quintus seems to recommend cooking up new dirt, *ad hominem* attacks are not always fallacious, as Cicero's exposure of Catiline's crimes demonstrated. Conversely, attorneys introduce testimony of good citizenship to defend their clients: "How could a loving father rob a bank?"

8. *Argumentum ad misericordium* ("argument toward pity"). A kind of reverse *ad hominem*, which also ignores the question. The lawyer appeals to the starving family to evade the question of guilt. Appeals to pity, of course, are far from illogical concerning support for the poor, the bereft, the victims of disaster.

9. *Argumentum ad populum* ("argument toward the people"). The *ad hominem* shifts to a social type or group of people, appealing to prejudices about race, sex, religion, class, or the like. Stereotyping appeals *ad populum*. Canada interned thousands of West Coast Japanese Canadians as untrustworthy enemies after Japan attacked Pearl Harbor. Edmund Wilson's "spinster" for a twenty-year-old unmarried

woman is a loaded *ad populum*, as is his assuming that all such women are sexually obsessed. Frequent *ad populum* fallacies are appeals to one's birthplace as a guarantee of excellence ("I was born in the cradle of democracy"—a physical impossibility to boot) or to social class as bad ("His immense wealth is entirely in wildcat oil").

10. *Guilt by association.* A form of *ad populum.* The reasoning is that of a false syllogism:

> X votes against criminalizing the possession of marijuana.
> Medpot hold rallies against restrictions on possession.
> X is a member of Medpot.

Because X and Medpot concur on one point does not mean they concur on all. This is our old *one* and *all* again, in formal logic called "the fallacy of the undistributed middle term." It is all too frequent in political infighting, easily recognized as unfair and, unfortunately, easily accepted by proponents.

11. *Argumentum ad ignorantum* ("argument toward ignorance"). Assuming that lack of evidence proves its opposite: UFOs exist because no one has proved that they don't, or ghosts do not exist because no one has proved that they do. For years, the tobacco industry argued that smoking was not a cause of cancer because no one had yet shown that it was.

12. *The bandwagon.* "Everyone does it, so it must be OK." Slavery held sway on "bandwagon" grounds, as have smoking and drinking and a great deal of our behaviour at the polls.

13. *The complex question.* "Have you stopped beating your wife?" is the classic example. Either "yes" or "no" traps the answerer, if he is guiltless. "Yes" says that he has beaten his wife. "No" says that he has beaten his wife and continues to do so. The only escape is to answer, "No—because I never started." Political questions take subtler form: "Jones opposes these nuclear plants and therefore opposes promoting the industry and the jobs the plants would create." To defend Jones, you would point to his opposition to radiation and unnecessary hazards, and show that other means of generating electricity would also promote industry and jobs.

Suggested Exercises

1. After each of the following assertions, write two or three short questions that will challenge its assumptions, questions like "Good for what? Throwing? Fertilizer?" For example: *Girls are brighter than boys.* "At what age? All girls? In chess? In physics?" In the questions, probe and distinguish among your facts, opinions, beliefs, and preferences.
   a. Men are superior to women.
   b. The backfield made some mistakes.
   c. Communism means violent repression.
   d. Don't trust anyone over thirty.
   e. All people are equal.
   f. The big companies are ruining the environment.
   g. Travel is educational.
   h. Our brand of cigarette is free of tar.
   i. The right will prevail.
   j. A long run is good for you.

2. Each of the following statements contains at least one fallacious citation of authority. Identify it, and explain how it involves one or several of these reasons: outside field, not accurately presented, not representative, out of date.
   a. According to Charles Morton, a distinguished seventeenth-century theologian and schoolmaster, the swallows of England disappear to the dark side of the moon in winter.
   b. Einstein states that everything is relative.
   c. War between capitalists and communists is inevitable, as Karl Marx shows.
   d. Government should legalize drugs; after all, neuroscientist Michael Gazzinga recommends legalization.
   e. "Fluff is Canada's finest bubble bath," says Patrick Roy.

3. Each of the following statistical statements is fallacious in one or several ways, either omitting something necessary for full understanding or generalizing in unsupported ways. Identify and explain the statistical fallacies.
   a. This car gets fifteen kilometres per litre.
   b. Fifty percent of his snapshots are poor.
   c. Twenty-nine persons were injured when a local bus skidded on an icy road near Weston and overturned. Two were hospitalized. Twenty-seven were treated and released.
   d. Women support this book one hundred percent, but fifty percent of Canadian males are drug addicts. (In a class of five women and ten men, all the women and five of the men vote to write about a book entitled *Say "No" to Drugs.*)

4. If baseball is in season, go to the sports page and write a brief explanation of the statistics on batting averages, RBIs, and so forth. Can you find any fallacies—things the statistics do not tell? Or do the same with another sport or subject where statistics are common.

5. Explain the following fallacious analogies and inductive leaps.
   a. The brain is like a computer. Scientists have demonstrated that it, like the computer, works through electrical impulses.
   b. This woman has ten sweaters; that woman has ten sweaters. They are equally rich in sweaters.
   c. At sixty, Ethel retires with investments and savings worth more than $500,000. She has nothing to worry about for the rest of her life.
   d. Every time the Boilers play a post-season game, they lose. They will lose this one.
   e. English majors are poor mathematicians.
   f. I studied hard. I answered every question. None of my answers was wrong. I have read my exam over again and again and can still see no reason for getting only a C.

6. Name and explain the fallacy in each of the following.
   a. Jones is rich. He must be dishonest.
   b. Either she worked hard for her money, or she is just plain lucky.
   c. The best things in life are free, like free love.
   d. Sunshine breeds flies, because when the sun shines the flies come out.
   e. If they have no bread, let them eat cake. Cake is both tastier and richer in calories.
   f. This is another example of American imperialism.
   g. Smith's canned-soup empire reaches farther than the Roman empire.
   h. *Home Improvement* is North America's most popular sit-com. It is clearly the best.
   i. He is innocent. His record is spotless. The jury found him not guilty.
   j. Women are the most exploited people in the history of the world.

Writing Good Sentences

All this time you have been writing sentences, as naturally as breathing, and perhaps with as little variation. But remember that, in drafting your essay, you are not only trying to convey your thoughts in an orderly fashion; you are also aiming at clarity, vigour, and interest in expressing those thoughts. So now it is time to take a close look at the varieties of the sentence. Some varieties can be shaggy and tangled indeed. But they are all offshoots of the simple active sentence, the basic English genus *John hits Joe*, with action moving straight from subject through verb to object.

This subject–verb–object sentence can be infinitely grafted and contorted, but it really has only two general varieties: (1) the "loose, or strung-along," in Aristotle's phrase, and (2) the periodic. English naturally runs "loose," or "cumulative." Our thoughts are naturally strung along from subject through verb to object, with whatever comes to mind added as it comes. The loose sentence puts its subject and verb early. But we can also use the periodic sentence characteristic of our Latin and Germanic ancestry, where ideas hang in the air like girders until all interconnections are locked by the final word, at the period: "John, the best student in the class, the tallest and most handsome, hits Joe." A periodic sentence, in other words, is one that suspends its meaning until the end, usually with subject and verb widely separated, and the verb as near the end as possible.

So we have two varieties of the English sentence. The piece-by-piece and the periodic species represent two ways of thought: the first, the natural stringing of thoughts as they come; the second, the more careful contrivance of emphasis and suspense.

The Simple Sentence
Use the Simple Active Sentence, Loosely Periodic

Your best sentences will be hybrids of the loose and the periodic. First, learn to use active verbs ("John *hits* Joe"), which will keep you within the simple active pattern with all parts showing (subject–verb–object), as opposed to a verb in the passive voice ("Joe *is hit* by John"), which puts everything backwards and uses more words. Then learn to give your native strung-along sentence a touch of periodicity and suspense.

Any change in normal order can give you unusual emphasis, as when you move the object ahead of the subject:

> That I like.
> The house itself she hated, but the yard was grand.
> Nature I loved; and next to Nature, Art.

Most often, we expect our ideas one at a time, in normal succession— "John hits Joe"—and with anything further added, in proper sequence, at the end—"a friendly punch on the shoulder." Change this fixed way of thinking, and you immediately put your readers on the alert for a pleasant surprise. Consequently, some of your best sentences will be simple, active ones sprung wide with phrases colouring subject, verb, object, or all three, in various ways.

You may, for instance, effectively complicate the subject:

> King Lear, proud, old, and childish, probably aware that his grip on the kingdom is beginning to slip, devises a foolish plan.

Or the verb:

> A good speech usually begins quietly, proceeds sensibly, gathers momentum, and finally moves even the most indifferent audience.

Or the object:

> Her notebooks contain marvellous comments on the turtle in the backyard, the flowers and weeds, the great elm by the drive, the road, the earth, the stars, and the men and women of the village.

Compound and Complex Sentences
Learn the Difference

A compound sentence links simple sentences with a coordinating conjunction (*and, but, or, nor, yet, still, for, so*) or with a colon or a semicolon. You make a complex one by hooking lesser sentences onto the main sentence with *that, which, who,* or one of the many other subordinating connectives like *although, because, where, when, after, if.* The compound sentence *coordinates*, treating everything on the same level; the complex *subordinates*, putting everything else somewhere below its one main self-sufficient idea. The compound links ideas one after the other, as in the basic simple sentence; the complex is a simple sentence elaborated by clauses instead of merely by phrases. The compound represents the strung-along way of thinking; the complex usually represents the periodic.

Avoid Simple-Minded Compounds

Essentially the compound sentence is simple-minded, a set of clauses on a string—a child's description of a birthday party, for instance: "We got paper hats and we pinned the tail on the donkey and we had chocolate ice cream and Randy sat on a piece of cake and I won third prize." *And . . . and . . . and.*

But this way of thinking is always useful for pacing related thoughts, and for breaking the staccato of simple statement. It often briskly connects cause and effect:

> The clock struck five, and the office was suddenly empty.
> The solipsist relates all knowledge to his own being, and the
>   demonstrable commonwealth of human nature dissolves
>   before his dogged timidity.

The compound sentence is built on the most enduring of colloquial patterns—the simple sequence of things said as they occur to the mind. It has the pace, the immediacy, and the dramatic effect of talk. Hemingway, for instance, often gets all the numb tension of a shell-shocked mind by reducing his character's thoughts all to one level, in compound sentences something like this: "It was a good night and I sat at a table and . . . and . . . and. . . ."

Think of the compound sentence in terms of its conjunctions—the words that yoke its clauses—and of the accompanying punctuation. Here are three basic groups of conjunctions that will help you sort out and punctuate your compound thoughts.

Group I   The three common coordinating conjunctions: *and, but,* and *or* (*nor*). Put a comma before each.

> I like her, and I don't mind saying so.
> Art is long, but life is short.
> Win this point, or the game is lost.

Group II Conjunctive adverbs: *therefore, moreover, however, nevertheless, consequently, furthermore.* Put a semicolon before, and a comma after, each.

> Nations indeed seem to have a kind of biological span like human life, from rebellious youth, through caution, to decay; consequently, predictions of doom are not uncommon.

Group III Some in-betweeners—*yet, still, so*—which sometimes take a comma, sometimes a semicolon, depending on your pace and emphasis.

> We long for the good old days, yet we overlook the disadvantages.
> People long for the good old days; yet they rarely take into account the inaccuracy of human memory.
> The preparation had been halfhearted and hasty, so the meeting was wretched.
> Rome declined into the pleasures of its circuses and couches; so the tough barbarians conquered.

Try Compounding Without Conjunctions

Though the conjunction usually governs its compound sentence, two powerful coordinators remain—the semicolon and the colon alone. For contrasts, the semicolon is the prince of coordinators:

> The novel concentrates on character; the film intensifies the   Semicolon
> violence.
> Golf demands the best of time and space; tennis, the best of personal energy.
> The government tries to get the most out of taxes; the individual tries to get out of the most taxes.

The colon similarly pulls two "sentences" together without the blessing of conjunction, period, or capital. But it signals amplification, not contrast: the second clause explains the first.

> A house with an aging furnace costs more than the asking   Colon
> price suggests: forty dollars more a month in fuel means about three hundred twenty dollars more a year.
> Each year, thousands of hectares of forest vanish: vanishing forests mean more carbon dioxide and less oxygen.
> Sports at any age are beneficial: they keep your pulses hopping.

Learn to Subordinate

You probably write compound sentences almost without thinking. But the subordinations of the complex usually require some thought. Indeed, you are ranking closely related thoughts, arranging the lesser ones so that they bear effectively on your main thought. You must first pick your most important idea. You must then change mere sequence into subordination—ordering your lesser thoughts *sub*, or below, the main idea. The childish birthday sentence, then, might come out something like this:

> *After* we got paper hats and ate chocolate ice cream, *after* Randy sat on a piece of cake and everyone pinned the tail on the donkey, **I won third prize**.

You do the trick with connectives—with any word, like *after* in the sentence above, indicating time, place, cause, or other qualification.

> *If* they try, *if* they fail, **they are still great** *because* their spirit is unbeaten.

You daily achieve subtler levels of subordination with the three relative pronouns *that, which, who*, and with the conjunction *that. That, which*, and *who* connect thoughts so closely related as to seem almost equal, but actually each tucks a clause (subject and verb) into some larger idea:

Relative Pronoun
> The car, *which* runs perfectly, is not worth selling.
> The car *that* runs perfectly is worth keeping.

Subordinating Conjunction
> He thought *that* the car would run forever.
> He thought [*that* omitted but understood] the car would run forever.

But the subordinating conjunctions and adverbs (*although, if, because, since, until, where, when, as if, so that*) really put subordinates in their places. Look at *when* in this sentence of E.B. White's from *Charlotte's Web*:

Adverbs
> Next morning *when* the first light came into the sky and the sparrows stirred in the trees, *when* the cows rattled their chains and the rooster crowed and the early automobiles went whispering along the road, Wilbur awoke and looked for Charlotte.

Here the simple *when*, used only twice, has regimented five subordinate clauses, all of equal rank, into their proper station below that of the main clause, "Wilbur awoke and looked for Charlotte." You can vary the ranking intricately and still keep it straight:

Although some claim *that* time is an illusion, *because* we have no absolute chronometer, *although* the mind cannot effectively grasp time, *because* the mind itself is a kind of timeless presence almost oblivious to seconds and hours, *although* the time of our solar system may be only an instant in the universe at large, **we still cannot quite deny** *that* some progression of universal time is passing over us, *if* only we could measure it.

Complex sentences are, at their best, really simple sentences gloriously elaborated with subordinate thoughts. The following beautiful and elaborate sentence from an essay by Rohinton Mistry is all built on the simple sentence "It was a door":

> It was a multicultural door, a good door, a strong and faithful door; a movable barricade of weight and substance, forming a bulwark against thieves, encyclopaedia pedlars, real-estate agents, and the winter cold; a benevolent barrier to keep in the warmth of the hearth, the dog, two children, cooking smells, and the memories of a happy family.[1]

Even a short sentence may be complex, attaining a remarkably varied suspense. Notice how the simple statement "I allowed myself" is skilfully elaborated in this sentence by the late Wolcott Gibbs of the *New Yorker*:

> Twice in my life, for reasons that escape me now, though I'm sure they were discreditable, I allowed myself to be persuaded that I ought to take a hand in turning out a musical comedy.

Try for Still Closer Connections: Modify

Your subordinating *ifs* and *whens* have really been modifying—that is, limiting—the things you have attached them to. But there is a smoother way. It is an adjectival sort of thing, a shoulder-to-shoulder operation, a neat trick with no need for shouting, a stone to a stone with no need for mortar. You simply put clauses and phrases up against a noun, instead of attaching them with a subordinator. This sort of modification includes the following constructions, all using the same close masonry: (1) appositives, (2) relatives understood, (3) adjectives-with-phrase, (4) participles, (5) absolutes.

Appositives   Those phrases about shoulders and tricks and stones, above, are all in apposition with *sort of thing*, and they are grammatically subordinate to it. *Apposition* means "put to" or "add to"—putting an equivalent beside, like two peas in a pod—hence these phrases are nearly

---

[1] Rohinton Mistry, "Searching for Stevenson," in *Writing Away*, 189. Copyright © 1993 by Rohinton Mistry. Reprinted with permission of the author.

coordinate and interchangeable. They are compressions of a series of sentences ("It is an adjectival sort of thing. It is a neat trick . . .," and so forth) set side by side, "stone to stone." Mere contact does the work of the verb *is* and its subject *it*. English often does the same with subordinate clauses, omitting the *who is* or *that is* and putting the rest directly into apposition. "The William who is the Conqueror" becomes "William the Conqueror." "The Jack who is the heavy hitter" becomes "Jack the heavy hitter." These, incidentally, are called *restrictive* appositions, because they restrict to a particular designation the nouns they modify, setting this William and this Jack apart from all others (with no separating commas). Similarly, you can make nonrestrictive appositives from nonrestrictive clauses, clauses that simply add information (between commas). "Smith, who is a woman to be reckoned with, . . ." becomes "Smith, a woman to be reckoned with, . . ." "Jones, who is our manager in Liverpool, . . ." becomes "Jones, our manager in Liverpool, . . ." Restrictive or nonrestrictive, close contact neatly makes your point.

Relatives Understood   You can often achieve the same economy, as I have already hinted, by omitting the relative pronouns *that, which*, and *who* with their verbs, thus gaining a compression both colloquial and classic:

> A compression [that is] both colloquial and classic. . . .
> The house, [which was] facing north, had a superb view.
> The specimens [that] she had collected. . . .
> The friends [whom] he [had] left behind. . . .

Adjectives-with-Phrase   This construction is also appositive and adjectival. It is neat and useful:

> The law was passed, *thick with provisions and codicils, heavy with implications.*
> There was the lake, *smooth in the morning air.*

Participles   Participles—when acting as adjectives—are extremely supple subordinators. Consider this sequence of six simple sentences:

> He had been thrown.
> He had accepted.
> He felt a need.
> He demanded money.
> He failed.
> He chose not to struggle.

Richard Wright, in *Native Son*, subordinates the first five of these to the sixth with participles. He elaborates the complete thought into a forceful sentence that runs for eighty-nine words with perfect clarity:

> *Having been thrown* by an accidental murder into a position where he had sensed a possible order and meaning in his relations with the people about him; *having accepted* the moral guilt and responsibility for that murder because it had made him feel free for the first time in his life; *having felt* in his heart some obscure need to be at home with people and *having demanded* ransom money to enable him to do it—*having* done all this and *failed*, he chose not to struggle any more.

These participles have the same adjectival force:

> Dead to the world, *wrapped* in sweet dreams, *untroubled* by bills, he slept till noon.

Notice that the participles operate exactly as the adjective *dead* does.

Beware of dangling participles. They may trip you, as they have tripped others. The participle, with its adjectival urge, may grab the first noun that comes along, with shocking results:

> Bowing to the crowd, the bull caught him unawares.
> Observing quietly from the bank, the beavers made several errors in judgment.
> Squandering everything at the track, the money was never repaid.
> What we need is a list of teachers broken down alphabetically.

Move the participle next to its intended noun or pronoun; you will have to supply this word if inadvertence or the passive voice has omitted it entirely. Recast the sentence for good alignment when necessary. You may also save the day by changing a present participle to a past, as in the third example below, or, perhaps better, by activating the sentence, as in the fourth example:

> The bull caught him unawares as he bowed to the crowd.
> Observing quietly from the bank, they saw the beavers make several errors in judgment.
> Squandered at the track, the money was never repaid.
> Having squandered everything at the track, she never repaid the money.
> What we need is an alphabetical list of teachers.

Gerunds, which look like present participles but act as nouns, are also good economizers. The two sentences "He had been thrown" and "It was unpleasant" can become one, with a gerund as subject: "*Having been thrown* was unpleasant." Gerunds also serve as objects of verbs and prepositions:

> She hated *going* home.
> By *driving* carefully, they increased their fuel efficiency.

Absolutes   The absolute phrase has a great potential of polished economy. It stands grammatically "absolute" or alone, modifying only through proximity, like an apposition. Many an absolute is simply a prepositional phrase with the preposition dropped:

> He ran up the stairs, [with] *a bouquet of roses under his arm,* and rang the bell.
> She walked slowly, [with] *her camera ready.*

The ablative absolute (*ablative* means "removed") is absolutely removed from the main clause, modifying only by proximity. It is a kind of brusque condensation, something like "*The road completed,* Caesar moved his camp." But it survives in the best of circles. And it is actually more common than you may suppose. For example, a newspaper article stated that "the Prince had fled the country, *his hopes of a negotiated peace shattered.*" The *hopes shattered* pattern (noun plus participle) marks the ablative absolute (also called, because of the noun, a nominative absolute). The idea might have been more conventionally subordinated: "since his hopes were shattered" or "with his hopes shattered." But the ablative absolute accomplishes the subordination with economy and style.

Take a regular subordinate clause: "*When* the road *was* completed." Cut the subordinator and reduce the verb. You now have an ablative absolute, a phrase that stands absolutely alone, shorn of both its connective *when* and its full predication: "*The road completed,* Caesar moved his camp." Basically a noun and a participle, or noun and adjective, it is a kind of grammatical shorthand, a telegram: *ROAD COMPLETED CAESAR MOVED*—most said in fewest words, speed with high compression. This is its appeal and its power:

> The cat froze, *its back arched, its eyes frantic.*
> *All things considered,* the plan would work.
> The *dishes washed,* the *baby bathed* and *asleep,* the last *ashtray emptied,* they could at last relax.

Parallel Construction
Use Parallels to Strengthen Equivalent Ideas

No long complex sentence will hold up without parallel construction. Parallelling can be very simple. Any word will seek its own kind, noun to noun, adjective to adjective, infinitive to infinitive. The simplest series of things automatically runs parallel:

> shoes and ships and sealing wax
> I came, I saw, I conquered
> to be or not to be
> a dull, dark, and soundless day
> mediocre work, cowardly work, disastrous work

But they very easily run out of parallel too, and this you must learn to prevent. The last item especially may slip out of line, as in this series: "friendly, kind, unobtrusive, and *a bore.*" The noun *bore* has jumped off the track laid by the preceding parallel adjectives. Your train of equivalent ideas should all be of the same grammatical kind to carry their equivalence clearly, to strengthen it: either parallel adjectives—*friendly, kind, unobtrusive,* and *boring*—or all nouns—*a friend, a saint, a diplomat,* and *a bore.* Your parallelling articles and prepositions should govern a series as a whole, or should accompany *every* item:

> *a* hat, cane, pair of gloves, and mustache
> *a* hat, *a* cane, *a* pair of gloves, and *a* mustache
> *by* land, sea, or air
> *by* land, *by* sea, or *by* air

Verbs also frequently intrude to throw a series of adjectives (or nouns) out of parallel:

> FAULTY: The woman was *attractive, intelligent,* and *knew* how to express her ideas.
> IMPROVED: The woman was *attractive, intelligent,* and *articulate,* knowing how to express her ideas.

Watch the Parallelling of Pairs

Pairs should be pairs, not odds and ends. Notice how the faulty pairs in these sentences have been corrected:

> She liked *the theatre and dancing* [the theatre and the dance].
> They were all *athletic or leaders on campus* [athletes or leaders on campus].
> They wanted *peace without being disgraced* [peace without dishonour].
> He was *shy but a creative man* [shy but creative].

Check your terms on both sides of your coordinating conjunctions (*and, but, or*) and see that they match:

necessary [adjective]

Orientation week seems both worthwhile [adjective] and ~~a necessity~~ [noun].

that

He prayed that they would leave and ~the telephone would not ring.

Learn to Use Parallelling Coordinators

The sentence above about "orientation week" has used one of a number of useful (and tricky) parallel constructions: *both–and, either–or, not only–but also, not–but, first–second–third, as well as.* This last one is similar to *and*, a simple link between two equivalents, but it often goes wrong:

> One should take care of one's physical self [noun] *as well as* being [participle] able to read and write.

Again, the pair should be matched: "one's *physical self* as well as one's *intellectual self*," or "one's physical *self* as well as one's *ability* to read and write"—though this second is still slightly unbalanced, in rhetoric if not in grammar. The best cure would probably extend the underlying antithesis, the basic parallel:

> One should take care of one's physical self as well as one's intellectual self, of one's ability to survive as well as to read and write.

With the *either–or*s and the *not only–but also*s, you continue the principle of pairing. The *either* and the *not only* are merely signposts of what is coming: two equivalents linked by a coordinating conjunction (*or* or *but*). Beware of putting the signs in the wrong place—too soon for the turn:

> She either is an absolute nerd or a fool!

> Neither in time nor space...

> He not only likes the country but the city, too.

In these examples, the thought got ahead of itself, as in talk. Just make sure that the word following each of the two coordinators is of the same kind, preposition for preposition, article for article, adjective for adjective—for even with signs well placed, the parallel can skid:

The students not only are organizing [present participle]
social activities, but also are ~~interested in~~ *discussing* [passive construction] political questions.

Put identical parts in parallel places; fill in the blanks with the same parts of speech: "not only _____, but also _____."

Beginning with *not only*, a common habit, always takes more words as it duplicates subject and verb, inviting a comma splice and frequently misaligning a parallel:

> POOR: *Not only* are human beings limited in their minds and in their position in the universe, they are also limited in their physical powers.
> IMPROVED: Human beings are limited *not only* in their minds and in their position in the universe, *but also* in their physical powers. [*22 words for 24*]

The following sentence avoids the comma splice but still must duplicate subject and verb:

> POOR: *Not only* are the names similar, but the two men also share some similarities of character.
> IMPROVED: The two men share similarities *not only* in name *but also* in character. [*13 words for 16*]

The following experienced writer avoids the usual comma splice with a semicolon but makes a dubious parallel:

> POOR: *Not only* was the right badly splintered into traditional conservatives, economic liberals, and several other factions; the left made its weakest showing in half a century.
> IMPROVED: The right was badly splintered . . ., and the left. . . .

You similarly parallel the words following numerical coordinators:

> However variously he expressed himself, he unquestionably thought, first, *that* everyone could get ahead; second, *that* workers generally were paid more than they earned; and, third, *that* laws enforcing a minimum wage were positively undemocratic.
>
> Numerical Coordinates
>
> For a number of reasons, he decided (1) *that* she did not like it, (2) *that* he would not like it, (3) *that* they would be better off without it. [Note that the parentheses around the numbers operate exactly as any parentheses, and need no additional punctuation, even if you omit the first half of the parenthesis: "3) *that* they. . . ."]
>
> My objections are obvious: (1) *it* is unnecessary, (2) *it* costs too much, and (3) *it* won't work.

In parallels of this kind, *that* is usually the problem, since you may easily, and properly, omit it when there is only one clause and no confusion:

> . . . he unquestionably thought everyone could get ahead.

If second and third clauses occur, as your thought moves along, you may have to go back and put up the first signpost:

> . . . he unquestionably thought ~~that~~ everyone could get ahead,
>
> that workers . . ., and that laws. . . .

Enough of *that*. Remember simply that equivalent thoughts demand parallel constructions. Notice the clear and massive strategy in the following sentence from the concluding chapter of Freud's last book, *An Outline of Psychoanalysis*. Freud is not only summing up the previous discussion, but also expressing the quintessence of his life's work. He is pulling everything together in a single sentence. Each of the parallel *which* clauses gathers up, in proper order, an entire chapter of his book (notice the parallel force in repeating *picture*, and the summarizing dash):

> The picture of an ego which mediates between the id and the external world, which takes over the instinctual demands of the former in order to bring them to satisfaction, which perceives things in the latter and uses them as memories, which, intent upon its self-preservation, is on guard against excessive claims from both directions, and which is governed in all its decisions by the injunctions of a modified pleasure principle—this picture actually applies to the ego only up to the end of the first period of childhood, till about the age of five.

Such precision is hard to match. This is what parallel thinking brings—balance and control and an eye for sentences that seem intellectual totalities, as if struck out all at once from the uncut rock. Francis Bacon's sentences can seem like this (notice how he drops the verb after establishing his pattern):

> For a crowd is not company, and faces are but a gallery of pictures, and talk but a tinkling cymbal, where there is no love.
>
> Reading maketh a full man; conference a ready man; and writing an exact man.

Commas would work well in the second example (see page 246):

> Reading maketh a full man; conference, a ready man; and writing, an exact man.

The Long and Short of It

Your style will emerge once you can manage some length of sentence, some intricacy of subordination, some vigour of parallel, and some play of long against short, of amplitude against brevity. Try the very long sentence, and the very short. Short sentences are the meatiest:

> Money talks.
> The mass of men lead lives of quiet desperation.
> The more selfish the man, the more anguished the failure.

Experiment with the Fragment

The fragment is close to conversation. It is the laconic reply, the pointed afterthought, the quiet exclamation, the telling question. Try to cut and place it clearly (usually at beginnings and ends of paragraphs) so as not to lead your reader to expect a full sentence, or to suspect a poor writer:

> Not at all.
> First, a look behind the scenes.
> Expert within limits, that is.
> Enough of that.

The fragment, of course, usually counts as an error. Readers expect a sentence and get only a fragment of one: you leave them hanging in air, waiting for the second shoe to fall, or the voice to drop, with the thought completed, at the period. A *rhetorical* fragment—the effective and persuasive one—leaves them satisfied: *Of course.* The *grammatical* fragment leaves them unsatisfied: *When the vote was counted.* A question hangs in the air: *What* happened? Who won? Who got mad? Each of the following typical grammatical fragments—italicized—could be cured by attaching it, with a comma, to its governing sentence:

> He dropped his teeth. *Which had cost five hundred dollars.*
> A good example is Rohinton Mistry. *A writer who can drama-tize the human condition.*
> Cleopatra is the stronger. *Trying to create Antony in her own Egyptian image.*

The grammatical, or *accidental*, fragment usually follows its governing sentence, as in the examples above.

Here is a paragraph with rhetorical fragments placed at the surest and most emphatic places, beginning and end, with a faulty grammatical fragment, to illustrate the difference, still wandering in the middle (all fragments in italics):

> *Not quite.* The battle, as it proved, still had two bloody hours to run. B Company, presumed lost by allies and enemy alike, had finally worked through the jungle and flanking outposts, virtually intact. *Tired but fully equipped.* They now brought the full force of surprise and weaponry to bear on the attackers' weakened right flank. The attack turned to meet the surprise. The defenders, heartened, increased their pressure. Reinforcements by helicopter completed the flaming drama. *Curtains for the assault on Won Thang.*

That floating fragment in the middle needs to be attached to the sentence of which it is really a part, either the one before or the one following.

> EITHER: B Company, presumed lost by allies and enemy alike, had finally worked through the jungle and flanking outposts, virtually intact, *tired but fully equipped.*
>
> OR: *Tired but fully equipped,* they now brought the full force. . . .

But the point here about rhetorical fragments is to use their short, conversational staccato as one of your means to vary the rhythm of your long and longer sentences, playing long against short.

Develop a Rhythm of Long and Short

The conversational flow between long and short makes a passage move. Study the subordinations, the parallels, and the play of short and long in this elegant passage of Virginia Woolf's—after you have read it once for sheer enjoyment. She is writing of Lord Chesterfield's famous letters to Philip Stanhope, his illegitimate son:

Subordinate, Long — But while we amuse ourselves with this brilliant nobleman and his views on life we are aware, and the letters owe much of their fascination to this consciousness, of a dumb yet sub-

Short; Long — stantial figure on the farther side of the page. Philip Stanhope is always there. It is true that he says nothing, but we feel his presence in Dresden, in Berlin, in Paris, opening the letters and pouring over them and looking dolefully at the thick packets which have been accumulating year after year since he

Short; Shorter — was a child of seven. He had grown into a rather serious, rather stout, rather short young man. He had a taste for for-

Longer; Long — eign politics. A little serious reading was rather to his liking. And by every post the letters came—urbane, polished, brilliant, imploring and commanding him to learn to dance, to learn to carve, to consider the management of his legs, and to seduce a lady of fashion. He did his best. He worked very hard in the school of the Graces, but their service was too exacting. He sat down halfway up the steep stairs which lead to the glittering hall with all the mirrors. He could not do it. He failed in the House of Commons; he subsided into some small post in Ratisbon; he died untimely. He left it to his widow to break the news which he had lacked the heart or the courage to tell his father—that he had been married all these years to a lady of low birth, who had borne him children.

Short; Longer

Short Parallels Long

    The Earl took the blow like a gentleman. His letter to his daughter-in-law is a model of urbanity. He began the education of his grandsons. . . .[2]

Short; Longer

Those are some sentences to copy. We immediately feel the rhythmic play of periodic and loose, parallel and simple, long and short. Such orchestration takes years of practice, but you can always begin.

---

[2] Virginia Woolf, *The Second Common Reader* (Harcourt Brace Jovanovich, 1932).

Suggested Exercises

These work best in short spurts in the classroom.

1. Warm up by writing two or three sentences that differ from your usual style. Try the following:
   a. A simple sentence elaborated—as much as possible, even ridiculously—by interruptive words or phrases, or by modifying the subject, the verb, or the object, or all three. See who can write the longest coherent sentence.
   b. A compound sentence balanced for contrast on a semicolon.
   c. A compound sentence with colon pointing to its explanatory second half.
   d. A compound sentence with conjunctive adverb (*therefore, however, moreover,* etc.), punctuated with semicolon and comma.
   e. Now write a usual complex sentence with a subordinating clause beginning *who* or *which* ("Tim Shields, who . . ."; "The course, which . . ."). Then revise that clause into an appositive phrase (see pages 113–14).
   f. A sentence modified by adjective-with-phrase ("The law passed, thick with provisions . . .").
   g. A sentence with an absolute ("The Prince fled, his hopes shattered . . .").

2. Write a one-hundred-word sentence (yes, you can do it!) with only one independent clause and with everything else subordinated. You can start with a string of parallel clauses: "When I get up in the morning, when I look at my bleary eyes in the mirror, when I think of the paper still to be done . . .," or "After . . ., after . . ., after. . . ." See how far you can run before you must bring in your main subject and verb.

3. Write a sentence beginning *not only*, then revise it by moving the *not only* along into the sentence to make the best parallel.

4. Correct the faulty parallelism in the following sentences from students' papers, and clean up any wordiness you find.
   a. A student follows not only a special course of training, but among the studies and social activities finds a liberal education.
   b. Either the critics attacked the book for its triteness, or it was criticized for its lack of organization.
   c. This is not only the case with the young voters of Canada, but also of the adult ones.
   d. Certain things are not actually taught in the classroom. They are learning how to get along with others, to depend on oneself, and managing one's own affairs.
   e. Knowing Greek and Roman antiquity is not just learning to speak their language but also their culture.

5. In the following famous sentence of Bacon's, straighten the faulty parallels and fill out all the phrasing implied by them: *Histories make men wise; poets witty; the mathematics subtle; natural philosophy deep; moral grave; logic and rhetoric able to contend.*

6. To discover how far parallelism might take you, write a parody of the following passage from Samuel Johnson, matching him phrase for phrase and sentence for sentence. Pick out two ball players, two actors, two rock stars, or the like, and have some fun. Simply substitute your terms for Johnson's, leaving everything else as it is, where it fits. ("Of genius, that power that constitutes a ball player; that quality without which fielding is cold and batting is inert. . . ." "Of glamour, that power which constitutes an actor. . . .")

> Of genius, that power which constitutes a poet; that quality without which judgement is cold and knowledge is inert; that energy which collects, combines, amplifies, and animates—the superiority must, with some hesitation, be allowed to Dryden. It is not to be inferred that of this poetical vigour Pope had only a little, because Dryden had more, for every other writer since Milton must give place to Pope; and even of Dryden it must be said that if he has brighter paragraphs, he has not better poems. Dryden's performances were always hasty, either excited by some external occasion, or extorted by domestick necessity; he composed without consideration, and published without correction. What his mind could supply at call, or gather in one excursion, was all that he sought, and all that he gave. The dilatory caution of Pope enabled him to condense his sentiments, to multiply his images, and to accumulate all that study might produce, or chance might supply. If the flights of Dryden therefore are higher, Pope continues longer on the wing. If of Dryden's fire the blaze is brighter, of Pope's the heat is more regular and constant. Dryden often surpasses expectation, and Pope never falls below it. Dryden is read with frequent astonishment, and Pope with perpetual delight.

7. Write a paragraph beginning and ending with a deliberate rhetorical fragment.

8. Write an imitation of the passage from Virginia Woolf on pages 122–23, choosing your own subject but matching the pattern, lengths, and rhythms of her sentences, sentence for sentence, if you can. At any rate, aim toward effective rhythms of long and short.

Correcting Wordy Sentences

Now let us contemplate evil—or at least the innocently awful, the bad habits that waste our words, fog our thoughts, and wreck our delivery. Our thoughts are naturally roundabout, our phrases naturally second-hand. Our satisfaction in merely getting something down on paper naturally blinds us to our errors and ineptitudes. It hypnotizes us into believing we have said what we meant, when our words actually say something else: "Every seat in the house was filled to capacity." Two ways of expressing your thought, two clichés, have collided: *every seat was taken* and *the house was filled to capacity.* Cut the excess verbiage, and the absurd accident vanishes: "Every seat was taken." Good sentences come from constant practice in correcting the bad. Remember that clarifying wordy writing is one of the major tasks in revising your final draft (Stage 5).

Count Your Words

Writing is devilish; the general sin is wordiness. We put down the first thought that comes, we miss the best order, and we then need lengths of *is*es, *of*s, *by*s, and *which*es—words virtually meaningless in themselves—to wire our meaningful words together again. Look for the two or three words that carry your meaning; then see if you can rearrange them to speak for themselves, cutting out all the little useless wirings:

> WORDY: This is the young woman who was elected to be president by the class.
> BETTER: This is the young woman the class elected president. [*9 words for 14*]
> OR: The class elected this young woman president. [*7 words for 14*]

See if you can't promote a noun into a verb, and cut overlaps in meaning:

> WORDY: Last week, the gold stampede in Europe reached near
> panic proportions.
> BETTER: Last week, Europe's gold speculators almost *stamped-
> ed.* [*7 words for 11*]

When you convert the noun *stampede* into the verb *stampeded,* you suddenly discover you have already said "near panic proportions," and you
can drop it entirely: stampedes *are* panics. That ungrammatical and inaccurate *near* is usually a symptom of wordiness, probably because it reveals
a general inattention to meanings: the writer is not, as the word seems to
say, visualizing a hand reaching near something called "panic." A "near
miss" says what it means: the opposite of a far or wide one. But what is a
far panic? That awful *near* has driven *almost* and *nearly* from our daily
papers and weekly magazines. Use them, and you will save some words
and seem remarkably fresh. A *virtual* or *virtually* also comes in handy.
Stop splitting hairs with "a near-mystical experience" and risk a little
hyperbole: "a mystical experience"—that *-al* handles the approximation,
and your readers will admire your verve.

   You can frequently also reduce other tautologies, those useless repetitions of the same idea in different words:

each separate incident	→	each incident
many different ways	→	many ways
dash quickly	→	dash

As these examples show, the basic cure for wordiness is to count the words
in any suspected sentence or phrase—and to make each word count. If
you can rephrase to save even one word, your sentence will be clearer. And
seek the active verb: "John *hits* Joe."

Shun the Passive Voice

The passive voice is more wordy and deadly than most people imagine, or
it would not be so persistent.

> PASSIVE: It was voted that there would be a drive for the clean-
> ing up of the people's park. [*17 words*]
> ACTIVE: We [the town, the council] voted for a drive to clean
> up the people's park. [*11 or 12 words, depending on subject*]

The passive voice puts the cart before the horse: the object of the action
first, then the harnessing verb, running backward, then the driver

forgotten, and the whole contraption at a standstill. The passive voice is simply "passive" action, the normal action backward: object–verb–subject (with the true subject usually forgotten) instead of subject–verb–object—"Joe is hit by John" instead of "John hits Joe."

The passive voice liquidates and buries the active individual, along with most of the awful truth. Our massed, scientific, and bureaucratic society is so addicted to it that you must constantly alert yourself against its drowsy, impersonal pomp. The simple English sentence is active; it *moves* from subject through verb to object: "The dean's office has turned down your proposal." But the impersonal bureau emits instead a passive smoke-screen, and the student sees no one at all to help him:

> It has been decided that your proposal for independent study
> is not sufficiently in line with the prescribed qualifications as
> outlined by the university in the calendar.

Committees often write this way, and the effect on academic writing, as the professor goes from committee to desk to classroom, is astounding. "It was moved that a meeting would be held," the secretary writes, to avoid pinning the rap on anybody. So writes the professor, so writes the student.

I reluctantly admit that the passive voice has certain uses. In fact, your meaning sometimes demands the passive voice; the agent may be better under cover—insignificant, or unknown, or mysterious. The active "Shrapnel hit him" seems to belie the uncanny impersonality of "He was hit by shrapnel." The broad forces of history similarly demand the passive: "The West was opened in 1848." Moreover, you may sometimes need the passive voice to place your true subject, the hero of the piece, where you can modify him conveniently: "Joe was hit by John, who, in spite of all. . . ." And sometimes it simply is more convenient: "This subject–verb–object sentence can be infinitely contorted." You can, of course, find a number of passive constructions in this book, which preaches against them, because they can also space out a thought that comes too fast and thick. In trying to describe periodic sentences, for instance (page 108), I changed "until all interconnections lock in the final word" (active) to ". . . are locked by the final word" (passive). The *lock* seemed too tight, especially with *in*, and the locking seemed contrary to the ways buildings *are built*. Yes, the passive has its uses.

But it is wordy. It puts useless words in a sentence. Its dullness derives as much from its extra words as from its impersonality. The best way to prune is with the active voice, cutting the passive and its fungus as you go. Notice the effect on these typical and real samples:

PASSIVE: Public concern *has also been given* a tremendous impetus by the findings of the Canadian government's inquiry into the military's conduct in Somalia, and other investigations into the military's handling of peacekeeping missions *have been called for.*

ACTIVE: The inquiry into the Canadian military's conduct in Somalia *has aroused* public concern, and the government *has begun* to examine other Canadian peacekeeping missions. [*24 words for 37*]

PASSIVE: The algal mats *are made up of* the interwoven filaments of several genera.

ACTIVE: The interwoven filaments of several genera *make up* the algal mats. [*11 words for 13*]

PASSIVE: Many of the remedies *would* probably *be shown to be* faith cures.

ACTIVE: Many of the remedies *were* probably faith cures. [*8 words for 12*]

PASSIVE: Anxiety and emotional conflict *are lessened* when latency sets in. The total personality *is oriented* in a repressive, inhibitory fashion so as to maintain the barriers, and what Freud has called "psychic dams," against psychosexual impulses.

ACTIVE: When latency sets in, anxiety and emotional conflict *lessen.* The personality *inhibits* itself, maintaining its barriers—Freud's "psychic dams"—against psychosexual impulses. [*22 words for 36*]

Check the Stretchers

To be, itself, frequently ought not to be:

He seems [to be] upset about something.
She considered him [to be] perfect.
This appears [to be] difficult.

Above all, keep your sentences awake by not putting them into those favourite stretchers of the passivists, *There is . . . that, It is . . . that,* and the like:

Moreover, [there is] one segment of the population [that] never seeks employment.
[There are] many women [who] never marry.
[There] is nothing wrong with it. [Nothing is. . . .]
[It is] his last book [that] shows his genius best.
[It is] this [that] is important.

Cut every *it* not referring to something. Next to activating your passive verbs, and cutting any passive *there is* and *it is,* perhaps nothing so improves your prose as to go through it systematically also deleting every *to be,* every *which, that, who,* and *whom* not needed for utter clarity or for spacing out a thought. All your sentences will feel better.

Beware the Of-and-Which Disease

The passive sentence frequently breaks out in a rash of *ofs* and *whiches,* and even the active sentence may suffer. Diagnosis: something like sleeping sickness. *Withs, ins, tos,* and *bys* also inflamed. Surgery imperative. Here is an actual case:

> Many biological journals, especially those *which* regularly publish new scientific names, now state *in* each issue the exact date *of* publication *of* the preceding issue. *In* dealing *with* journals *which* do not follow this practice, or *with* volumes *which* are issued individually, the biologist often needs *to* resort *to* indexes . . . *in order to* determine the actual date *of* publication *of* a particular name.

Note *of publication of* twice over, and the three *whiches.* The passage is a sleeping beauty. The longer you look at it, the more useless little attendants you see. Note the inevitable passive voice (*which are issued*) in spite of the author's active efforts. The *ofs* accompany extra nouns, *publication* repeating *publish,* for instance. Remedy: (1) eliminate *ofs* and their nouns; (2) change *which* clauses into participles; (3) change nouns into verbs. You can cut more than a third of this passage without touching the sense:

> Many biological journals, especially those regularly *publishing* new scientific names, now give the date of each preceding issue. With journals not *following* this practice, and with some books, the biologist must turn to indexes . . . *to date* a particular name. [*39 words for 63*]

I repeat: you can cut most *whiches,* one way or another, with no loss of blood. Participles can modify their antecedents directly, since they are verbal adjectives, without an intervening *which*: "a car *which was* going south" is "a car going south"; "a train *which is* moving" is "a moving train." Similarly with the adjective itself: "a song *that was* popular last year" is "a song popular last year"; "a person *who is* attractive" is "an attractive person." Beware of this whole crowd: *who are, that was, which are.*

If you need a relative clause, remember *that. That* is still best for restrictive clauses, those necessary to definition: "A house that faces north is cool" (a participle would save a word: "A house facing north is cool"). *That* is tolerable; *which* is downright oppressive. *Which* should signal the nonrestrictive clause (the afterthought): "The house, which faces north, is a good buy." Here you need *which*. Even restrictive clauses must turn to *which* when complicated parallels arise. "He preaches the fellowship of humanity *that* everyone affirms" elaborates like this: "He preaches the fellowship of humanity *which* everyone affirms, *which* all the great philosophies support, but *for which* few can make any immediate concession." Nevertheless, if you need relatives, a *that* will often ease your sentence and save you from the *whiches*.

Verbs and their derivatives, especially present participles and gerunds, can also help to cure a string of *ofs*. Alfred North Whitehead, usually of clear mind, once produced this linked sausage: "Education is the acquisition *of* the art *of* the utilization *of* knowledge." Anything to get around the three *ofs* and the three heavy nouns would have been better: "Education instills the art of using knowledge"—"Education teaches us to use knowledge well." Find an active verb for *is the acquisition of,* and shift *the utilization of* into some verbal form: the gerund *using,* or the infinitive *to use.* Shun the *-tions*! Simply change your surplus *-tions* and *ofs*—along with your *which* phrases—into verbs, or verbals (*to use, learning*). You will save words, and activate your sentences.

Avoid "The Use Of"

In fact, both *use,* as a noun, and *use,* as a verb, are dangerously wordy words. Since *using* is one of our most basic concepts, other words in your sentence will already contain it.

> He uses rationalization. [He rationalizes.]
> She uses the device of foreshadowing. [She foreshadows.]
> Through [the use of] logic, he persuades.
> His [use of] dialogue is effective.

The utilization of and *utilize* are only horrendous extremes of the same pestilence, to be stamped out completely.

Break the Noun Habit

Passive writing adores the noun, modifying nouns with nouns in pairs, and even in denser clusters—which then become official jargon. Break up these logjams; let the language flow; make one noun of the pair an adjective:

> NOUN PAIR: *Air pollution* is not as marked in Saskatoon.
> NOUN PLUS ADJECTIVE: *Air* is not so *polluted* in Saskatoon.
> [*7 words for 8*]

Or convert one noun to a verb:

> NOUN PAIR: *Consumer demand* is falling in the area of services.
> NOUN PLUS VERB: Consumers *are demanding* fewer services.
> [*5 words for 9*]

Of course, nouns have long served English as adjectives: as in "*rail*road," "*railroad* station," "*court*house," and "*noun* habit." But modern prose has aggravated the tendency beyond belief; and we get such monstrosities as *child sex education course* and *child sex education curriculum publication deadline reminder*—whole strings of nothing but nouns. Education, sociology, and psychology produce the worst noun-stringers, the hardest for you not to copy if you take these courses. But we have all caught the habit. The nouns *level* and *quality*, used as adjectives, have produced a rash of redundancies. A meeting of "high officials" has now unfortunately become a meeting of "high-*level* officials." The "finest cloth" these days is always "finest *quality* cloth." Drop those two redundant nouns and you will make a good start, and will sound surprisingly original. In fact, using the noun *quality* as an adjective has become almost obsessive—*quality food, quality wine, quality service, quality entertainment, high-quality drilling equipment*—blurring all distinctions of *good, fine, excellent, superb, superior,* in one dull and inaccurate cliché. A good rule is: *Don't use nouns as adjectives.* You can drop many an excess noun:

WORDY	DIRECT
advance notice	notice
long in size	long
puzzling in nature	puzzling
of an indefinite nature	indefinite
of a peculiar kind	peculiar
in order to	to
by means of	by
in relation to	with
in connection with	with
1998-model car	1998 car
at this point in time	at this time; now

Wherever possible, find the equivalent adjective:

of great importance	important
highest significance level	highest significant level
government spending	governmental spending

reaction fixation	reactional fixation
teaching excellence	excellent teaching
encourage teaching quality	encourage good teaching

Or change the noun to its related participle:

advance placement	advanced placement
uniform police	uniformed police
poison arrow	poisoned arrow

Or make the noun possessive:

reader interest	reader's interest
veterans insurance	veterans' insurance

Or try a cautious *of*:

colour lipstick	colour of lipstick
significance level	level of significance

Of our many misused nouns, *type* often uselessly intrudes. Advertisers talk of *detergent-type cleansers* instead of *detergents*; educators, of *apprentice-type situations* instead of *apprenticeships*; journalists, of *fascist-type organizations* instead of *fascistic organizations*. We have forgotten that making the individual stand for the type is the simplest and oldest of metaphors: "Give us this day our daily bread." A twentieth-century supplicant might have written "bread-type food."

The active sentence transmits the message by putting each word unmistakably in its place, a noun as a noun, an adjective as an adjective, with the verb—no stationary *is*—really carrying the weight. After a flood, a newspaper produced this apparently succinct and dramatic sentence: "Dead animals cause water pollution." (The word *cause*, incidentally, indicates wasted words.) That noun *water* as an adjective throws the meaning off and takes 25 percent more words than the essential active message: "Dead animals pollute water." As you read your way into the sentence, it seems to say *dead animals cause water* (which is true enough), and then you must readjust your thoughts to accommodate *pollution*. The simplest change is from *water pollution* (noun–noun) to *polluted water* (adjective–noun), clarifying each word's function. But the supreme solution is to make *pollute* the verb it is, and the sentence a simple active message in which no word misspeaks itself. Here are the possibilities, in a scale from most active and clearest to most passive and wordiest, which may serve to chart your troubles if you get tangled in causes and nouns:

> Dead animals pollute water.
> Dead animals cause polluted water.
> Dead animals cause water pollution.
> Dead animals are a factor in causing the pollution of water.

> Dead animals are a serious factor in causing the water pollu-
> tion situation.
>
> Dead farm-type animals are a danger factor in causing the
> post-flood clearance and water pollution situation.

So the message should now be clear. Write simple active sentences, out-manoeuvring all passive eddies, all shallow *is*es, *of*s, *which*es, and *that*s, all overlappings, all rocky clusters of nouns: they take you off your course, delay your delivery, and wreck many a straight and gallant thought.

Avoid Excessive Distinctions and Definitions

Too many distinctions, too many nouns, and too much Latin make pea soup:

> Reading is a processing skill of symbolic reasoning sustained
> by the interfacilitation of an intricate hierarchy of substrata
> factors that have been mobilized as a psychological working
> system and pressed into service in accordance with the pur-
> pose of the reader.

This comes from an educator, with the wrong kind of education. He is saying:

> Reading is a process of symbolic reasoning aided by an intri-
> cate network of ideas and motives. [*16 words for 40*]

Except with crucial assumptions and implications (see pages 87–90), try *not* to define your terms. If you do, you are probably either evading the toil of finding the right word, or defining the obvious:

> Let us agree to use the word *signal* as an abbreviation for the
> phrase "the simplest kind of sign." (This agrees fairly well with
> the customary meaning of the word *signal*.)

That came from a renowned semanticist, an authority on the meanings of words. The customary meaning of a word *is* its meaning, and uncustomary meanings come only from careful punning. Don't underestimate your readers, as this semanticist did.

The definer of words is usually a bad writer. Our semanticist contin-ues, trying to get his signals straight and grinding out about three parts sawdust to every one of meat. In the following excerpt, I have bracketed his sawdust. Read the sentence first as he wrote it; then read it again, omitting the bracketed words:

> The moral of such examples is that all intelligent criticism [of any instance] of language [in use] must begin with understanding [of] the motives [and purposes] of the speaker [in that situation].

Here, each of the bracketed phrases is already implied in the others. Attempting to be precise, the writer has beclouded himself. Naturally, the speaker would be "in that situation"; naturally, a sampling of language would be "an instance" of language "in use." *Motives* may not be *purposes*, but the difference here is insignificant. Our semanticist's next sentence deserves some kind of immortality. He means "Muddy language makes trouble":

> Unfortunately, the type of case that causes trouble in practise is that in which the kind of use made of language is not transparently clear. . . .

Legal documents are infamous for their obscurity. Read any insurance policy to see the effects of jargon mixed with verbosity.

Clearly, transparency is hard. Writing is hard. It requires constant attention to meanings and constant pruning. Count your words, and make your words count.

Suggested Exercises

1. Clear up the blurred ideas, and grammar, in these sentences from students' papers and official prose, making each word say what it means and counting your words to make sure your version has fewer.

    a. Tree pruning may be done in any season of the year. [11 words]
    b. After reading a dozen books, the subject is still as puzzling as ever. [13]
    c. They were unable to locate my cheque, as well as their cashier department. [13]
    d. The courses listed herein are those which meet the university-level requirements which were stated above. [16]
    e. Tapes can be used in the Audio Room by individual students for their suggested listening assignments. [16]
    f. My counter was for refunds for which the customer had already paid for. [13]
    g. Entrance was gained by means of the skylight. [8]
    h. The reason we give this test is because we are anxious to know whether or not you have reflexes that are sufficiently fast to allow you to be a safe worker. [31]
    i. Spring thaw makes roads most susceptible to pavement breakup. [9]

2. Find in your textbooks, or elsewhere, a passage suffering from the passive voice, the of-and-which disease, the the-use-of contagion, and the noun habit (for example, "which shows the effect of age and intelligence level upon the use of the reflexes and the emergence of child behaviour difficulties"), and rewrite it in clear English.

3. Recast these sentences in the active voice, clearing out all passive constructions, saving as many words as you can, and indicating the number saved:

    a. The particular topic chosen by the instructor for study in his section of English 102 must be approved by the Steering Committee. [Start with "The Steering Committee," and don't forget the economy of an apostrophe-s. I managed 14 words for 22.]
    b. Avoidance of such blunders should not be considered a virtue for which the student is to be commended, any more than he would be praised for not wiping his hands on the tablecloth or polishing his shoes with the guest towels. [Begin "We should not"; try *avoiding* for *avoidance*. I dropped *virtue* as redundant and scored 27 for 41.]
    c. The first respect in which too much variation seems to exist is in the care with which writing assignments are made. ["First, care in assigning"—8 for 21.]
    d. The remaining variations that will be mentioned are concerned not with the assignment of papers but with the marking and grading of them. ["Finally, I will mention"—14 for 23.]
    e. The difference between restrictives and nonrestrictives can also be better approached through a study of the different contours that mark the utterance of the two kinds of elements than through

confusing attempts to differentiate the two by meaning. ["One can differentiate restrictives"—I managed 13 for 38. The writer is dead wrong, incidentally: meaning is the true differentiator. See pages 238–40.]

4. Eliminate the italicized words in the following passages, together with all their accompanying wordiness, indicating the number of words saved (my figures again are merely guides; other solutions that come close are quite good).

   a. *There is* a certain tendency to defend one's own position *which* will cause the opponent's argument *to be* ignored. [13 words for 19]

   b. *It is* the other requirements *that* present obstacles, some *of which* may prove insurmountable in the teaching of certain subjects. [11 for 20]

   c. In the sort of literature-centred course being discussed here, *there is* usually a general understanding *that* themes will be based on the various literary works *that* are studied, the theory being *that* both the instruction in literature and *that* in writing will be made more effective by this interrelationship. [21 for 50]

   d. The person *whom* he met was an expert *who was* able to teach the fundamentals quickly. [13 for 16]

   e. They will take a pride *which is* wholly justifiable in being able to command a prose style *that is* lucid and supple. [13 for 22]

5. To culminate this chapter, clear up the wordiness, especially the italicized patches, in these two official statements, one from an eminent linguist, one from an eminent publisher.

   a. The work *which is* reported *in this* study *is* an investigation *of* language *within* the social context *of* the community *in which it is* spoken. *It is* a study *of* a linguistic structure *which is* unusually complex, but no more than the social structure of the city *in which it* functions. [I tried two versions, as I chased out the *which*es; 29 and 22 words for 51.]

   b. Methods *which are* unique to the historian *are illustrated* throughout the volume *in order* to show how history *is written* and how historians work. The historian's approach to his subject, *which* leads to the asking of provocative questions and to a new understanding of complex events, situations, and personalities, *is probed.* The manner *in which* the historian reduces masses of chaotic fact—and occasional fancy— to reliable meaning, and the way *in which* he formulates explanations and tests them *is examined and clarified* for the student. *It is its* emphasis on historical method *which* distinguishes this book from other source readings in western civilization. The problems *which are examined* concern *themselves with* subjects *which are dealt with by* most courses in western civilization. [66 for 123. The all-time winner from a student is 45 words.]

Words

Here is the word. Sesquipedalian or short, magniloquent or low, Latin or Anglo-Saxon, Celtic, Danish, French, Spanish, Hindustani, Dutch, Italian, Portuguese, Choctaw, Swahili, Chinese, Hebrew, Turkish, Greek, Inuktitut—English contains them all, a million words at our disposal, if we are disposed to use them. No language is richer than English. But our spoken vocabularies average only about 2800 words, our expository vocabularies probably fewer than 8000. We all have a way to go to possess our heritage.

Vocabulary
Build Your Stock Systematically

If you can increase your hoard, you increase your chances of finding the right word when you need it, especially during revision (Stage 5), when you are focusing solely on the clarity, economy, and precision of your expression. Read as widely as you can, and look words up the second or third time you meet them. I once knew a man who swore he learned three new words a day from his reading by using each at least once in conversation. I didn't ask him about *polyphiloprogenitive* or *antidisestablishmentarianism*. It depends a little on the crowd. But the idea is sound. The bigger the vocabulary, the more various the ideas one can get across with it— the more the shades and intensities of meaning.

The big vocabulary also needs the little word. The vocabularian often stands on a Latin cloud and forgets the Anglo-Saxon ground—the common ground between writer and audience. So do not forget the little things, the *stuff, lint, get, twig, snap, go, mud, coax.* Hundreds of small words not in immediate vogue can refresh your vocabulary. The Norse and Anglo-Saxon adjectives in -y (*muggy, scrawny, drowsy*), for instance, rarely appear in sober print. The minute the beginner tries to sound dignified, in comes a misty layer of words a few feet off the ground and nowhere near heaven, the same two dozen or so, most of them verbs. One or two will do no harm, but any accumulation is fatal—words like *depart* instead of *go*. Avoid the big ones; go for the little ones after the dash:

accompany — go with	place — put
appeared — looked or seemed	possess — have
arrive — come	prepare — get ready
become — get	questioned — asked
cause — make	receive — get
cease — stop	relate — tell
complete — finish	remain — stay
continue — keep on	remove — take off
delve — dig	retire — go to bed
discover — find	return — go back
indicate — say	secure — get
individual — person	transform — change
locate — find	verify — check

Persons for *people* is also faintly stuffy. I add one treasured noun: *manner* for *way*. The question, as always, is one of meaning. *Manner* is something with a flourish; *way* is the usual way. But the beginner makes no distinction, losing the normal *way*, and the meaning, in a false flourish of *manners*. Similarly, "She *placed* her keys on the table" is usually not what the writer means (*place* connotes *arrange*). *Delve* is something that happens only when students try to dig. *Get* and *got* may be too colloquial for constant use, but a discreet one or two can limber many a stiff sentence. Therefore, use the elegant Latin along with the commonplace Anglo-Saxon, but shun the frayed gentility of *secure* and *place* and *remain*.

Through the centuries, English has added Latin derivatives alongside the Anglo-Saxon words already there, keeping the old with the new: after the Anglo-Saxon *deor* (now *deer*) came the *beast* and then the *brute*, both from Latin through French, and the *animal* straight from Rome. We have the Anglo-Saxon *cow*, *sheep*, and *pig* alongside Latin (through French) *beef*, *mutton*, and *pork*. Although we use more Anglo-Saxon in assembling our sentences (*to*, *by*, *with*, *though*, *is*), well over half our total vocabulary comes one way or another from Latin. The things of this world tend to be Anglo-Saxon (*man*, *house*, *stone*, *wind*, *rain*); the abstract qualities, Latin and French (*value*, *duty*, *contemplation*).

Most of our big words are Latin and Greek. Your reading acquaints you with them; your dictionary will show you their prefixes and roots. Learn the common prefixes and roots (see Exercise 3 at the end of this chapter), and you can handle all kinds of foreigners at first encounter:

con-cession — going along with
ex-clude — lock out

pre-fer — carry before
sub-version — turning under
trans-late — carry across
claustro-phobia — dread of being locked in
hydro-phobia — dread of water
ailuro-philia — love of cats
megalo-cephalic — bigheaded
micro-meter — little measurer

You can even, for fun, coin a word to suit the occasion: *megalopede* (big-footed). You can remember that *intramural* means "within the (school) walls," and that "intermural sports," which is the frequent mispronunciation and misspelling, would mean something like "wall battling wall," a physical absurdity.

Besides owning a good dictionary, you should refer, with caution, to a thesaurus—a treasury of synonyms ("together-names")—in which you can find the word you couldn't think of. The danger lies in raiding this treasury too enthusiastically. Checking for meaning in a dictionary will help assure that you have expanded, not distorted, your vocabulary.

Abstract and Concrete
Learn Their Powers, Separate and Combined

Every good stylist has perceived, in one way or another, the distinction between the abstract and the concrete. Tangible things—things we can touch—are *concrete*; their qualities, along with all our emotional, intellectual, and spiritual states, are *abstract*. The rule for a good style is to be concrete, to illustrate tangibly your general propositions, to use *shoes* and *ships* and *sealing wax* instead of *commercial concomitants*.

But abstraction, a "drawing out from," is the very nature of thought. Thought moves from concrete to abstract. In fact, *all* words are abstractions. *Stick* is a generalization of all sticks, the crooked and the straight, the long and the short, the peeled and the shaggy. No word fits its object like a glove, because words are not things: words represent ideas of things. They are the means by which we class eggs and tents and trees so that we can handle them as ideas—not as actual things but as *kinds* or *classes* of things.

Abstract words can attain a power of their own, as the rhetorician heightens attention to their meanings. This ability, of course, does not come easily or soon. I repeat, you need to be as concrete as you can, to illustrate tangibly, to pin your abstractions down to specifics. But once you have learned this, you can move on to the rhetoric of abstraction, which is a kind of squeezing of abstract words for their specific juice

Abraham Lincoln does exactly this when he concentrates on *dedication* six times within the ten sentences of his dedication at Gettysburg: "We have come to *dedicate*. . . . It is rather for us to be here *dedicated*. . . ." Similarly, Eliot refers to "faces/Distracted from distraction by distraction" (*Four Quartets*). Abstractions can, in fact, operate beautifully as specifics: "As a knight, Richard the Lion-Hearted was a *triumph*; as a king, he was a *disaster*." Many rhetorical patterns likewise concentrate on abstract essences:

> . . . tribulation works patience, and patience experience, and
> experience hope. (Rom. 5.3–4)
> The humble are proud of their humility.
> Care in your youth so you may live without care.

An able writer like Samuel Johnson can make a virtual poetry of abstractions, as he alliterates and balances them against each other (I have capitalized the alliterations and italicized the balances):

> Dryden's performances were always hasty, either *Excited* by
> some *External occasion*, or *Extorted* by some *domestic necessity*,
> he *ComPosed without Consideration* and *Published without*
> *Correction*.

Notice especially how *excited* ("called forth") and *extorted* ("twisted out"), so alike in sound and form, so alike in making Dryden write, nevertheless contrast their opposite essential meanings.

So before we disparage abstraction, we should acknowledge its rhetorical power, and we should understand that it is an essential distillation, a primary and natural and continual mental process. Without it, we could not make four of two and two. So we make abstractions of abstractions to handle bigger and bigger groups of ideas. *Egg* becomes *food*, and *food* becomes *nourishment*. We also classify all the psychic and physical qualities we can recognize: *candour, truth, anger, beauty, negligence, temperament*. But because our thoughts drift upward, we need always to look for the word that will bring them nearer earth, that will make our abstractions seem visible and tangible, that will make them graspable—mentioning a *handle*, or a *pin*, or an *egg*, alongside our abstraction, for instance.

But the writer's ultimate skill perhaps lies in making a single object represent its whole abstract class. I have paired each abstraction below with its concrete translation:

ABSTRACT: *Friendliness* is the salesperson's best asset.
CONCRETE: *A smile* is the salesperson's best asset.

ABSTRACT: *Administration of proper proteins* might have saved John Keats.
CONCRETE: *A good steak* might have saved John Keats.

ABSTRACT: To *understand* the world by *observing all of its geological details. . . .*
CONCRETE: To *see* the world in *a grain of sand.* . . .

Denotation and Connotation

Denotation is the concrete shade of meaning for the general abstract connotation. When we look up synonyms in our dictionary—*shake, tremble, quake, quiver, shiver, shudder, wobble*—we see that all of them specify, or *denote*, the same thing: a shaking motion. But each also *connotes* a different kind of shake. We move from the denotation, "a shaking," to the connotations of different shakings. These connotations have certain emotional attachments: *tremble* (fear), *quiver* (excitement), *shiver* (coldness), *shudder* (horror), *wobble* (imbalance). In short, words *denote* things, acts, moods, whatever: *tree, house, running, anger.* But they also *connote* an attitude toward these things. *Tree* is a purely neutral denotation, but *oak* connotes sturdiness and *willow* sadness, in addition to denoting different trees. Contexts also add connotations. "Christ died on the tree," for instance, connotes the whole expanse of agony and sacrifice with which medieval Christianity endowed the word. *A House Is Not a Home*, wrote a certain woman, playing on the warm connotation of *home* and a specific denotation: a house of prostitution. *Woman* and *lady* both denote the human female, but carry connotations awakened in differing contexts:

A *woman* usually outlives a man. (denotation)
She is a very able *woman.* (positive connotation)
She is his *woman.* (negative connotation)
She acts more like a *lady* than a *lady* of pleasure. (positive and negative connotations)

Inclusive and Nonsexist Language

Using inclusive language (words that do not denote or connote sexist, racist, religious, cultural, or ageist bias) is important. Obviously, insulting terms, like *frog* for French or *dago* for Italian, are unacceptable. Others are not so obvious, like *Eskimo* for Inuit (the word in Chippewa means "eater of raw meat"). The terms *Negro* and *coloured* have given way to *Black* or, in some circles, *African–Canadian* or *African–American*. Usage can change both denotations and connotations over time, and sensitivity to a group's preference is a basic and necessary courtesy. Homophobic language and racial or sexual stereotyping also suggest a small-minded bigotry that can destroy the effectiveness of your writing.

Use nonsexist words, like *customer, voter, patient, applicant,* or *officer,* and avoid unnecessary references to gender:

> EXCLUSIVE: Any reasonable *man* would vote for this candidate.
> INCLUSIVE: Any reasonable *voter* would choose this candidate.

> EXCLUSIVE: The *woman lawyer* cross-examined the witness.
> INCLUSIVE: The *lawyer* cross-examined the witness.

To avoid having to use a singular pronoun to refer to an unspecified person, you can sometimes recast your sentence using the plural:

> EXCLUSIVE: Each student will present *his* paper in class.
> INCLUSIVE: All students will present *their* papers in class.

The use of double pronouns (*he/she* or *s/he*) is awkward, although *he or she* can be appropriate at times:

> EXCLUSIVE: The winner of the Giller Prize, to be announced tonight, will have *his* picture in the newspaper tomorrow.
> INCLUSIVE: The winner of the Giller Prize, to be announced tonight, will have *his or her* picture in the newspaper tomorrow.

Avoid unnecessary feminine identifications, like *poetess* or *authoress*; even the familiar *actress* and *waitress* are giving way to the unisex *actor* and *waiter*. Replace sexist occupational terms—*fireman, salesman, cleaning lady, mailman*—with neutral words—*firefighter, salesperson, janitor, letter carrier*. *Chairman* is a male designation; not only will women not accept such sexism in our vocabulary, but neither will any man who recognizes the latent inequality suggested. The terms *chair* and *chairperson* have gained wide acceptance. Finally, refer to a woman by her own name, not her husband's—*Natalie Riopelle*, not *Mrs. Marc Riopelle*—and use *Ms.* instead of *Mrs.* unless told to do otherwise by the woman herself. Sensitivity, a bit of reflection, and common sense will answer most problems in this area.

Euphemism

Substituting positive for negative connotations is *euphemism* ("good speaking"). Ironically, it is an effective kind of understatement: "She drove *a little fast*"; "He *imbibed occasionally*." But it also grows straight and unadorned from our social tact as we avoid hurting others and from our private defences as we sugarcoat our shortcomings. We constantly say *passed away* for *died* and, with our pets, *put to sleep* for *killed*. *Powder room, rest room, ladies' room,* and *men's room* are among the common euphemisms for *washroom,* itself a euphemism for *toilet.* Politics, as George Orwell points out, is a constant game of euphemism to cover mistakes and atrocities:

> Things like the continuance of British rule in India, the Russian purges and deportations, the dropping of the atomic bombs on Japan, can indeed be defended, but only by arguments which are too brutal for most people to face, and which do not square with the professed aims of political parties. Thus political language has to consist largely of euphemism, question-begging and sheer cloudy vagueness. Defenceless villages are bombarded from the air, the inhabitants driven out into the countryside, the cattle machine-gunned, the huts set on fire with incendiary bullets: this is called *pacification.* Millions of peasants are robbed of their farms and sent trudging along the roads with no more than they can carry: this is called *transfer of population* or *rectification of frontiers.* People are imprisoned for years without trial, or shot in the back of the neck or sent to die of scurvy in Arctic lumber camps: this is called *elimination of unreliable elements.*[1]

Since euphemism veils stark particulars in generality, we should steer clear of euphemisms if we can, except for irony. Give the particulars as clearly as possible without hurting or antagonizing your readers. Your writing, as Orwell suggests, will be livelier and truer.

---

[1] George Orwell, "Politics and the English Language," in *Shooting an Elephant and Other Essays.* Copyright © Mark Hamilton as the Literary Executor of the Estate of the Late Sonia Brownell Orwell. Reprinted by permission of Martin Secker & Warburg Limited and A.M. Heath & Co. Ltd.

Metaphor
Bring Your Words to Life

As you have probably noticed, I frequently use metaphors—the most useful way of making our abstractions concrete. The word is Greek for "transfer" (*meta* equals *trans* equals *across*; *phor* equals *fer* equals *ferry*). Metaphors illustrate our general ideas at a single stroke. Many of our common words are metaphors—*grasp* for "understanding," for instance, which compares the mind to something with hands, *transferring* the physical picture of the clutching hand to the invisible mental act.

Metaphor seems to work at about four levels, each with a different clarity and force. Suppose you wrote "He swelled and displayed his finery." You have transferred to a man the qualities of a peacock to make his appearance and personality vivid. You have chosen one of the four ways to make this transfer (I italicize the distinguishing signals):

SIMILE:	He was *like* a peacock.
	He displayed himself *as* a peacock does.
	He displayed himself *as if* he were a peacock.
PLAIN METAPHOR:	He *was* a peacock.
IMPLIED METAPHOR:	He swelled and displayed his finery.
	He swelled, and ruffled his plumage.
	He swelled, ruffling his plumage.
DEAD METAPHOR:	He strutted.

Simile   The simile is the most obvious form the metaphor can take, and hence would seem elementary. But it has powers of its own, particularly where the writer seems to be trying urgently to express the inexpressible, comparing his subject to several different possibilities, no one wholly adequate. In *The Sound and the Fury*, Faulkner thus describes two jaybirds (my italics):

> . . . [they] whirled up on the blast *like gaudy scraps of cloth or paper* and lodged in the mulberries, . . . screaming into the wind that *ripped* their harsh cries onward and away *like scraps of paper or of cloth* in turn.

The simile has a high poetic energy. D.H. Lawrence uses it frequently, as here in *The Plumed Serpent* (my italics):

The lake was quite black, *like a great pit*. The wind suddenly blew with violence, with a strange ripping sound in the mango trees, *as if some membrane in the air were being ripped*.

Plain Metaphor   The plain metaphor makes its comparison in one imaginative leap. It is shorthand for "as if he were a peacock"; it pretends, by exaggeration (*hyperbole*), that he *is* a peacock. We move instinctively to this kind of exaggerated comparison as we try to convey our impressions with all their emotional impact. "He was a maniac at Frisbee," we might say, or "a dynamo." The metaphor is probably our most common figure of speech: *the pigs, the swine, a plum, a gem, a phantom of delight, a shot in the arm*. It may be humorous or bitter; it may be simply and aptly visual: "The road was a ribbon of silver." Thoreau extends a metaphor through several sentences in one of his most famous passages:

> Time is but a stream I go a-fishing in. I drink at it; but while I drink I see the sandy bottom and detect how shallow it is. Its thin current slides away, but eternity remains. I would drink deeper; fish in the sky, whose bottom is pebbly with stars.

Implied Metaphor   The implied metaphor is even more widely used. It operates most often among the verbs, as in *swelled, displayed*, and *ruffled*, the verbs suggesting "peacock." Most ideas can suggest analogues of physical processes or natural history. Give your television system *tentacles* reaching into every home, and you have compared television to an octopus, with all its lethal and wiry suggestions. You can have your school spirit *fall below zero*, and you have implied that your school spirit is like temperature, registered on a thermometer in a sudden chill. Malcolm Cowley writes metaphorically about Hawthorne's style, first in a direct simile (*like a footprint*) and then in a metaphor implying that phrases are people walking at different speeds:

> He dreamed in words, while walking along the seashore or under the pines, till the words fitted themselves to his stride. The result was that his eighteenth-century English developed into a natural, a *walked*, style, with a phrase for every step and a comma after every phrase like a footprint in the sand. Sometimes the phrases hurry, sometimes they loiter, sometimes they march to drums.[2]

---

[2] Malcolm Cowley, ed., *The Portable Hawthorne* (New York: Viking, 1948).

Dead Metaphor   The art of resuscitation is the metaphorist's finest skill. It comes from liking words and paying attention to what they say. Simply add onto the dead metaphor enough implied metaphors to get the circulation going again: "He strutted, swelling and ruffling his plumage." *He strutted* means by itself "walked in a pompous manner." By bringing the metaphor back to life, we keep the general meaning but also restore the physical picture of a peacock puffing up and spreading his feathers. We recognize *strut* concretely and truly for the first time. We know the word, and we know the man. We have an image of him, a posture strongly suggestive of a peacock.

Perhaps the best dead metaphors to revive are those in proverbial clichés. See what Thoreau does (in his *Journal*) with *spur of the moment*:

> I feel the spur of the moment thrust deep into my side. The present is an inexorable rider.

Or again, when in *Walden* he speaks of wanting "to improve *the nick of time*, and notch it on my stick too," and of not being *thrown off the track* "by every nutshell and mosquito's wing that falls on the rails." In each case, he takes the proverbial phrase literally and physically, adding an attribute or two to bring the old metaphor back alive.

You can go too far, of course. Your metaphors can be too thick and vivid, and the obvious pun brings a howl of protest. I have myself advised scholars against metaphors because they are so often overworked and so often tangled in physical impossibilities, becoming "mixed" metaphors. "The violent population explosion has paved the way for new intellectual growth" looks pretty good—until you realize that explosions do not pave, and that new vegetation does not grow up through solid pavement. Changing *paved* to *cleared* would clear the confusion. "He will have a hard road to hoe" confuses two colloquial metaphors into physical absurdity.

The metaphor, then, is your most potent device. It makes your thought concrete and your writing vivid. It tells in an instant how your subject looks to you. But it is dangerous. It should be quiet, almost unnoticed, with all details agreeing, and all absolutely consistent with the natural universe.

Allusion
Illuminate the Dim with a Familiar Light

Allusions also illustrate your general idea by referring it to something else, making it take your reader as Wellington took Waterloo, making you the

Mickey Mantle of the essay, or the Mickey Mouse. Allusions depend on common knowledge. Like the metaphor, they illustrate the remote with the familiar—a familiar place, or event, or personage. "He looked . . . like a Japanese Humphrey Bogart," writes William Bittner of French author Albert Camus, and we instantly see a face like the one we know so well (a glance at Camus's picture confirms this allusion as surprisingly accurate). Perhaps the most effective allusions depend on a knowledge of literature. When Thoreau writes that "the winter of man's discontent was thawing as well as the earth," we get a secret pleasure from recognizing this as an allusive borrowing from the opening lines of Shakespeare's *Richard III*: "Now is the winter of our discontent / Made glorious summer by this sun of York." Thoreau flatters us by assuming we are as well read as he. We need not catch the allusion to enjoy his point, but if we catch it, we feel a sudden fellowship of knowledge with him. We now see the full metaphorical force, Thoreau's and Shakespeare's both, heightened as it is by our remembrance of Richard Crookback's twisted discontent, an allusive illustration of all our pitiful resentments now thawing with the spring.

Allusions can also be humorous. The hero of Peter De Vries's "The Vale of Laughter," alluding to Lot's wife looking back on Sodom (Gen. 19:26) as he contemplates adultery for a moment, decides on the path toward home and honour:

> If you look back, you turn into a pillar of salt. If you look ahead, you turn into a pillar of society.

Diction
Reach for Both the High and the Low

"What we need is a mixed diction," said Aristotle, and his point remains true twenty-four centuries and several languages later. The aim of style, he says, is to be clear but distinguished. For clarity, we need common, current words; but, used alone, these are commonplace, and as ephemeral as everyday talk. For distinction, we need words not heard every minute, unusual words, large words, foreign words, metaphors; but, used alone, these become bogs, vapours, or at worst, gibberish. What we need is a diction that weds the popular with the dignified, the clear current with the sedgy margins of language and thought.

Not too low, not too high; not too simple, not too hard—an easy breadth of idea and vocabulary. English is peculiarly well endowed for this Aristotelian mixture. The long abstract Latin words and the short concrete Anglo-Saxon ones give you all the range you need. For most of your ideas, you can find Latin and Anglo-Saxon partners. In fact, for many ideas, you can find a whole spectrum of synonyms from Latin through French to Anglo-Saxon, from general to specific—from *intrepidity* to *fortitude* to *valour* to *courage* to *bravery* to *pluck* to *guts*. Each of these *denotes* or specifies the same thing: being brave. But each has a different *connotation*, or aura of meaning (see page 142). You can choose the high word for high effect, or you can get tough with Anglo-Saxon specifics. But you do not want all Anglo-Saxon, and you must especially guard against sobriety's luring you into all Latin. Tune your diction agreeably between the two extremes.

Indeed, the two extremes generate incomparable zip when tumbled side by side, as in *incomparable zip, inconsequential snip, megalomaniacal creep*, and the like. Rhythm and surprise conspire to set up the huge adjective first, then to add the small noun, like a monumental kick. Here is a passage from Edward Dahlberg's *Can These Bones Live*, which I opened completely at random to see how the large fell with the small (my italics):

> Christ walks on a *visionary sea*; Myshkin . . . has his ecstatic premonition of infinity when he has an *epileptic fit*. We know the inward size of an artist by his *dimensional thirst*. . . .

This mixing of large Latin and small Anglo-Saxon, as John Crowe Ransom has noted, is what gives Shakespeare much of his power:

> This my hand will rather
> The multitudinous seas incarnadine,
> Making the green one red.
> (*Macbeth* 2.2.60–62)

The short Anglo-Saxon *seas* works sharply between the two magnificent Latin words, as do the three short Anglo-Saxons that bring the big passage to rest, contrasting the Anglo-Saxon *red* with its big Latin kin, *incarnadine*. William Faulkner, who soaked himself in Shakespeare, gets much the same power from the same mixture. He is describing a very old Black woman in *The Sound and the Fury* (the title itself comes from *Macbeth*). She has been fat, but now she is wrinkled and completely shrunken except for her stomach:

> . . . a paunch almost dropsical, as though muscle and tissue had been courage or fortitude which the days or the years had consumed until only the indomitable skeleton was left rising like a ruin or a landmark above the somnolent and impervious guts. . . .

The impact of that short, ugly Anglo-Saxon *guts*, with its slang metaphorical pun, is almost unbearably moving. And the impact would be nothing, the effect slurring, without the grand Latin preparation.

A good diction takes work. It exploits the natural, but does not come naturally. It demands a wary eye for the way meanings sprout, and it demands the courage to prune. It has the warmth of human concern. It is a cut above the commonplace, a cut above the inaccuracies and circumlocutions of speech, yet within easy reach. Clarity is the first aim; economy, the second; grace, the third; dignity, the fourth. Our writing should be a little strange, a little out of the ordinary, a little beautiful, with words and phrases not met every day but seeming as right and natural as grass. A good diction takes care and cultivation.

It can be overcultivated. It may seem to call attention to itself rather than to its subject. Suddenly we are aware of the writer at work, and a little too pleased with himself or herself, reaching for the elegant cliché and the showy phrase. Some readers find this very fault with my own writing, though I do really try to saddle my maverick love of metaphor. If I strike you in this way, you can use me profitably as a bad example along with the following passage. I have italicized elements that individually may have a certain effectiveness, but that cumulatively become mannerism, as if the writer were watching himself gesture in a mirror. Some of his phrases are redundant; some are trite. Everything is somehow cosy and grandiose, and a little too nautical:

> *There's* little excitement *ashore* when merchant ships from *far-away* India, Nationalist China, or Egypt *knife through* the *gentle swells* of Virginia's Hampton Roads. This *unconcern* may simply reflect the *nonchalance* of people who live by *one of the world's great seaports.* Or perhaps *it's just* that *folk* who *dwell* in the *home towns* of atomic submarines and Mercury astronauts are not likely to be impressed by a visiting freighter, *from however distant a realm.* . . . *Upstream a bit* and also *to port,* the mouth of the Elizabeth River leads to Portsmouth and a major naval shipyard. *To starboard lies* Hampton, where at Langley Air Force Base the National Aeronautics and Space Administration prepares to send a man *into the heavens.*

Suggested Exercises

1. As a warm-up, clear the example on page 150 of its overdone phrases.

2. Revise the following sentences to make them more vivid and distinct by replacing as many of the abstract terms as possible with concrete terms.
   a. For the better part of a year, she was without gainful employment.
   b. Of the students who go to university outside their own province, seventy percent do not go back after completing their studies.
   c. A sizable proportion of those people who use long-distance movers are large-corporation employees whose moving expenses are entirely underwritten by their companies.
   d. His great-grandfather once ran successfully for high public office, but he never served because his opponent mortally wounded him in a duel with pistols.
   e. There was a severe disturbance at Headingly Jail one day in the spring—convicts, armed with makeshift weapons, took some of the prison personnel hostage.
   f. Her husband had one extramarital relationship after another and finally disappeared with a hotel dining-room employee in one of our larger western cities.
   g. Rejected by the military because of an impairment of his vision, Ernest became a journalist with an Ottawa newspaper.
   h. Disadvantaged people are often maltreated by the very social-service agencies ostensibly designed to help them.
   i. The newspaper reported that a small foreign car had overturned on the expressway just north of town.
   j. The new contract offers almost no change in the fringe-benefit package.

3. Look up in your dictionary six of the Latin and Greek constituents listed below. Illustrate each with several English derivatives closely translated, as in these two examples: (1) *con-* (with): *convince* (conquer with), *conclude* (shut with), *concur* (run with); (2) *chron-* (time): *chronic* (lasting a long time), *chronicle* (a record of the time), *chronometer* (time-measurer).

   LATIN: *a- (ab-), ad-, ante-, bene-, bi-, circum-, con-, contra-, di- (dis-), e- (ex-), in-* (two meanings), *inter-, intra-, mal-, multi-, ob-, per-, post-, pre-, pro-, retro-, semi-, sub- (sur-), super-, trans-, ultra-*

   GREEK: *a- (an-), -agogue, allo-, anthropo-, anti-, apo-, arch-, auto-, batho-, bio-, cata-, cephalo-, chron-, -cracy, demo-, dia-, dyna-, dys-, ecto-, epi-, eu-, -gen, geo-, -gon, -gony, graph-, gyn-, hemi-, hepta-, hetero-, hexa-, homo-, hydr-, hyper-, hypo-, log-, mega-, -meter, micro-, mono-, morph-, -nomy, -nym, -pathy, penta-, -phagy, phil-, -phobe (-phobia), -phone, poly-, pseudo-, psyche-, -scope, soph-, stereo-, sym- (syn-), tele-, tetra-, theo-, thermo-, tri-, zoo-*

4. Revise the following sentences so as to clear up the illogical or unnatural connections in their metaphors and similes.

a. The violent population explosion has paved the way for new intellectual growth.

b. The book causes a shock, like a bucket of icy water suddenly thrown on a fire.

c. The whole social fabric will become unstuck.

d. The tangled web of Jane's business crumbled under its own weight.

e. His last week had mirrored his future, like a hand writing on the wall.

f. The recent economic picture, which seemed to spell prosperity, has wilted beyond repair.

g. They were tickled to death by the thunderous applause.

h. Stream of consciousness fiction has gone out of phase with the new castles in the air of fantasy.

i. The murmured protests drifted from the convention floor to the podium, cracking the façade of her imperturbability.

j. Richard was ecstatic with his success. He had scaled the mountain of difficulties and from here on out he could sail with the breeze.

k. She pitches a high profile that sometimes backfires.

5. Write a sentence for each of the following dead metaphors, bringing it to life by adding implied metaphorical detail, as in "She bridled, *snorting and tossing her mane*," or by adding a simile, as in "He was dead wrong, *laid out like a corpse on a slab*."

a.	dead centre	**e.**	pinned down	**h.**	sharp as a tack
b.	stick to	**f.**	whined	**i.**	purred
c.	reflected	**g.**	ran for office	**j.**	yawned
d.	take a course				

6. Write a sentence for each of the following, in which you allude either humorously or seriously to

a. a famous—or infamous—person (Caesar, Cleopatra, Mulroney, Stalin, Picasso, Bogart)

b. a famous event (building the Canadian Pacific Railroad, the Battle of Waterloo, Confederation, the Battle of the Bulge, the signing of the Magna Carta, Cartier's arrival in Canada, the Somalia affair)

c. a notable place (Athens, Rome, Paris, London Bridge, Jerusalem, the Vatican)

d. this famous passage from Shakespeare, by quietly borrowing some of its phrases:

> To be, or not to be—that is the question:
> Whether 'tis nobler in the mind to suffer
> The slings and arrows of outrageous fortune,
> Or to take arms against a sea of troubles,
> And by opposing end them.
> (*Hamlet* 3.1.56–60)

7. Write a paragraph in which you mix your diction as effectively as you can, with the big Latin word and the little Anglo-Saxon word, the formal word and just the right touch of slang, working in at least two combinations of the extremes, on the pattern of *multitudinous seas, diversionary thrust, incomparable zip*, underlining these for your instructor's convenience.

8. Write a *terrible essay.* Have some fun with this perennial favourite, in which you reinforce your sense for clear, figurative, and meaningful words by writing the muddiest and wordiest essay you can invent, gloriously working out all your bad habits. Organize in the usual way, with a thesis, a good beginning, middle, and end, but parody the worst kind of sociological and bureaucratic prose. Here are the rules:

   a. Put *everything* in the passive voice.

   b. Modify nouns *only* with nouns, preferably in strings of three or four, never with adjectives: *governmental spending* becomes *government-level spending*; an *excellent idea* becomes *quality program concept.*

   c. Use only big abstract nouns—as many *-tions* as possible.

   d. Use no participles: not *dripping faucets* but *faucets which drip*; and use as many *whiches* as possible.

   e. Use as many words as possible to say the least.

   f. Work in as many trite and wordy expressions as possible: *needless to say, all things being equal, due to the fact that, in terms of, as far as that is concerned.*

   g. Sprinkle heavily with *-wise*-type and *type*-type expressions, and say *hopefully* every three or four sentences, along with *near-perfect, near-hysterical,* and the other woolly *nears.*

   h. Compile and use a basic terrible vocabulary: *situation, aspect, function, factor, phase, process, procedure, utilize, the use of,* and so on. The class may well cooperate in this.

9. Refine your sense of diction and meanings still further by writing an *ironic essay,* saying the opposite of what you mean, as in "The party was a dazzling success," "The Rockheads are the solidest group in town," or "Our team is the best in the West."

Research

Now you need to consolidate and advance. Instead of eight or nine hundred words, you will write three thousand. Instead of a self-propelled debate or independent literary analysis, you will write a scholarly argument or explain the results of a scholarly investigation. You have already learned to follow the steps in the writing process, from choosing your subject to revising your final draft. Now, you will also learn to use the library and electronic technology, and to take notes and give citations. You will learn the ways of scholarship. You will learn to acknowledge your predecessors as you distinguish yourself, to make not only a bibliography but also a contribution.

The research paper is very likely not what you think it is. *Research* suggests that a *search* has been done. Searching is the first step in the process that leads to the research paper. It is writer-centred, and it implies that you have examined the directly relevant sources likely to clarify your area of concern. This process should enable you to discover a realistic subject, a question that resulted from your search of relevant sources. Only by discovering as much as you need to know to proceed legitimately will you make yourself ready to do *research*. Even when you think you are able to conduct legitimate research, you will often find it is necessary to return to the searching stage to eliminate some ignorance that hinders your progress. Imagine what could happen to a student in a chemistry laboratory if he or she began to experiment with various chemical combinations without first knowing a great deal about the properties of the substances and the potential results of their combination; an explosion or the creation of a deadly gas could kill the student. Ignorance as the starting point of research can lead to disaster.

You are looking, usually, where others have looked before; but you hope to see something they have not. Research is not combining a paragraph from the *Encyclopaedia Britannica* and a paragraph from the *Canadian Encyclopedia* with a slick pinch from *Maclean's*. That's robbery. Nor is it research even if you carefully change each phrase and acknowledge the source. That's drudgery. Even in some high circles, I am afraid, such scavenging is called research. It is not. It is simply a cloudier condensation of what you have done in school as a "report"—sanctioned plagiarism to teach something about ants or Ankara, a studious, if tedious, compiling of what is already known. That such material is new to you is not the issue: it is already in the public stock.

Choosing Your Subject
Pick Something That Interests You

First, identify an area of interest that suits the occasion out of which the need to write a research paper arose (Stage 1). You need not shake the world. Such topics as "Television for Teens," "College Versus University," "Excluding Television from Trials," or the changing valuation of a former popular idol or book well suit the research paper. Bigger topics, of course, will try your mettle: affirmative action, abortion, federal versus provincial powers, or the protection of endangered species in conflict with public need. The whole question of governmental versus private endeavour affords many lively issues for searching, researching, and taking a position, perhaps even in your own locality.

You can stir your own interests and turn up a number of good ideas to investigate by reading newspapers and by browsing through current magazines—such as *Maclean's, Saturday Night, Canadian Forum, Newsweek, Psychology Today, Equinox, Atlantic Monthly*—informational CD-ROMs, and many another source. The Internet and the World Wide Web, if available to you, are teeming with possibilities. Other good sources are interviews on television, film documentaries, and even arguments in the coffee shop or bar.

Work with a Thesis

Once you have discovered a subject that interests you and you know enough about it to pursue a research project confidently, lean toward your inclination regarding it and write a tentative thesis sentence—that is, assert a position that responds to the subject question you are researching (Stage 2). Though tentative, any stand *for* or *against* (for an argumentative paper), or the assertion of a point or series of related points (for an expository essay), will save you time in further searching and researching, and help you establish manageable bounds.

Since you will be dealing mostly with facts in the public stock and with ideas with other people's names on them, what can you do to avoid copycatting? You move from facts and old ideas to new ideas. In other words, you begin by inquiring what is *already* known about a problematic area for investigation (searching), and then, as you collect inferences and judgments, you begin to perceive fallacies, to form conclusions of your own, to reinforce or to change your working thesis (researching). Here the range is infinite. Every old idea needs new assertion. Every new assertion needs judgment. Here you are in the area of values, where everyone is in favour of virtue but in doubt about what is virtuous. Your best area of research is in some controversial issue, where you can add, and document, a new judgment of "right" or "wrong," or on a topic that you realize needs study and clarification, where a process of investigation and discovery can bring fresh insight or new knowledge.

Unless you have a working hypothesis to keep your purpose alive as you collect, or at least a *clear question to be answered*, you may collect forever, forever hoping for a purpose. If you have a thesis, you will learn—and then overcome—the temptations of collecting only the supporting evidence and ignoring the obverse facts and whispers of conscience. If further facts and good arguments persuade you to the other side of an argument, or cause you to alter your understanding of the problem and your response to it, so much the better. You will be the stronger for it.

Persuade Your Readers

You do not search primarily for facts. You do not aim to summarize everything ever said on the subject. You aim to convince your readers that the thesis you believe in is right, or to bring them to a deeper understanding of your subject. You persuade them by (1) letting them see that you have been thoroughly around the subject and that you know what is known of it and thought of it, (2) showing them where the wrongs are wrong, and (3) citing the rights as right. *Your* opinion, *your* thesis, is what you are showing; all your quotations from all the authorities in the world are subservient to *your* demonstration or explanation. You are the reigning authority. You have, for the moment, the longest perspective and the last word. So, pick a subject, and move into the library.

Using the Library
Start with the Encyclopedias

Find the *Encyclopaedia Britannica*, or Microsoft's *Encarta*, or another comprehensive encyclopedia, and you are well on your way. Such a reference will handily survey your subject and guide you to your sources. It is not, usually, a basic source in itself, but each article will refer you, at the end, to several authorities. If someone's initials appear at the end, look them up in the contributors' list. The authors of the articles are authorities themselves; you should mention them in your paper, and also look them up to see what books they have written on the subject. Furthermore, the contributors' list may name some works, which will swell your bibliography and aid your research. The index will also refer you to data scattered through all the volumes. Under "medicine, history of," for instance, the *Britannica* directs you to topics all the way from alchemy to Navajo rites to women's role in primitive cultures. Other encyclopedias, such as *Collier's Encyclopedia*, though less celebrated, will here and there challenge *Britannica*'s reign, and the one-volume *Columbia Encyclopedia* is a fine shorter reference. The *Canadian Encyclopedia* provides in-depth coverage of Canadian topics.

The World Almanac and Book of Facts, a paperback lode of news and statistics (issued yearly since 1868), can provide a factual nugget for almost any subject. Information from Statistics Canada is available both in various printed publications and on the Internet. Other good references are *Webster's Biographical Dictionary*, the *Dictionary of Canadian Biography*, and *Webster's New Geographical Dictionary*, their concise entries lead quickly to thousands of people and places. And don't overlook the atlases: *The Times Atlas of the World*, the *Reader's Digest Atlas of Canada*, *The Historical Atlas of Canada*. Another treasure-trove is *The Oxford English Dictionary* (twelve volumes and supplements—abbreviated *OED* in footnotes), which gives the date a word first appeared in print and traces changing usages through the years.

At this point, it would be advisable to consult your reference librarian to find out what electronic resources are available that would help you in your search and research. The *OED* is now on CD-ROM, which your library may own, along with dozens of other aids to research. Get advice and probably a handout from the reference room summarizing your library's electronic resources. Explore them. You will find many encyclopedias, outlines, atlases, and dictionaries providing more intensive coverage than the general works on the arts, history, philosophy, literature, the social sciences, the natural sciences, business, and technology. Instructors in subjects you may be exploring can guide you to the best references. For a list of Canadian reference sources, see pages 216–18.

Discover Your Library's Catalogue

The on-line public-access catalogue has probably banished your library's card catalogue to the basement, where its cards can still provide some details not included on-line—author's vital dates, first editions, a book's contents, perhaps. Nevertheless, the on-line system has wonderfully simplified the task of research. It gives a book's or periodical's call number, its location, whether it is checked out, and when it is due. The system may also include access to the catalogues in other convenient libraries. Your library may also connect with national databases in a variety of subjects from anthropology to zoos. With a computer and modem, you probably can consult your library's catalogue from where you sit. You can search by author, title, call number, subject, or keyword. You can even scout two subjects simultaneously. If you are interested in the effect of drugs on divorce, for instance, you can ask your computer to show titles containing both words.

Discover the Indexes to Periodicals and Newspapers

Indexes to periodicals do for articles what the on-line catalogue does for books. Your on-line catalogue will tell you, by call number, where to find the indexes in an index or reference room. Many indexes are now computerized on CD-ROMs; your librarian will tell you where to find these. Some index by subject only, others by subject and author. Begin with the *Reader's Guide to Periodical Literature*—an index of articles (and portraits and poems) in more than a hundred magazines. This treasure is now on CD-ROM, but find the *Guide* itself so that you can begin with the most recent issue. Look up your subject, and make yourself a bibliographical card for each title—spelling out the abbreviations of titles and dates according to the key just inside the front cover. If you don't spell them out fully, your cards may be mysteries to you when you sit down to write. Be sure to get the volume number, which you will need for your "Works Cited." You can drop back a few issues and years to collect more articles;

and if your subject belongs to the recent past, you can drop back to the right year and track your subject forward. (*Poole's Index to Periodical Literature* provides similar guidance to American and English periodicals from 1802 to 1906, if you are doing historical research.) The *Canadian Periodical Index* and *Canadian News Index* are useful guides to Canadian materials.

The *Social Sciences Citation Index* and the *Humanities Index* do for scholarly journals what the *Reader's Guide* does for the popular ones. The *Expanded Academic Index* includes the sciences, social sciences, and humanities, beginning in 1989. If you are searching for an essay that may be in a book rather than in a magazine, your guide is the *Essay and General Literature Index*. The *Citation Index*, published annually in six volumes for the arts and humanities and another six for the social sciences, gives all the citations *within* scholarly articles—an almost overwhelming supply of titles on your subject. Add to these the *Book Review Digest* (since 1905), the *Book Review Index* (since 1965), the *Biography Index* (which nicely collects scattered references, since 1946), and *Current Biography Yearbook* (since 1940), and you will probably need no more. But if you want more, consult the American Library Association's *Guide to Reference Books*, which is also a valuable guide to encyclopedias and dictionaries. For research in English and American literature, Nancy L. Baker's and Nancy Huling's *Research Guide for Undergraduates* is a great help. Helpful reviews of research in Canadian literature are published regularly in the journal *Canadian Literature*. Your reference librarian can direct you to other Canadian reference works and bibliographies.

Taking Notes from Sources

Plan on some ten or fifteen sources for your three thousand words of text. As you find each source in a catalogue or reference guide, begin to take notes. Put the author (last name first) on one line, and the title of the work on the next, leaving space to fill in the details of publication when you get to the work itself—for books, place of publication, publisher, and date; for magazine articles, volume number, date, and pages. Italicize (that is, underscore) titles of books and magazines; put titles of articles *within* books and magazines in quotation marks. The catalogue will supply the call numbers and much of the other publishing data you need; but check and complete all your publishing data when you finally get the book or magazine in your hands, putting a light check mark in pencil to assure yourself that your information is authoritative, that quotations are word for word and all your publishing data accurate, safe to check your finished paper against. Get the author's name as it appears on the title page, adding details in brackets, if helpful: Smith, D[elmar] P[rince]. The *Reader's Guide*, for instance, gives only the author's last name and initials, which you can fill out only when you have found the article itself. Get all the information, to save repeated trips to the library. You will simplify some of the publishing data for your "Works Cited" (see pages 168 and following), but get it all down now to be sure.

One method of organizing your bibliography is to use index cards. As you pick up an author or two, and some titles, start a bibliographical card for each title. Such cards are easily organized and reorganized as you add or delete titles in your "Works Cited." Of course, if you are lucky enough to have a laptop computer, or if you transfer handwritten notes to your computer, you can use your software's cut-and-paste or sort functions to organize your entries.

Take Brief Notes

Keep your notes brief. Read quickly, with an eye for the general idea and the telling point. Holding a clear thesis in mind will guide and limit your note taking. Some of your sources will need no more than the briefest summary: "Violently opposed, recommends complete abolition." This violent and undistinguished author will appear in your paper only among several others in a single footnote to one of your sentences:

> Opposition, of course, has been tenacious and emphatic.[2]

Suppose you are writing a paper denying an interpretation of Louis Riel as a saviour of minority rights. John Coulter, you find, says he was. Here is a perfect piece of opposition, a con, to set your thesis against, to explain and qualify. But don't copy too much. Summarize the author's point, jot down some facts you might use, and copy down directly, within distinct quotation marks, only the most quotable phrases, such as his calling Riel a "dark and haunting symbol." Or suppose you want to explain the narrative technique of Margaret Laurence's short stories based on her experiences growing up in Manitoba, and you find that she has written an essay about her approach to telling those stories. This provides an ideal starting point for developing your explanation, especially through illustrations from her works. (Each of these examples is developed fully in the model student essays reproduced later in this chapter.)

Take care with page numbers. When your passage runs from one page to the next—from 29 over onto 30, for instance—put "(29–30)" after it, *but also mark the exact point where the page changed.* You might want to use only part of the passage and then be uncertain as to which of the pages contained it. An inverted L-bracket (or another symbol of your choice) and the number "30" after the last word of page 29 will do nicely: "All had ⌐ **30** occurred earlier." Do the same even when the page changes in midword with a hyphen: "having con- ⌐ **21** vinced no one."

We all have our own preferred methods of taking and organizing notes. These methods may vary depending on whether you are working at the library, where you will need notepaper or note cards, or at home, where you may be able to work directly on a computer. I have found that the economy of taking notes directly on bibliographical cards is well worth the slight clutter. Limiting yourself to what you can put on the front and back of one bibliographical card will restrain your notes to the sharp and manageable. You can always add another note card if you must. If you find one source offering a number of irresistible quotations, put each one separately on a card (with author's name on each), so you can rearrange them later for writing.

When preparing a research paper on a piece of literature, you will also need a bibliographical entry for the edition you are using, and notes for summaries and quotations from the work itself.

Take Care Against Plagiarism

Plagiarism is stealing another's words or ideas and passing them off as your own. Since in research you will be dealing with what others have written, and with a number of ideas already stated and shared, plagiarism, inadvertent or intentional, may seem hard to avoid. But simple honesty will guide you, and care in your note taking will protect you. Actually, care against plagiarizing will make your research self-evidently more solid and thorough.

If you borrow an idea, declare your source (see pages 166–68 for ways of citation). If you have an idea of your own and then discover that someone has beaten you to it, swallow your disappointment and mention your predecessor, seeing what more you can add to get back some of your own. Or you can keep even more of your own by saying, in a footnote, "I discover that James Smith agrees with me on this point," explaining, if possible, what Smith has overlooked, or his differing emphasis, and again giving a full citation of Smith's article for reference.

In taking notes, copy out possible quotations accurately, with full details of source and page, and mark them clearly so that you will know they are quotations later. Quote them directly in your paper, and include the page number from the work your "Works Cited" will fully identify:

> According to Freud, establishing the ego is a kind of "reclamation work, like the draining of the Zuyder Zee" (112).

Notice that I have quoted the shortest possible segment of Freud's sentence to get the sharpest focus, and that I have run it into my own sentence within quotation marks. You would indent and double-space a long quotation, and omit the quotation marks; for further details, see page 168.

Or you may quote indirectly, rephrasing unmistakably in your own words:

> Freud likens psychotherapy to reclaiming territory from the sea (112).

The danger lies in copying out phrases from your source as you summarize what it says, and then incorporating them in your essay, with or without realizing that those phrases are not yours. The solution is, again, to take down and mark quotations accurately in your notes, or to summarize succinctly in your own words, words as far away from the original as possible, keeping the two as distinct as you can, so that nothing from your source will leak through your notes, unmarked, into your paper, arousing your reader's suspicions. Remember that the word *plagiarism* comes from the Latin word for kidnapping (from *plaga*, "net"), and that it is indeed a crime—one that can bring lawsuits and expulsions from university. Remember, too, that your instructor can almost invariably detect changes in your vocabulary and style that indicate a kidnapping of someone else's brainchild. Be honest, and your papers and prose will reflect that honesty.

Using the Computer for Research

In the past decade, the use of computers and other electronic devices, sources, and services has somewhat changed the way students can approach the research essay. Documenting materials drawn from unconventional sources and services, however, has become problematic. You should know how to take advantage of the newer resources available for searching and researching and have a way of referring to these materials that is not too awkward or complicated.

The computer can be useful for writing research essays in a number of ways, some of which we have already considered in Chapter 1. Three important additional uses are

1. to access guides to possible research sources and materials contained on CD-ROMs held in or obtainable through your school's library (for example, bibliographies of scholarly books and articles published during a specific period, like the annual *MLA International Bibliography of Books and Articles on the Modern Languages and Literatures*)

2. to access databases (such as ERIC or NEWSBANK, which provide the full texts of cited articles on microfiche), on-line databases (such as DIALOG), or particular works available on the Internet and the World Wide Web

3. to access other information available in or through the library or, where they exist, larger computer centres or campus computer networks

Using CD-ROMs (compact computer discs that contain as much as 250,000 pages of information on "read-only" memory) requires a minimum knowledge of computer operation, a level most of today's students surpassed long ago. Your librarian or computer centre adviser can provide help, if necessary. Many basic tools, like encyclopedias and unabridged dictionaries (the *Oxford English Dictionary*, for example), are contained on CD-ROMs. Many essential bibliographical tools are also available, and your reference librarian is on staff specifically to help you to use them. Learn to use your library's on-line catalogue to discover what it has and what it can obtain for you.

Far more complex and problematic is the use of the Internet and the Web for research purposes. The main problem is to know the reliability of the information acquired. You could easily be misled into using false or questionable data or unreliable opinions simply because they have been published in what appears to be a credible form. The quality of materials on the Internet varies greatly, and there is no certain or consistent means yet available to evaluate sources. Finally, computerized sources change so often and rapidly that finding up-to-date and reliable data can be difficult, and trying to cite them in a useful way can cause headaches.

A number of handbooks explain the uses of the Internet and its related resources. One of the best Canadian books is the *Canadian Internet Handbook* (Prentice Hall Canada). It is revised and updated on a regular basis. Of particular value is Chapter 9, "Undertaking Research on the Internet." If you intend to connect to the Internet at home, you will have to sign up with a good Internet Service Provider (ISP). Then you must learn to use the search systems that help you "browse" your way into and around the Internet; you must define your search terms exactly and decide ahead of time where you are going to look for data.

Learning to use the Internet on your own will require time and careful study, and the possibility that you will easily discover solid research data is somewhat debatable. It is best that you consult your reference librarian or computer centre adviser, or someone thoroughly knowledgeable in the use of computers for research in your field, to assure the validity and efficiency of your efforts.

Your First Draft
Plot Your Course

Formal outlines, especially those made too early in the game, can take more time than they are worth, but a long paper with notes demands some planning (Stage 3). First, draft a beginning paragraph, incorporating your thesis. Then read through your notes, arranging them roughly in the order you think you will use them, getting the opposition off the street first. If your thesis is strongly argumentative, you can sort into three piles: pros, cons, and "in-betweens" (often simple facts). Now, by way of outline, you can simply make three or four general headings on a sheet of paper, with ample space between, in which you can jot down your sources in the order, pro and con, that is best for your argument. Our paper on Louis Riel would block out something like this:

PRO	CON

I. Riel, the historical figure

	Revising Riel's image (Morton)
But other commentators (Pannekeok)	

II. Riel in Manitoba

Riel's contribution (Thomas)	
	But Flanagan—Riel "inflexible"; execution of Scott

III. Riel's mental state

Riel: self and cause identified
(Flanagan)
Unbalanced mind (Wallace)

Name "David" (Flanagan)

IV. Riel in Saskatchewan

Métis situation and the Battle
of Batoche—surveys and land
claims (Laurence and Stanley)

The trial (Morton, Flanagan)

The trial and execution
(Coulter, Anthony, Stanley)

V. Confusion of views—newspapers

Riel as mythical hero
(*Montreal Gazette, Winnipeg
Free Press*)

Riel as mythical rebel
(*Toronto Star*)

VI. The real Riel—a mystery

Outline More Fully for the Finished Product

You can easily refine this rough blocking into a full topic outline, one that displays your points logically, not necessarily in the actual sequence of your writing. You can make this outline best after your first draft has stretched and squeezed your material into handsomer shape. The principle of outlining is to rank equivalent headings—keeping your headings all as nouns, or noun phrases, to make the ranks apparent as in the full outline of our sample paper (page 178).

But *begin to write soon.* You have already begun to write, of course, in getting your thesis down on paper, and then drafting a first paragraph to hold it. Now that you have blocked out your argument or explanation, however roughly, plunge into your first draft (Stage 4).

Put in Your References as You Go

The Modern Language Association of America, in conformity with many journals in the social sciences and sciences, recommends a system of citations that simplifies your job considerably. A list of "Works Cited" at the end of your paper—the usual bibliography—now replaces all footnotes merely identifying a work. Previously, on first mention, you would have made the following footnote:

[1] Geraldine Anthony, *John Coulter* (Boston: Twayne, 1976), p. 61.

Now you save all that for your "Works Cited," where you would have had to repeat it anyway. You skip the footnote altogether, putting in your paper no more than the author's name and the page number, omitting the old and unnecessary *p.*:

> According to Geraldine Anthony, "Coulter's Canadian plays emphasize that spirit of rebellion against injustice so familiar to the heart of an Irishman" (61).

If you have two "Works Cited" entries for the same author, simply include a short title in addition to the usual page number:

> The handling of the Scott execution, for Flanagan, shows Riel to have been "inflexible" (*Louis* 29).

More details on the system will follow in a moment. But the old bother of including a footnote for every citation has vanished. All you do is mention your author's name—last name alone suffices—and then add the page number in parentheses where you usually would have put a footnote number. Now you limit your footnotes to your own commentary or explanation, which of course may include references to other authors and works, or even quotations, which would be handled in the same way. If you are working on a computer, you can put these few footnotes directly into your draft, using your software's footnote function, which automatically numbers your notes in sequence. Here you can easily check them against your text and revise them, if necessary, for your final draft. If you are typing or writing by hand, put your notes, unnumbered, directly in your running text, surrounding them with triple parentheses—(((...)))—

the easiest distinction you can make, and numbering them for your final gathering at the end of your paper.

Your Final Draft
Reset Your Long Quotations

Your final draft will change in many ways, as the rewriting polishes up your phrases and turns up new and better ideas. But some changes are merely presentational. The quotation marks around the *long* quotations will disappear, since you will indent, *without quotation marks*, all quotations of more than fifty words, keeping them double-spaced, and setting them off by triple-spacing above and below. You will do the same with shorter quotations, if you want to give them special emphasis, and also with passages of poetry. You will move your few footnotes, double-spaced, onto a page (or pages) headed "Notes," to follow your text, before "Works Cited."

Differentiate Those Page Numbers

Notice that you cite, or quote, in three different ways: (1) indirect quotation or reference, (2) direct quotation in your running text, and (3) direct quotation set apart from your running text and indented. Accordingly, you punctuate the page reference in three slightly different ways:

1. With an indirect quotation or reference, you simply include the page number within the parentheses, like any parentheses, *within* the sentence, or within the phrase—that is, *before* any and all punctuation marks:

    . . . as Anderson (291) and others believe, but not. . . .

    . . . as others, including Anderson (291), believe.

    Anderson believes the evidence inconclusive (291).

2. With a direct quotation in your running text, put the page-parentheses *after* the closing quotation mark but *before* the punctuation, thus including the parentheses within *your* sentence.

    He thinks them "quite daffy" (213), but concedes. . . .

    As Belweather says, "Many of these proposals for investigation are quite daffy" (213).

3. But when you indent a double-spaced quotation, you *omit* quotation marks and put the page reference *after* the final period and a few spaces farther along—with no period following it:

> . . . revealing a culture, a commonly shared, learned, and
>
> remembered history as a group, which it transmits through
>
> the generations. (218)

What if an author has more than one work? I repeat for clarity. Simply devise a short label for each. Suppose Samuelson has both a book and an article you want to cite—I'm making these up: *Physiological Differences in Simian Primates* and "The Oral and Nasal Physiology of *Pongo Pygmaeus.*" Your references then might read:

> Samuelson finds the neocortex inadequate for language (*Physiological* 291), and "the larynx is too high" ("Oral" 13).

The Details of "Works Cited"

Many instructors in the humanities endorse the citational style detailed in the *MLA Handbook for Writers of Research Papers, Theses, and Dissertations* (compiled by the Modern Language Association of America). The instructions below are based on that style.

Include only those works you *have* cited. Don't pad. Handle these with care so that your readers can find what you found, and you too can find it again. Note that the system condenses most publishers' names: "Breakwater Books Limited" becomes "Breakwater"; "Alfred A. Knopf" becomes "Knopf." Spacing is like this:

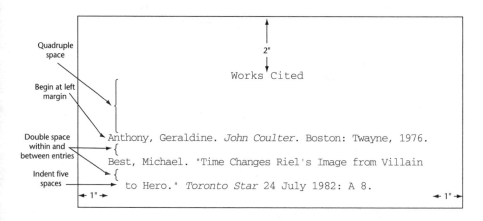

A "Bibliography," following the older style, would be nearly identical for books, adding only the publisher's full name—"Boston: Twayne Publishers, 1976." The style for an article would also be punctuated differently:

> Best, Michael. "Time Changes Riel's Image from Villain to Hero." *Toronto Star,* 24 July 1982, A 8.

Books

You indicate books that give no place (n.p.) or date of publication (n.d.) as follows:

> Segal, Annette. *The Question of Rights.* N.p.: Bell, n.d.

When listing other works by the same author, use three hyphens and a period instead of repeating the name:

> Bercuson, David Jay, and J.L. Granatstein. *The Collins Dictionary of Canadian History, 1867 to the Present.* Don Mills, ON: Collins, 1988.
>
> ---. *Dictionary of Canadian Military History.* Toronto: Oxford UP, 1992.

Two Authors; More Than One Entry for Same Author(s)

Bercuson and Granatstein also wrote the second entry, which alphabetizes second by title. ("UP" is the standard abbreviation for "University Press.") If Bercuson alone had written *Dictionary of Canadian Military History,* it would come first, with his name in full, and the *Collins Dictionary* entry would follow as it stands, with both names in full.

Books that are monographs in a series look like this:

> Stanton, Mary Emma. *Newspaper Comics: A Social History.* Univ. of Someplace Studies in Language and Literature, No. 37. Placeville, Som.: U of Someplace P, 1995.

Periodicals

With scholarly journals that number their pages consecutively throughout the year, you give the volume number, the year, and the pages an article covers, with no comma following title and all in Arabic numbers, but with a space after the colon. If each issue begins again at page 1, you also include the issue number, after the volume:

> Thomas, Gillian. "Lifton's Law and the Teaching of Litera-
> ture." *Dalhousie Review* 66.1–2 (1986): 14–21.

With weekly and monthly magazines that begin numbering their pages anew with each issue, give the full date:

> Soderstrom, Mary. "Not *pure laine*, but *sans-mitaines*." *Books
> in Canada* June 1997: 5–7.

Newspapers

Newspaper articles sometimes need more detail. Alphabetize by title—by *Power* in the following item:

> "Power is the Canadian dilemma." Editorial. *Globe and Mail*
> 28 June 1997: D6.

You have added "Editorial" after the title. Here again the full date is necessary. The "D6" indicates "Section D, page 6." Give the section and page number just as it appears in the newspapers—4.6, 8*B,* or *D-*4.

If the article has a by-line, you include the author. If the article is mostly an interview with one authority, bracket that authority as your key, since you will be quoting him or her in your essay:

> [Mills, Jay.] "Chipmunks Are Funny People." Associated Press
> News Release. *Back Creek Evening Star* 15 Oct. 1997: A4,
> A8.

Source Within Source

When you find a useful quotation, or a complete essay, within another source or collection, include both in your "Works Cited." At the end of the entry to the original source, use the abbreviation *Qtd.* ("Quoted") and a short reference to direct the reader to the secondary source in which you found the quotation or essay:

> Quigley, E. "Particular Poetry." *Rune* 6 (Spring 1980): 30–53.
> Qtd. in Kroetsch.

You then also cite Kroetsch fully in your "Works Cited":

> Kroetsch, Robert. *The Lovely Treachery of Words.* Toronto:
> Oxford UP, 1989.

You treat an article within a series of volumes in the same way:

> Thomas, Lewis H. "Louis Riel." In *Dictionary of Canadian Biography* XI.

Again, cite the *Dictionary* fully in your "Works Cited." You may simplify citations of articles in encyclopedias:

> Peters, Arnold. "Medicine." *Encyclopaedia Britannica.* 11th ed. 1911.
>
> "Expo 67." *Canadian Encyclopedia.* 1985 ed.

You need neither volume nor page numbers in alphabetized encyclopedias, only the edition you are citing. The entry on "Medicine" is initialled "A.P.," and you have looked up the author's name in the contributors' list. The article on Expo 67 is anonymous, to be alphabetized in your "Works Cited" under *E.*

Editions

Alphabetize editions by the author's name, but cite the editor:

> Shakespeare, William. *Romeo and Juliet.* In *An Essential Shakespeare.* Ed. Russell Fraser. New York: Prentice Hall, 1972.

But alphabetize by the editor when you have referred to his or her introduction and notes:

> Byatt, A.S., ed. *The Mill on the Floss.* By George Eliot. With introduction and notes. Toronto: Penguin, 1979.
>
> Weaver, Robert. Introduction. *The End of the World and Other Stories.* By Mavis Gallant. Toronto: McClelland and Stewart, 1974.

In the second entry, Weaver has contributed only an "Introduction" with no editor specified, and you have referred only to his remarks. If, on the other hand, you quote from both the novel and Weaver, you would list by *Gallant*:

> Gallant, Mavis. *The End of the World and Other Stories.* With introduction by Robert Weaver. Toronto: McClelland and Stewart, 1974.

Other Details

The following example shows where to put the period when the title of an article ends in a quotation. The original title would have had double quotation marks around the poem.

> Gillies, George L. "Henry Smith's 'Electra.'" *Speculation* 2 (1881): 490–98.

The next entries bracket useful details not appearing in the published work. But keep famous initials as initials: T.S. Eliot, H.G. Wells, D.H. Lawrence.

> Schwartz, P[aul] F[riedrich]. *A Quartet of Thoughts.* New York: Appleton, 1943.

> [Lewes, George H.] "Percy Bysshe Shelley." *Westminster Review* 35 (1841): 303–44.

Government documents, pamphlets, and other oddities require common sense:

> Canada. Parliamentary Committee on Equality Rights. *Equality for All.* 33rd Parl., 1st sess. Ottawa: Queen's Printer for Canada, 1984–85.

> *Briefly from CANCOPY.* Newsletter. Vol. 7, No. 2. Toronto: CANCOPY, 1997.

> The Aphrodite Drawings *by Kate Brown.* Exhibit notes (photocopied). Toronto: Women's Art Resource Centre, 24 Sept. to 7 Oct. 1997.

Briefly include the details to help others hunt them down.

Recordings, films, and CD-ROMs also require some ingenuity. Do not cite microfilms and other reproductions of things in print. Simply cite the book, article, or newspaper as if you had it in hand. But other media are forms of publication in themselves, to be cited as clearly as possible:

Recording
> Cockburn, Bruce. *The Charity of Night.* Toronto: True North, 1997.

CD-ROM
> *The 1998 Canadian and World Encyclopedia.* CD-ROM. Toronto: McClelland and Stewart, 1997.

Film
> *Double Happiness.* Mina Shum, dir. First Generation Films, 1995.

If you are citing the director's work, list the film by director instead of title. Add any other information that may be appropriate to your context: actors, cinematographer, and so on:

> Shum, Mina, dir. *Double Happiness.* With Sandra Oh. First Generation Films, 1995.

Other nonprint items follow the same pattern. For videotapes and film-strips, the medium is usually indicated after the title.

Citing On-Line Sources

Electronic sources sometimes will not give the usual information (author, page number, etc.), so you must adapt your note to the material—for example, giving the site and date. The citation of on-line sources should include the following, where applicable and available:

- author
- title of work
- title of the site or database
- publication information (publisher, date)
- page numbers
- medium (*On-line*)
- the service provider or network you used
- date you accessed the article
- address at which the article is available

Following the standard MLA style,[1] entries in your "Works Cited" would look something like this:

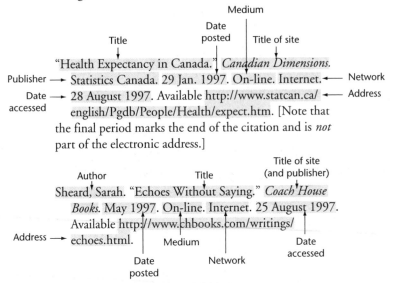

[1] The Alliance for Computers and Writing (ACW) offers guidelines that cover a variety of electronic sources that may not be easy to cite in the MLA style. See *The Scott, Foresman Handbook for Writers*, 4th edition, by Hairston and Ruszkiewicz (671–75) for a more complete explanation of the ACW system of citation.

Abbreviations

Omit Unnecessary Abbreviations

Do not use these old favourites:

- ibid.—*ibidem* ("in the same place"), meaning the title and page recently cited. Instead, *use the author's last name and page*, preferably phrased as part of your text: ". . . as Claeburn also makes clear (28)."

- op. cit.—*opere citato* ("in the work cited"), meaning a work referred to again after several others have intervened. Again, *use the author's last name and page*: ". . . too small for vocalization (Adams 911)."

- loc. cit.—*loco citato* ("in the place cited"). Simply repeat the page number: ". . . as Smith says (31). He cites, however, some notable exceptions (31)."

- p., pp.—"page, pages." These old standbys are now redundant: omit them completely. As we have seen, the number alone within parentheses suffices in the text, as it does in "Works Cited" as well.

- l., ll.—"line, lines." These you would probably not need anyway, since they concern certain kinds of literary and textual scholarship, but, as you see, they are confusing, since they look like the numerals 1 and 11. If you ever need them, just write "line" and "lines."

Use Only Conventional Abbreviations

The following conventional abbreviations remain useful (do *not* italicize them):

- cf.—*confer* ("bring together," or "compare"); do not use for "see."

- et al.—*et alii* ("and others"); does not mean "and all"; use after the first author in multiple authorships: "Ronald Elkins et al."

Two more Latin terms (not abbreviations), also not italicized, are equally handy:

- passim—"throughout the work; here and there." Use instead of page references when a writer makes the same point in many places within a single work; use also for statistics you have compiled from observations and tables scattered throughout the work.

- sic—"so", "this is so"; always in brackets—[sic]—because used only within quotations following some misspelling or other surprising detail to show that it really was there, was "so" in the original, and that the mistake is not yours.

Other useful abbreviations are

- c. *or* ca.—*circa,* "about" (c. 1709)
- ch., chs.—chapter, chapters, with Arabic numerals (ch. 12)
- ed.—edited by, edition, editor
- ms., mss.—manuscript, manuscripts
- n.d.—no date given
- n.p.—no place of publication given
- rev.—revised
- tr., trans.—translated by
- vol., vols.—volume, volumes (use only with books: *Forsythe Saga,* vol. 3.)

A footnote using some of these might go like this:

> [3] See Donald Allenberg et al., *Population* 308–12; cf. Weiss 60. Dillon, passim, takes a position even more conservative than Weiss's. See also A.H. Hawkins 71–83 and ch. 10. Records sufficient for broad comparisons begin only ca. 1850.

Abbreviate Plays and Long Poems After First Mention

After first mention, refer to plays and long poems directly in your text, within parentheses—abbreviated, with no commas, and with Arabic numerals. Italicize the title (underscore on typewriter or in handwriting): *Merch.* 2.4.72–75 (this is *The Merchant of Venice,* Act II, scene iv, lines 72–75), *Caesar* 5.3.6, *Ham.* 1.1.23, *Iliad* 9.93 (= Book IX, line 93), *PL* 4.918 (= *Paradise Lost,* Book IV, line 918). Notice: no comma between short title and numbers; periods and no spaces between numbers. Use the numbers alone if you have already mentioned the title, or have clearly implied it, as in repeated quotations from the same work. Your "Works Cited" will contain the edition you are using.

Abbreviate Books of the Bible, Even the First Time

The Bible and its books, though capitalized as ordinary titles, are never italicized; the same applies to other sacred texts (Koran, Vedas, etc.). Spell them out in your running text: "The Bible begins with Genesis." You refer to them also directly in your text, in the same style used for plays and long poems: Mark 16.6; Jer. 4.24; 1 Sam. 18.33. You can find the accepted abbreviations and forms in some dictionaries and style guides. Make biblical references like this:

> There is still nothing new under the sun (Eccl. 1.9); man still does not live by bread alone (Matt. 4.4).

> As Ecclesiastes tells us, "there is no new thing under the sun" (1.9).

As noted above, I have based these instructions on *The MLA Handbook for Writers of Research Papers, Theses, and Dissertations* (compiled by the Modern Language Association of America), following the customs for work in literature and the humanities. Some of the social and natural sciences continue to use slightly different conventions. An article would look like this in a botanical bibliography (no quotation marks, no parentheses, fewer capitals):

> Mann, K.H. 1973. Seaweeds: their productivity and strategy for growth. *Science* 182:975–81.

This article might be referred to in the text as (Mann, 1973), or simply as, say, (14), if the bibliographic entries are not alphabetized but numbered (for example, "14. K.H. Mann, *Science.* 182:975–81"—title of article omitted). For papers in the social and natural sciences, consult your instructor about the correct style, or style manual, to follow.

A good general manual is Kate L. Turabian's *A Manual for Writers of Term Papers, Theses, and Dissertations* (University of Chicago Press). A larger reference popular with scholars and editors is *The Chicago Manual of Style*, also published by the University of Chicago Press. Both the *MLA Handbook* and the *Chicago Manual* list other manuals for the various disciplines—engineering, geology, linguistics, psychology, and medicine, for example.

Sample Research Papers

Here are two complete research papers, with everything laid out in typescript and properly spaced, as if you had done it.

Argumentative Essay

The first writer has followed his own interest in Canadian history, as anyone might explore an interest in automobiles, kites, piccolos, or whatever. The writer has found a lively argumentative area, right down the alley of his personal curiosity about Louis Riel's place in Canada's development. The marginal notes reveal (1) the structure of this pro–con essay—the alternation of cons and pros, the examples that support the argument, the appeals to authority; (2) the structure of the paragraphs—the funnel to the thesis in the opening paragraph, the topic sentences in middle paragraphs, the conclusion that broadens out from a restatement of the thesis; and (3) the mechanics of the essay—the source citations, the footnotes.

This paper combines title page with outline; perhaps more common is the separate title page, which we will see in the second paper (page 199).

Within the essay, notice especially how the three footnotes contain only authorial amplification (pages 179, 187, 188), and how the writer easily refers to his sources, both in his notes and in his text. He has chosen to use footnotes instead of gathering the notes at the end of his paper.

Note also the spacing of "Works Cited," with the hanging indentation five spaces in for clear distinction, but otherwise everything double-spaced (pages 195–97). Anonymous titles fall into alphabetical place among the alphabetized authors, with no "Anon." crowding them all in at the beginning.

Michel Laflamme
English 0312
Professor Gamache
April 1, 19--

          Was Riel a Madman or a Hero?

Thesis: Although both his defenders and detractors
may remain unconvinced, the evidence suggests that
Louis Riel was neither an unblemished hero and martyr nor an insane revolutionary, and that the myth
has, in fact, far outdistanced the reality of his
character and deeds.

I.   Riel, the historical figure: the conflicting
     views of him and his actions

II. His role in Manitoba
     A. The establishment of the province, 1869–70
        1. The Métis vs. the new settlers
        2. The Manitoba Act
     B. The execution of Scott
     C. The loss of power and exile

III. Riel's mental problems

IV. Riel in Saskatchewan
     A. His mental state
     B. The Battle of Batoche
     C. Trial and execution

V.   The real Riel vs. the myth

Was Riel a Madman or a Hero?

Louis Riel, leader of the Métis uprisings in later Opening Invitation
nineteenth-century Manitoba and Saskatchewan, has
been characterized as both hero and madman, sedi-
tionist and political idealist. In recent years, with
the growth of the human rights movement in North
America and the concomitant growth of consciousness
of minorities and their often oppressed situations,
Riel's character and career have undergone re-assess- Funnelling to Thesis
ment, some claim revision, in order to rectify what
has been called, by Riel's current defenders, a grave
misrepresentation of history. The treatment of Riel,
and of the Métis generally, is singled out as a clear
instance of Canadian racism and a chronicle of injustice.[1] Perhaps these claims are true, but their truth
or falsity does not necessarily clarify the truth about
the enigmatic Riel. Although both his defend- Thesis
ers and his detractors may remain unconvinced, the
evidence suggests that he was really neither an
unblemished hero nor an insane revolutionary; his
myth has, in fact, far outdistanced the reality of
his character and deeds.

[1] This conflict of views has been discussed often,
in particular by Hartwell Bowsfield in the selection
of essays he edited, *Louis Riel: The Rebel and the
Hero* and in *Louis Riel: Rebel of the Western Frontier
or Victim of Politics and Prejudice*; George F.G.
Stanley in his pamphlet *Louis Riel, Patriot or Rebel?*
is also useful.

The case against Riel has been developed from a number of sources; among the more important are the historical record, as interpreted by writers convinced of the efficacy of a Canadian national destiny and of the dangers of Riel's vision for the Métis people, and the evidence of Riel's personal life, including his psychological breakdown, which reflects the image of a very complex and troubled

personality. But the same sources have also been used to argue Riel's heroism and to prove he was driven by the highest of ideals. His detractors consider such readings of the record, however, as attempts to

revise history. Desmond Morton, for example, considers the re-assessment of the Riel case revisionist:

> Each generation rewrites history to suit its own purposes and Riel, as a man with a powerful sense of his own importance, might well be satisfied that he is getting his due. But other ancestors also have their rights. If Canadians in 1985 want to pardon Riel to please voters in Quebec or the West, they should not harbor the illusion that they are righting some savage injustice of the past. ("Reflections" F 2)

For Morton, evidently the actions of Riel, as a leader of the Métis people during the events in

Manitoba preceding its establishment, in 1870, as a Canadian province and in Saskatchewan in 1885, leading to his trial and execution for "levying war upon Her Majesty"--high treason--justified the treatment accorded him by the Government of Canada and its leader, Sir John A. Macdonald.

But other commentators vigorously disagree with Morton's kind of assessment, urging the view that Riel's goals in both Manitoba and Saskatchewan were reasonable and properly motivated by a perception of what was best for the Métis and for Westerners generally. The historian Fritz Pannekeok discusses the genuine fear of the Métis that **"union with Canada would mean a Protestant supremacy" (67).** He points out that "bigots . . . sought to discredit the Catholic Church, their morals, and their lifestyles, and the Canadians who invaded the [Métis] settlement in the later 1860s confirmed the fears of the Métis" **(67).** The unrest of the people of Assiniboia (the earlier name of the territory) was also fuelled by the realization of the long-established residents "that although their settlement was still isolated, it was the object of expansionist aspirations on the part of both the United States and Canada" **(Thomas 737).** New settlers were endangering the way of life of the older inhabitants; little heed was being paid to their needs and fears, or to the conflicts among racially, linguistically, and religiously different

[Margin annotations: Topic Sentence (Pro); Quotation Marks, Page in Parentheses, Period After; Same Page Repeated; Further Evidence]

groups, each seeking to establish itself while antagonizing the others.

Topic
Sentence   **In 1870, Riel was a major contributor to the
negotiations that produced the Manitoba Act of the
Canadian Parliament establishing the new province,
but because of his decision to sentence to death
Thomas Scott, a man "determined to foment civil war
to eliminate Métis power" (Thomas 740), he destroyed
any future he might have had in the new province.** He
was driven into exile. According to Lewis Thomas, **the**

Pro   **fears of the Métis, those noted by Pannekeok, were
justified: the Ontario militia volunteers, in
Manitoba as part of a Canadian force sent to establish order, "seemed bent on nothing short of assas-
sinating all the Métis" (742).** They gave vent to
their anger over Scott's execution and the hatred
English Canadians harboured against the French-
speaking Métis. Riel, elected twice to the Canadian
Parliament as member for the district of Provencher,
was expelled from the House of Commons, and, in 1875,
he was banished from the country for five years. This
happened despite the fact that, in 1871, he had
offered to help repel an attempted Fenian invasion
with the purpose to annex Manitoba to the United
States. He had supported Canada despite its apparent
rejection of him and the Métis people. Thus, argue
those who support Riel, he was a victim of injustice
and racism. **However, other evidence and interpreta-**

tions of Riel's action in Manitoba offered by Thomas Flanagan, a noted Riel scholar, suggest a less positive view. The handling of the Scott execution, for Flanagan, shows Riel to have been "inflexible" (*Louis* 29). He comments:

> The execution was a ghastly mistake. For one thing it was morally repugnant because of the procedures followed. Scott was hastily tried for an unclear offense; he had no legal assistance nor did he enjoy any other benefits of fair play. He could not even understand the proceedings, which were conducted in French. The alleged legal deficiencies of Riel's own trial fifteen years later pale by comparison. (*Louis* 30)

In analysing Riel's character, Flanagan also suggests that idealism was not the only driving motive behind Riel's actions: "Riel was an ambitious man, but his ambition was fused with his dedication to the cause of his people" (*Louis* 30). This fusion amounted to the identification of Riel's self with his cause. Flanagan says, "If the two [self and cause] become identified in the mind of the individual, it becomes difficult, even impossible, for him to remain objective about himself. Any action, no matter how reprehensible it may seem to outsiders, can be justified for the sake of the cause" (*Louis* 30). So it was that Riel ordered, unjustly and for evidently political reasons (according to Flanagan, to show that his "government possessed the sovereignty of a state" and to "'make Canada respect us'" [*Louis* 291]), that a man be put to death.

This episode in Riel's life demonstrated his character. In Flanagan's opinion, he had shown "considerable political acumen, as well as [an] unfortunate streak of stubbornness. . . . Unquestionably he enjoyed the role he played. Politics was his natural métier, for it allowed him to exercise his very great oratorical and persuasive gifts. He also relished the exercise of power and the prestige that went with it" (*Louis* 31). It also suggests that there is some truth in W. Stewart Wallace's assertion that "Riel was a man of some ability, but of an unbalanced mind" (631). By the time Manitoba became Canada's fifth province, he was but twenty-six years of age; his later activities as leader of the 1885 uprising were the unfortunate fulfilment of the promise of his youth.

The story of the Métis unrest in Saskatchewan in some ways repeats the Manitoba episode, but with greater extremes of behaviour both by Riel and by his

opponents. **Again the evidence suggests that his actions cannot be interpreted simply as those of a heroic leader or of an egocentric madman.** According to Morton, "No one else [other than Riel] had the capacity, the influence or the imagination to orchestrate so massive and dangerous an act of resistance to Canada's transcontinental drive" ("Some" A 12). This view seems to imply that, by resisting Canada's expansion, Riel was behaving unreasonably. To the Métis of today, "the battle Riel waged against the federal government of 1885 is still being fought" ("Métis Vow" A 20). What he fought, they say, was "against Ottawa's indifference to western grievances" ("Métis Vow" A 20). Each of these views has some supporting evidence, but neither, alone, accurately or justly explains Riel.

After Riel left Manitoba for Montana in 1875, where he became an American citizen in 1883, he experienced a series of mental crises. He had previous difficulties of this kind in his early years, and in December 1874, during a visit to Washington, D.C., he "had experienced a mystical vision and an uncontrollable emotional seizure" (Thomas 745). **He was committed to mental asylums of Longue Pointe and Beauport, in Quebec, between 1876 and 1878, during which time he adopted the name of "David,"** which he signed with inverted commas--suggesting that this use was metaphorical and that Riel was not suffering a delusion.

In his essay on Riel's use of the name, Flanagan suggests, with evidence to support the possibility,

Evidence:
Specific
Illustration

that Louis may have chosen to use "David" as an alias while a fugitive; or, perhaps, he chose that name because he saw similarities between himself and the biblical David and between the Métis and the Jews (see "Louis Riel's Name" 50–51). Whatever the reason, it is clear he saw himself as a man with a mission--to secure a land for his people and to establish a peaceful relationship with nonfrancophones in the West and in Eastern Canada. The course of action he began early in 1885 was not intended to start an armed conflict; according to Joseph Kinsey Howard, Riel did not realize the differences that existed between the situations on the Saskatchewan and on the Red River:

Additional
Evidence:
Expert
Opinion
(Con)

Actually, though none but a few of his intimates knew it, Riel had now decided upon a dangerous gamble--establishment of a Provisional Government under the protection of Métis cavalry, as he had done in Rupert's Land. He looked upon this as a demonstration rather than as an act of war, and it had worked on Red River; he was convinced it was the only way to bring Ottawa to terms. But he was not thinking as clearly as he had fifteen years before; his judgment had been impaired by mental lapses, by years of brooding exile, and perhaps most of all by his emotional response to the enthusiasm with which his people had received him in Saskatchewan. (320)

If Howard is accurate, then Riel can hardly be thought of as a conscious rebel leading his people in fanatical dedication to an insane, religious delusion. It was this interpretation that, each for their own reasons, his defenders and his enemies suggested at the time (see Thomas 745). That Riel suffered from bouts of intense emotional stress is clear; that he was insane is not. He had been encouraged in the religious conviction of his role as saviour of his people by Bishop Bourget, and the need for him to play this role was also confirmed by the conviction of the Métis that "they had been abandoned by everyone who had temporal power" (Osler 186–87).

The loss of the Battle of Batoche had dire consequences for Riel and for the Métis. Such fears as the loss of their land resulting from the surveys of 1869 in Manitoba and the ignoring of their land claims in Saskatchewan were only a pale foreshadowing of what they had to fear after Batoche.[2] The rep-

---

[2] A fuller discussion of these surveys and land claims and the relevance to the Métis in Manitoba and in Saskatchewan, and therefore to Riel, is contained in George F.G. Stanley's biography of Riel (see *Louis Riel* 57–59, 295–99).

Footnote
Citing
Further
Evidence

resentation of the Métis heritage in the twentieth

century in such literary works as **Margaret Laurence's**
"The Loons," if they are even only partly valid
reflections of the current situation, certainly
argue the truth of the Métis's fears in the nineteenth century.[3] For Riel, the consequence was his
execution.

   **The trial of Riel has been discussed incessant-
ly, beginning with a flurry of pamphlets that began
appearing soon after his execution, highly emotional in their defence of the man and also highly vig-
orous in attacking the Macdonald government.** Some
sought to arouse American sympathy, since Riel had
become an American. The government, predictably,
published its own justification, for example, the
Interior Department's "Facts," published in 1887.
From the extensive list included with the *Dictionary
of Canadian Biography* Riel entry, it would appear
that the controversy caused the Riel story very early
to lose its reality as an historical event, to become
part of the mythology of Canada--with almost as many
permutations as can be found in Canadian society
itself (see Thomas 751).

   [3] A list in Lussier's collection of essays (see
198-200) of twenty-nine literary works dealing with
the Riel story is by no means complete. It does not,
in fact, include Laurence's.

Of all the things written about the Riel trial, **however, none has had the range of influence that John Coulter, the Irish-born dramatist, created through his plays on the subject, first performed in 1950, revived in 1975 and later broadcast on the CBC.** According to Geraldine Anthony, "Coulter's Canadian plays emphasize that spirit of rebellion against injustice so familiar to the heart of an Irishman" (61). He identified Riel's fight with that of the Irish against the British. In the 1975 program notes, as quoted by Anthony, Coulter called Riel a "dark and haunting symbol nagging our political conscience. . . . I see in his uprisings . . . the early beginnings of movements all over the world in which an emerging people . . . insist on being left alone to mature" (61). This assessment seems to ignore, at the least, Riel's own expressed political affinity for conservative rather than liberal movements (see Flanagan, "Political Thought" 154–57). It is clear that these plays did much to intensify the image of Riel as hero. After they reawakened interest in an apparent protector of an oppressed minority, particularly during the era of activism against the oppression of minorities of the sixties and seventies, the Riel of history was further obscured. They led to ceremonial honouring of Riel's burial place, by today's Métis and today's politicians, as the resting place of a "hero and martyr" deserving of a posthumous pardon from today's Canadian Parliament ("The Métis" B 4). It is this image that is being defended by such moves as MP Bill Yurko's private member's bill introduced in 1983 to grant Riel a pardon. According to Yurko, the hanging of the Métis's chief on Monday, November 15, 1885, is "a blot on Canadian justice" ("Independent" F 18).

But the research of such scholars as Flanagan and Morton seem to lead to another conclusion--that Riel's trial was not, as Coulter represents it, a travesty, but was well run and honestly conducted (see, e.g., Morton, "Reflections" F 2). Thomas calls the treason charge "a legal rationalization" (750), but even his account suggests that Riel had a good chance of avoiding a death sentence by following his lawyer's advice --to build an insanity plea. Not only did he not do as advised, he spoke in such clear and impassioned

Pro   terms on his own behalf that **he confounded all attempts to prove that he was "not an accountable being, that he was unable to distinguish between right and wrong on political and religious subjects"--the judgment of François Xavier Valade, one of the three doctors appointed to examine him (Thomas 751).** He was convicted by the jury "after one hour and twenty minutes [sic] deliberation" (Stanley, *Patriot* 22). One of the jurors, fifty years later, said, according to Stanley, "We tried Riel for treason, and he was hanged for the murder of Scott" (*Patriot* 23).

That the comment of the juror, if what he said
was true, suggests Riel was unjustly hanged is clear,
but that juror was only one man recalling distant
events; he may well have been falsely interpreting
the jury's feelings. Even if the jurors did feel he
should die for killing Scott, they may have been convinced at the trial that he was also guilty of treason. According to Morton, Riel's trial "was conducted . . . with painful propriety and respect for law
and procedure as they existed in 1885. . . . The verdict was inevitable" ("Reflections" F 2).

It is hard to deny, according to Stanley, that the
execution of Riel was "determined by political expe-
diency, that, in the final analysis, it represented
the careful assessment by the Canadian government of
the relative voting strengths and political loyalties
of the two racial groups in Canada" (*Patriot* 23). It
was also reported that Macdonald had said, "He shall
hang . . . though every dog in Quebec bark in his
favour" (Stanley, *Louis Riel* 367). No doubt, from the
evidence given by Stanley (*Louis Riel* 421) of the
Ontario pressure on Macdonald to uphold the death
sentence, the hatred of Protestant for Catholic and
of Englishman for Frenchman motivated many who influenced the prime minister after the trial in Regina.
No clear picture, either of justice done for proper
reasons or of persecution and martyrdom, emerges from
a review of the evidence.

**The confusion of views of Riel makes any assess-
ment of his proper place difficult.** He has become the
hero of a number of camps: to the Métis he is still
a beloved leader; to many French of Canada, he is the
symbol of their fight to preserve their language and
culture; to a number, he is the martyred victim of
Ontario Orangemen's hatred of Catholics and "Popery";
and to others, like John Coulter, he is the symbol
of the minorities' struggle to throw off the oppression of a ruling class. A brief look at recent newspaper accounts of reactions to Riel's story, increasingly prominent because of the 1985 centenary year of
his death, reveals the liveliness of each of the
facets of the Riel myth: in the *Montreal Gazette* it
is noted that a "school package [for Manitoba's
French-language schools] . . . concentrates on the
role played by Riel in the struggle for survival of
francophones in the West" ("Riel's Death" A 9); in
another issue of the same paper, the statements of
Métis leaders at his graveside call Riel "a hero and
a martyr" whose fight was for the Métis ("Métis Pay"
B 4). In a major Manitoba paper a story was printed,
during the separation referendum campaign, giving an
account of a group of *Oui* supporters (attending a
Canadian Labour Congress convention) who went to
Riel's gravesite and "honoured his gravestone with a
few *Oui* stickers and a couple of wreaths. . . . Louis
Laberge . . . [said], ' . . . To them, it was a ges-

ture that symbolized something. . . . Riel asked for
then what Quebecers are asking for now'" (Campbell
2). And in the *Toronto Star*, Michael Best reported
the words of the great-nephew of Riel: "He [Riel] was
an honorable man, who believed that what he was doing
was for the ultimate good of Canada as well as his
people. He shouldn't have been hung for that" (A 8).
The remarks of the historian Morton in the same paper
(cited above) certainly contrast with those of the
young Riel and also with the general tone of Best's
article.

What does become apparent from all these diverg- Expert
ing views is that the real Louis Riel is not their Opinions:
Summation
subject--it is the mythical Riel. An historian
referred to by Morton, Douglas Omran, "noted a few
years ago, Louis Riel has slowly become the Canadian
myth for all seasons" ("Reflections" F 2), and
Stanley, Riel's biographer, said, "By historical
accident rather than by design he became the symbol
of divisions as old as the Franco-British struggle
for the control of North America" (*Patriot* 24). He
also seems to have come to symbolize divisions of our
times as well, as Coulter's view and dramatized ren-
dering of the Riel trial suggest.

Riel's own declared motives, in particular those
that sprang from his religious and basically conservative beliefs, have tended to fade in the popular
image of him. Realizations of these facets of his

life and deeds seem only to be given importance by

Closing Statements: Conclusion from Evidence

historical scholars. **Which Riel is more important seems to depend on whether historical truth or dedication to a cause he can be identified with is more important. But even to the historian, the real Riel remains something of a mystery.**

Works Cited

Anthony, Geraldine. *John Coulter*. Boston: Twayne, 1976.

Best, Michael. "Time Changes Riel's Image from Villain to Hero." *Toronto Star* 24 July 1982: A 8.

Bowsfield, Hartwell, ed. *Louis Riel: Rebel of the Western Frontier or Victim of Politics and Prejudice.* Toronto: Copp Clark, 1969.

---. *Louis Riel: The Rebel and the Hero.* Toronto: Oxford UP, 1971.

Campbell, Ron. "Oui Backers Visit Riel Grave." *Winnipeg Free Press* 8 May 1980: 1.

Coulter, John. *The Crime of Louis Riel.* Toronto: Playwright's Co-op, 1976.

---. *The Trial of Louis Riel.* Ottawa: Oberon, 1968.

Flanagan, Thomas E. *Louis "David" Riel: Prophet of the New World.* Toronto: U of Toronto P, 1979.

---. "Louis Riel's Name 'David,'" in A.S. Lussier: 48–65.

---. "The Political Thought of Louis Riel," in A.S. Lussier: 131–160.

Howard, Joseph Kinsey. *Strange Empire: The Story of Louis Riel.* Toronto: Swan, 1952.

"Independent MP to Introduce Bill That Would Grant Riel a Pardon." *Montreal Gazette* 20 September 1983: F 18.

Laurence, Margaret. "The Loons." In *A Bird in the House*. Toronto: McClelland and Stewart, 1974: 114-27.

Lussier, A.S., ed. *Riel and the Métis: Riel Mini-Conference Papers*. Winnipeg: Manitoba Métis Federation, 1979.

"The Métis Pay Homage to Riel at Annual Graveside Ceremony." *Montreal Gazette* 17 November 1983: B 4.

"Métis Vow to Fight." *Vancouver Sun* 17 November 1983: A 20.

Morton, Desmond. "Reflections on the Centenary of Louis Riel's Execution." *Sunday Star* 13 January 1985: F 2.

---. "Some Reflections on Louis Riel." *Toronto Star* 2 August 1982: A 12.

Osler, E.B. *The Man Who Had to Hang: Louis Riel*. Toronto: Longman's Green, 1961.

Pannekeok, Fritz. "Some Comments on the Social Origins of the Riel Protest of 1869," in A.S. Lussier: 66-83.

"Riel's Death to Be Remembered." *Montreal Gazette* 12 October 1984: A 9.

Stanley, George F.G. "Riel, Louis (David)" *Encyclopedia Canadiana*. 1966 ed.

---. "Riel, Louis." *The Oxford Companion to Canadian History and Literature*. Ed. Norah Story. Toronto: Oxford UP, 1967: 712-13.

---. *Louis Riel.* Toronto: McGraw-Hill Ryerson, 1963.

---. *Louis Riel, Patriot or Rebel?* Ottawa: Canadian
Historical Association Booklets, 1970.

Thomas, Lewis H. "Riel." *Dictionary of Canadian
Biography*, 1881–1890.

Wallace, W. Stewart. "Riel, Louis." *The Macmillan
Dictionary of Canadian Biography.* London:
Macmillan, 1963.

Expository Essay

The Riel paper is a model for the pro–con argumentative essay, a kind you will often want to develop for your academic assignments in university or college. The following paper is a model for a basically expository essay, here on a literary subject. This kind of paper is also a frequently appropriate type for academic assignments. The explanations offered in the margins are not as technically informative as those provided for the Riel essay, since such duplication would be redundant. What they do provide are indications of the rhetorical elements in the essay. Note that this essay uses a simple title page without an outline, and gathers the notes at the end instead of using footnotes.

In examining Margaret Laurence's handling of narrative technique in her series of interconnected stories, together titled *A Bird in the House* (also the title of an individual story), the student author has searched and then researched the available materials on Laurence and the stories. She examined the library in her own and at least one other nearby university, and looked through the scholarly bibliographies and journals that would likely contain information on her topic. After considerable study, she concluded that the technique she calls "double narration" needed to be clarified so she could explain the effectiveness of its use, even though she found at least one scholar as well as an editor who argued against the idea that Laurence successfully implemented a double perspective on the events of the stories by using the technique she chose.

Double Narration in *A Bird in the House*

By Mandie Bzdell

ENG 1120D

Professor Gamache

December 8, 19--

Double Narration in *A Bird in the House*

Opening
Invitation Margaret Laurence's collection of eight framed stories known as *A Bird in the House* are united by
recurring characters, themes, a common setting, and,
most importantly, the narrative point of view. Both
the child and adult responses of Vanessa, the story-
teller, are conveyed as she recollects her experiences through ten years of childhood. The frame
adapted by Laurence is reminiscent of James Joyce's
in *Dubliners*: while he reflects the life of the Irish
in Dublin, using themes centred on their religious,
political, and cultural heritage, Laurence focuses on
the world of southern Manitoba (her fictional
Manawaka), on the life and heritage of European immi-
grants who settled there and the Native Canadians
they displaced. The narrative technique of her eight
Funnelling
to Subject stories is similar to Joyce's in his first three
tales. Her central concern is like that of Joyce's
earliest stories: the vision of a child remembering,
and more profoundly understanding as an adult, the
world of her own family and its particular inheri-
tance from the past as it influences the present and
the future.

Subject   A double perspective is developed by Vanessa
MacLeod, who recounts each story in the first person
from two different points in time; she speaks as a
wise, understanding adult and recalls the vision of
an observant, perceptive child. In each story Vanessa
recalls childhood events that took place at a par-

ticular point in her life or a series of connected events over several periods of her development in childhood or young adulthood. Her perceptions as a child are filtered by her larger comprehension as an adult, revealing the shaping influence of her family and cultural heritage on her adult outlook. This double narration develops a pattern of understanding people as opposed to the focus on a specific idea: "Margaret Laurence is not particularly interested in revealing a point or an idea--she is interested in revealing a revaluation of a character" (Thompson 233).

It is the development of the protagonist that highlights the effectiveness of Laurence's use of the "complex narrative perspective" (Davidson 95). Critics have discussed the effectiveness, or lack thereof, of what might be termed her technique of "double narration." Leona Gom, for example, thinks the two points of view, that is, of the child and the adult Vanessa, strain against each other sufficiently to cause "one of the greatest problems" in these narratives ("Laurence" 55). This technique, however, successfully reveals Vanessa's growth from a child's **Thesis** innocent, often confused, and sometimes mistaken awareness of people, to an adult, sympathetic understanding of their faults and their strengths.

An examination of three relationships she experiences as a child, one to her father, another to her **Method of Development** grandfather Connor, and the third to her childhood acquaintance, Piquette Tonnerre, can help to explain how the double narration works and can also help to Transition to the Body illustrate that it does work successfully; but to appreciate the effectiveness of Laurence's craft, a clear explanation of the double narration as technique and what it entails is a prerequisite.

Topic Sentence Laurence's essay "Time and the Narrative Voice" discusses double narration as literary technique and her reasons for using it. She contrasts the story structure of the novel with a framed series of short Definition stories. She explains that the themes, experiences, and interaction between characters in a novel compare to "a series of wavy lines, converging, separating, touching, drawing apart, but moving in a *horizontal* direction" ("Time" 128). Interconnected short stories, on the other hand, have flow-lines that "move very close together but parallel and in a *vertical* direction" ("Time" 128). Because each story in *A Bird in the House* traces a specific set of connected events, centred on some revelation Vanessa had of a member of her immediate family or someone from her Manawaka community, with no unrelated experience intersecting, even if from the same time frame, Laurence concludes that "the structure of these stories is a good deal simpler than that of a novel" ("Time" 128). To clarify the intent of Vanessa's narration, the author explains:

The narrative voice had to be that of an older
Vanessa, but at the same time the narration be
done in such a way that the ten-year-old would
be conveyed. The narrative voice, therefore,
had to speak as though from two points in
time, simultaneously. ("Time" 128)

Quotation
as Evidence

To reveal the thoughts of the young Vanessa, Laurence
makes the child a reporter who describes herself as "a
professional listener" sitting quietly "in plain
view" (*Bird* 18). Her curiosity as a child leads her
to eavesdrop in her grandparents' house by listening
through the upstairs stovepipes to conveniently
revealing conversations of other family members. She
observes more than her child self understands, which
Laurence indicates by tone and references to time;
for example, such narrative comments as "Two years Examples
ago . . . Yet now, when I had spoken . . ." (*Bird*
133), "Then . . . unable to take in the significance
of what he had said" (*Bird* 79), or "It was only when
I [had] . . . a self-consciousness I would not have
felt even the year before" (*Bird* 139) reveal the age
difference of the adult and child Vanessa. The child
indicates that she has heard but not understood. It
is these devices that Gom argues "Laurence is forced Opposed
Expert
Opinion
to overuse [--that is,] both the eavesdropping device
and the listening-but-not-understanding device. . ."
("Laurence" 55). Continuing her argument, Gom adds:

> The strain between the two Vanessas . . . often requires an unwilling suspension of disbelief on the part of the reader to accept both the understanding of the child and also the detailed and more objective recall of the older Vanessa, whom the reader never actually gets to meet and evaluate for himself. ("Laurence" 55)

Counter-Argument

Aside from the fact that it is not true the reader never "actually gets to meet the older Vanessa," Gom's argument, at best, exaggerates the difficulty for the reader to accept the two points of view without an "unwilling suspension of disbelief."[1] The primary job of the young Vanessa is to be reporter, enabling her to be a capable narrator (Morley 21), and in turn allowing the reader to learn about the story without the voice of the adult narrator interfering.

Despite the author's admission of difficulty with the narration (*Bird* 28), critics, with the exception **Support** of Gom, comment favourably on her technique. Hehner, for example, describes the technique as "almost perfect narration" (45). Clara Thomas attributes part of the success of double narration to the narrator's ability to guide the reader through portions of her life remembered at different developmental stages. She explains:

Vanessa, the narrator, provides a calmly consistent viewpoint as she looks back at her
child-self, who dealt with the circumstances
of her place and life buoyantly and with growing sensitivity. . . . Vanessa, the child,
sees all the surfaces and feels, confusedly,
all the swirling undercurrents, but she does
see as a child, through a glass darkly.
Vanessa, the adult, draws from each remembered
experience more than the sum of its surface
part. . . . (*Manawaka* 56)

This double perspective illustrates the revaluation
of the past shaping Vanessa's character as she
evolves to the comprehending, mature adult.

Thomas does indicate that there are some places
where Vanessa seems "a little too contrived," pointing out the child's comment, "My grandmother was a
Mitigated Baptist. I knew this because I heard my
father say, 'at least she's not an unmitigated
Baptist'" (*Bird* 23). The critic argues, however, that
Laurence's mistakes are rare (*Manawaka* 104-105).

Kertzer believes the narrative form, which he
calls "the memoir," binds the stories together on a
deeper level. He comments on her memoir form:
"Through confession, that is, honest self-revalua-
tion, Vanessa attempts to see life whole. What she
gradually pieces together throughout the stories is

(margin notes)
Thesis

Opposed
Evidence

Support;
Introduce
the Body

herself as she has developed over the years" (23). The repetitious piecing together of details creates a pattern of understanding with Vanessa maturing into a three-dimensional character rather than a childish, two-dimensional one. Thomas agrees:

Using an
Authority
for Support

> In every case the remembering charts some progress in Vanessa's experience, steps toward understanding, or those more difficult steps, toward acceptance when understanding is impossible. (*Margaret* 55)

The main character's acquired comprehension fits M.H. Abrams's description of a "flat" or two-dimensional character developed into a "round" or three-dimensional one (21). This additional dimension can be seen developed during one story that takes Vanessa through a series of events related to her growing understanding of the Métis girl, Piquette Tonnerre, and more fully illustrated through the parallel patterns of understanding revealed in several stories that concern her father and grandfather Connor.

Further
Example as
Evidence

Vanessa's relationship with her father, Ewen, is an example of increasing insight developed in the title story, "A Bird in the House," and in "To Set Our House in Order." Vanessa is not given much time with her father. In the latter story, Vanessa as a child finds her father's travel literature and discovers he had dreams of adventuring beyond Manawaka, dreams he sacrificed to compensate his mother for the death of his brother, Roderick. Only later, as an adult, does she realize fully the extent of his loss. In the title story, Ewen dies from the flu epidemic one winter when she is twelve, still a child with little understanding of death. Of the mixed emotions Vanessa feels, anger is the strongest. In her lack of understanding, she is convinced that she is responsible for her father's death because she allowed a sparrow trapped between the glasses of the window to come into the room. "A bird in the house means a death in the house," the hired girl, Noreen, reports to Vanessa after they let it loose outdoors (*Bird* 98). Shortly after Noreen's prediction, Ewen dies. In an angry reaction to her father's death Vanessa strikes Noreen. Like the bird, she is bat-tling to escape, yet the bird escapes. Vanessa is trapped. She cannot undo her father's death and believes from that point that she must have been responsible. The child cannot understand adequately.

Years later, Vanessa's eyes are opened while sorting through her father's desk. She discovers a letter and "a picture of a girl" whom her father met while fighting in the First World War in France. A new side of her father now revealed to her, she finds herself comparing their lives. She is in the same position as her father once had been: young, in love,

and anxious to leave Manawaka. In a moment of understanding, the older Vanessa realizes that her father
was a real person and she accepts that she was not
responsible for his premature death. When Vanessa
remarks, "I grieved for my father as though he had
just died now" (*Bird* 107), it is understood that she
is forgiving him for a deed he could not control: his
death.

This same pattern of understanding is repeated in
"The Loons" as it spans four periods in Vanessa's
life, the first beginning at age eleven. The story
introduces Piquette as a Tonnerre, a Métis family who
live on the outskirts of Manawaka. Piquette joins the
MacLeods on their vacation at Diamond Lake upon the
advice of Dr. MacLeod, who wants her to rest her
tubercular-infected leg. Excited by the prospect of
having someone with extensive knowledge of the outdoors, Vanessa naïvely associates the Métis girl with
"the people of Big Bear and Poundmaker, of Tecumseh,
of the Iroquois who had eaten Father Brébeuf's heart"
(*Bird* 112). Vanessa is disappointed by Piquette's
lack of interest in the outdoors. Four years later,
Vanessa meets Piquette at the Regal Café. Embarrassed
by their encounter, Vanessa listens to Piquette talk
about her travels to prairie cities and about her
intentions to marry a white man. Like the summer
spent together at the lake, Vanessa cannot relate to
Piquette. She is mature enough to recognize "a ter-

rifying hope" (*Bird* 117) in Piquette's eyes. Three years later, Vanessa's mother reports that Piquette and her two children died in a house fire. In the final narration, the adult Vanessa reminisces about the summer at Diamond Lake and Piquette not wanting to come to the lake to listen to the crying of the loons. "It seemed to me now that in some unconscious and totally unrecognised way, Piquette might have been the only one, after all, who had heard the crying of the loons" (*Bird* 122). The adult Vanessa associates the silence of the loons with the silence of the Métis people. With time she has developed a larger understanding of Piquette's social situation.

Vanessa's relationship with Grandfather Connor reveals her greatest growth in understanding. Grandfather Connor is an autocratic person, known as "an upright man" (*Bird* 16) and a pillar of the community. Vanessa, in her juvenile ignorance, detests him. She childishly refuses to admit she agrees with Grandfather's opinion, even when she knows that he is right. In "The Sound of Singing" for example, Grandfather throws his brother out for asking for money. Grandmother Connor tells her husband to go after him. Bewildered and upset at this, he turns to Vanessa for support. Vanessa knows that the point he is making about taking care of Uncle Dan with his hard-earned money is legitimate, yet she veers "sharply away from his touch" (*Bird* 39).

Another
Example as
Evidence

The tension between Vanessa and the "protago-nist's chief antagonist" (Davidson 99) is intensified when her family is forced to move into the brick house after the death of her father. At the age of seventeen, Vanessa finds herself in love with an air cadet who is stationed outside of Manawaka. Michael is visiting one night when Grandfather intervenes, telling Vanessa that she must go to bed. Embarrassed in front of her boyfriend by someone she hates, she is angry. Bitter words are exchanged. Grandfather Connor verbally attacks Vanessa's relationship: "'You ought to know better than run around with a fellow like this. I'll bet a nickel to a doughnut hole he's married.'" Vanessa retaliates: "I jumped. . . . Then I shouted at him, as though if I sounded all my trumpets loudly enough, his walls would quake and crumble" (*Bird* 184). The narration of the angry adolescent effectively conveys the tension between the two stubborn characters.

Her anger and hatred stay with her at twenty, after Grandfather Connor's death. The narrator explains, "I was not sorry that he was dead. I was only surprised. Perhaps I had really imagined that he was immortal. Perhaps he even was immortal, in ways which it would take me half a lifetime to comprehend" (*Bird* 189).

Twenty years later, Vanessa understands her grandfather better. In "The Mask of the Bear" she

explains, while observing a Haida bear mask, "I imagined I could see somewhere within that darkness a
look which I knew, a lurking bewilderment" (*Bird* 86).
In the ending of "Jericho's Brick Battlements"
Vanessa is forty, and returns to Manawaka. Upon view-
ing the brick house she realizes, "I had feared and
fought the old man, yet he proclaimed himself in my
veins" (*Bird* 191). She acknowledges the kinship and
makes peace inside of herself because she has accepted the relationship between Grandfather Connor and
herself, which has taken the adult Vanessa many years
of reflection to develop.

Following the pattern that Laurence traces in *A*   Conclusion
Bird in the House highlights the effectiveness of
double narration. Vanessa grows into a tolerant and
understanding human being as she gains insight into
her childhood experiences with family members and
with her fellow Manawakans, and it is precisely
because of the successful use of a double perspective conveyed through the narrative technique that
this revelation of Vanessa and of the people of her
world is achieved. Interestingly, when Laurence submitted her eight stories to be published as one complete work, the publishers did not want to publish
it right away. Judith Jones, the editor, believed
that the first-time reader would not be able to follow the inconsistent time sequence that the narration handled. She suggested "a continuous narrative

of them, not exactly a novel but something closer to a novel than a series of stories" (Davies 338).

Thesis Affirmed Laurence preferred to narrate the story from two points in time, thus allowing the reader to discover the effective growth of the main character, a kind of development that could only be done through double narration.

Notes

¹ Gom's assertion that the reader never meets the adult Vanessa ignores a number of instances where her adult experience is used to reveal the full impact of the child's experience. For example, she realizes the meaning of Grandfather Connor's bear cloak as she looks into the eyes of the Haida mask at the end of "The Mask of the Bear," and she discovers the significance of Piquette's death when she is grown to adulthood. These and other instances of Vanessa's adult experiences reveal her in an intimate way to the reader.

Explanatory
Endnote

Works Cited

Abrams, M.H. *A Glossary of Literary Terms.* 3rd ed.
Holt, Rinehart and Winston, 1971.

Davidson, A.E. "Cages and Escapes in Margaret
Laurence's *A Bird in the House.*" *University of
Windsor Review* Fall-Winter 1981: 94–96.

Davies, R.A. "'Half War/Half Peace': Margaret
Laurence and the Publishing of *A Bird in the
House.*" *English Studies in Canada* September 1981:
338–41.

Gom, Leona. "Laurence and the Use of Memory."
Canadian Literature 71 (1976): 54–55.

---. "Margaret Laurence and the First Person."
Dalhousie Review 55 (1975): 238–49.

Hehner, B. "River of Now and Then: Margaret
Laurence's Narratives." *Canadian Literature* 74
(1977): 45.

Kertzer, Jonathan. *That House in Manawaka: Margaret
Laurence's* A Bird in the House. Toronto: ECW,
1992.

Laurence, Margaret. *A Bird in the House.* Toronto:
McClelland and Stewart, 1970.

---. "Time and the Narrative Voice." In *The Narrative
Voice.* Ed. John Metcalf. Toronto: McGraw-Hill
Ryerson, 1972: 126-130.

Morley, P. "The Long Trek Home: Margaret Laurence's
    Stories." *Journal of Canadian Studies* 11 (1976):
    21-23.

Thomas,   Clara.   *Margaret   Laurence*.   Toronto:
    McClelland and Stewart, 1969.

---. *The Manawaka World of Margaret Laurence*.
    Toronto: McClelland and Stewart, 1975.

Thompson, K. "Review of *A Bird in the House*." In *A
    Place to Stand On*. Ed. George Woodcock. Edmonton:
    NeWest, 1983: 232-35.

Canadian Reference Sources

The following list is a selection of some basic Canadian reference sources available in printed form. Many of these books and periodicals will direct you to other sources, as your research leads you closer to your final thesis. Your reference librarian can suggest other sources, including CD-ROMs and Internet sites, both for preliminary searches and for in-depth research.

General Reference

The Canadian Encyclopedia. 2nd ed. Edmonton: Hurtig, 1988. Also available on CD-ROM, updated annually, from McClelland and Stewart (Toronto).

Dictionary of Canadian Biography. Toronto: University of Toronto Press. In progress; volumes published to date cover the years 1000–1870 and 1881–1900.

The Historical Atlas of Canada. 3 vols. Toronto: University of Toronto Press, 1987–93.

Ingles, Ernie. *Bibliography of Canadian Bibliographies.* 3rd ed. Toronto: University of Toronto Press, 1994.

Dictionaries

The Canadian Oxford Dictionary. Toronto: Oxford University Press, 1998.

Fee, Margery, and Janice McAlpine. *Guide to Canadian English Usage.* Toronto: Oxford University Press, 1997.

Gage Canadian Dictionary. Toronto: Gage Educational, 1997.

ITP Nelson Canadian Dictionary of the English Language. Toronto: ITP Nelson, 1997.

Annual Publications

Canada Year Book. Ottawa: Statistics Canada.

Canadian Almanac and Directory. Toronto: Copp Clark Professional. Provides a directory to governments; education; health care facilities;

courts and law firms; companies and associations in fields such as communication, finance, culture, sports, tourism, and transportation.

Canadian Book Review Annual. Toronto. Contains original reviews of new Canadian books.

Canadian Books in Print. Toronto: University of Toronto Press. Lists in-print Canadian books in English.

Canadian Who's Who. Toronto: University of Toronto Press.

Canadiana. Ottawa: National Library of Canada. Canada's official national bibliography lists publications of Canadian interest received by the National Library.

Colombo, John Robert, ed. *The Canadian Global Almanac.* Toronto: Macmillan.

Livres disponibles. Lists in-print Canadian books in French.

Who's Who of Canadian Women. Toronto: Who's Who Publications.

Periodicals

Books in Canada. Toronto. Discusses books in the social sciences and humanities.

Canadian Historical Review. Toronto: University of Toronto Press. Lists recent publications relating to Canadian history, economics, geography, statistics, education, religion, ethnology, and folklore.

Canadian Literature. Vancouver: University of British Columbia.

Essays on Canadian Writing. Toronto: ECW Press.

Journal of Canadian Studies/Revue d'études canadiennes. Peterborough: Trent University.

Literary Review of Canada. Toronto. Contains reviews of new Canadian books in fields such as history, politics, philosophy, literary criticism, and culture.

Prairie Forum: The Journal of the Canadian Plains Research Centre. Regina: University of Regina.

Queen's Quarterly. Kingston: Queen's University.

Quill & Quire. Toronto. The publishing industry's trade magazine.

University of Toronto Quarterly. Toronto: University of Toronto Press. Includes an annual review entitled "Letters in Canada."

Indexes

Canadian Index (formerly *Canadian Magazine Index*). Toronto: Micromedia.

Canadian News Index (formerly *Canadian Newspaper Index*). Toronto: Micromedia.

Canadian Periodical Index. Toronto: Gale Canada (formerly published by the Canadian Library Association).

Literature and the Arts

Benson, Eugene, and L.W. Conolly. *Oxford Companion to Canadian Theatre.* Toronto: Oxford University Press, 1989.

Benson, Eugene, and William Toye, eds. *Oxford Companion to Canadian Literature.* 2nd ed. Toronto: Oxford University Press, 1997.

Henighan, Tom. *Ideas of North: A Guide to Canadian Arts and Culture.* Vancouver: Raincoast, 1997.

Kallmann, Helmut, and Gilles Potvin, eds. *Encyclopedia of Music in Canada.* 2nd ed. Toronto: University of Toronto Press, 1992.

Klinck, Carl F. *Literary History of Canada: Canadian Literature in English.* 2nd ed. 4 vols. Toronto: University of Toronto Press, 1976–90.

Miska, John P. *Ethnic and Native Canadian Literature: A Bibliography.* Toronto: University of Toronto Press, 1990.

New, W.H. *A History of Canadian Literature.* Macmillan History of Literature. London: Macmillan Educational, 1989.

Suggested Exercises

1. Consult the current *World Almanac and Book of Facts* for the date of some memorable event—the sinking of the Titanic or the Lusitania, Lindbergh's flight over the Atlantic, Canada's entry into the Second World War, the founding of the United Nations, the great stock-market crash, or the like. Now go to another collection, like *Facts on File*, and some of the other almanacs and yearbooks for the year of your event; write an essay entitled, let us say, "1929"—a synopsis of the monumental and the quaint for that year, as lively and interesting as you can make it.

2. Look up some event of the recent past in the *Canadian News Index* or the *Canadian Global Almanac*. Write a paper on how the event is reported in the newspapers available in your library.

3. Choose a subject like the origin of man, the PLO, apartheid—anything that interests you—and compile a bibliographical list of the articles given in the *Reader's Guide*, beginning with the most recent issue and going backward in time until you have eight or ten titles. You may have to look under several headings, such as "archaeology," "anthropology," and "evolution," for the origin of man, under "Israel," "Lebanon," and others in addition to "PLO" itself, and under "South Africa," "racism," and "apartheid" itself for apartheid. Then look in the scholarly *Indexes* (see page 159), and make another bibliographical listing of your subject for the same period. Which articles appear in the *Humanities* or *Social Sciences Index* (or both) only? Which articles appear in the *Reader's Guide* only? Which appear in both the *Indexes* and the *Guide*? Write a brief commentary about the differences in coverage in these two (or three) indexes. What does comparing them tell you about research?

4. In the *Essay and General Literature Index*, look up three essays on Gerard Manley Hopkins published in anthologies between 1965 and 1969, recording each entry and then following it by full data on the book, with call number, from the library catalogue.

5. Select some well-known literary work: *Sunshine Sketches of a Little Town*, *David Copperfield*, *Alice in Wonderland*, *The Wind in the Willows*, *A Farewell to Arms*, *Ulysses*. Describe how thoroughly it is catalogued by your library. Check entries for author, title, and subject. How many editions does the library have? Is the work contained within any *Works*? How many entries treat it as a subject? Does your library own a first edition? This last may require that you find the date of the first edition by looking up your author in an encyclopedia, checking available critical or biographical books, and perhaps checking in the British Library's *General Catalogue of Printed Books* (or, for a twentieth-century book, *United States Catalog of Printed Books* or *Cumulative Book Index*) to discover the earliest cataloguing.

The Trouble with Grammar

You have chosen your subject, and narrowed it down to a focused thesis. You have researched your topic, and organized your thoughts. You have drafted your essay, and revised the final draft, relieved that your assignment is done. But wait!—you have forgotten something. The last stage of the writing process still lies ahead—proofreading. In this chapter and the next, we will look at some of the points to consider in adding the final polish to your paper.

Agreement: Subjects and Verbs

Disagreement is our trouble—especially between subjects and verbs. The English *s* troubles students who speak English as a second language. An *s* makes a plural noun—*grades, places, businesses*—but a singular verb—*gets, goes, operates*. With verbs, *s* signals only the third person singular (he, she, it), and is used only in the present tense:

	SINGULAR	PLURAL
FIRST PERSON	I get	we get
SECOND PERSON	you get	you get
THIRD PERSON	he, she, it get*s*	they get

The varied forms in our most frequent verb, *to be*, also cause trouble:

	SINGULAR	PLURAL
FIRST PERSON	I am	we are
SECOND PERSON	you are	you are
THIRD PERSON	he, she, it is	they are

So this is the most basic problem of agreement—matching singular subjects with singular verbs, plurals with plurals. First, find the verb, since that names the action—*sways* in the following sentence: "The poplar tree *sways* in the wind, dropping yellow leaves on the lawn." Then ask *who* or *what* sways, and you have your simple subject: *tree*, a singular noun. Then make sure that your singular subject matches its singular verb. You will have little trouble except when subject and verb are far apart, or when the number of the subject itself is doubtful. (Is *family* singular or plural? What about *none*? What about *neither he nor she*?)

> FAULTY: *Revision* of their views about markets and averages *are* mandatory. Subject and Verb Widely Separated
>
> REVISED: *Revision* of their views about markets and averages *is* mandatory.

Sidestep the plural constructions that fall between your singular subject and its verb:

> FAULTY: The *attention* of the students *wander* out the window. Mistaken Plurals
>
> REVISED: The *attention* of the students *wanders* out the window.
>
> FAULTY: The *plaster*, as well as the floors, *need* repair.
>
> REVISED: The *plaster*, as well as the floors, *needs* repair.

Collective nouns (*committee, jury, herd, group, family, kind, quartet*) are usually considered single units in Canada (although often plural in British usage); give them singular verbs, or plural members:

> FAULTY: Her *family* were ready. Collective Nouns
>
> REVISED: Her *family* was ready.
>
> FAULTY: The *jury have disagreed* among themselves.
>
> REVISED: The *jurors have disagreed* among themselves.
>
> FAULTY: These *kind* of muffins *are* delicious.
>
> REVISED: *These muffins are* delicious.
>
> REVISED: *This kind* of muffin *is* delicious.

Watch out for the indefinite pronouns—*each, neither, anyone, everyone, no one, none, everybody, nobody*. Each of these is (not *are*) singular in idea, yet each one flirts with the crowd from which it singles out its idea: each of *these*, either of *them*, none of *them*. Give all of them singular verbs.

> *None* of these men *is* a failure. Indefinite Pronouns
> *None* of the class, even the best prepared, *wants* the test.
> *Everybody*, including the high-school kids, *goes* to Andy's Café.
> *Neither* the right nor the left *supports* the issue.

None of them are is very common. From Shakespeare's time to ours, it has persisted alongside the more precise *none of them is*, which seems to have the edge in careful prose.

When one side of the *either–or* contrast is plural, you have a problem, conventionally solved by matching the verb to the nearer noun:

> Either the players or the coach *is* bad. "Either–Or"

Since *players is* disturbs some feelings for plurality, the best solution is probably to switch your nouns:

> Either the coach or the players *are* bad.

When both sides of the contrast are plural, the verb is naturally also plural:

> Neither the rights of man nor the needs of the commonwealth *are* relevant to the question.

Don't let a plural noun in the predicate lure you into a plural verb:

> FAULTY: His most faithful rooting *section are* his family and his girlfriend.
>
> REVISED: His most faithful rooting *section is* his family and his girlfriend.
>
> REVISED: His family and his girlfriend *are* his best rooting section.

Aligning the Verbs

Verbs have *tense* (past, present, future), *mood* (indicative, imperative, subjunctive), and *voice* (active, passive). These can sometimes slip out of line, as your thought slips, so a review should be useful here.

Use the Tense That Best Expresses Your Idea

Each tense (from Latin *tempus*, meaning time) has its own virtues for expressing what you want your sentences to say. Use the *present tense*, of course, to express present action: "Now she *knows*. She *is leaving*." Use the present also for habitual action: "He *sees* her every day," and for describing literary events: "Hamlet *finds* the king praying, but he *is* unable to act; he *lets* the opportunity slip." And use the present tense to express timeless facts: "The Greeks knew the world *is* round." The present can also serve for the future: "Classes *begin* next Monday." Apply the *past tense* to all action before the present:

> One day I *was watching* television when the phone *rang*. It *was* the police.
>
> In the centre of the cracked façade, the door *sagged*. Rubble *lay* all around the foundations.

Use the future tense for action expected after the present:

> He *will finish* it next year.
>
> When he *finishes* next year, . . . [The present functioning as future]

He *is going to finish* it next year. [The "present progressive" *is going* plus an infinitive, like *to finish,* commonly expresses the future.]

Use the *present perfect tense* for action completed ("perfected") but relevant to the present moment:

I *have gone* there before.
He *has sung* forty concerts.
She *has driven* there every day.

Use the *past perfect tense* to express "the past of the past":

When we *arrived* [past], they *had finished* [past perfect].

Similarly, use the *future perfect tense* to express "the past of the future":

When we *arrive* [future], they *will have finished* [future perfect].
You *will have worked* [future perfect] thirty hours by Christmas.
The flare *will signal* [future] that he *has started* [perfect].

Set your tense, then move your readers clearly forward or back from it as your thought requires:

Hamlet *finds* the king praying. He *had sworn* instant revenge the night before, but he *will achieve* it only by accident and about a week later. Here he *is* unable to act; he *loses* his best opportunity.

Shifting Tenses

But avoid mixtures like this: "Hamlet *finds* the king praying, but he *was* unable to act; he *let* the opportunity slip." Here, all the verbs should be in the present, corresponding to *finds.*

Confusing the past tense of *lie* with the verb *lay* is a frequent error. *Lie* is intransitive, taking no object: *Lie* down; I *lie* down; I *lay* down yesterday; I have *lain* down often. *Lay* is transitive, taking an object: I *lay* carpets; I *laid* one yesterday; I have *laid* them often. When someone says incorrectly, "He is *laying* down," ask yourself the impudent questions "Who is Down?" or "Is he laying goose feathers?"—and you might remember to say, and write: "He is *lying* down."

Irregular Verbs

The irregular verbs, like *lie,* frequently slip into disagreement, not because of the third-person *s,* but because their past tense and past participle do not always match in the regular way: "She *played*; she has *played.* She *won*;

she has *won*." Some of the irregulars also match: "He *bid*; he has *bid*." But most do not:

He arose.   He has *arisen*.
She *swam*.   She has *swum*.

Here are some to watch. Alternate forms are in parentheses. (Also see the Glossary in Chapter 14 for *hanged, hung*; *lay, lie*; *lighted, lit*; *rise, raise*; *set, sit*.)

PRESENT TENSE	PAST TENSE	PAST PARTICIPLE
arise	arose	arisen
awake	awoke	awaked (*but* was awakened)
bear	bore	borne
beat	beat	beaten
begin	began	begun
bid ("order")	bade	bidden
bid ("offer")	bid	bid
burst	burst	burst
drag	dragged (*not* drug)	dragged
fit	fitted (fit, *especially intransitively*)	fitted (*but* a fit person)
fling	flung	flung
get	got	got (gotten)
hang ("execute")	hanged	hanged
hang	hung	hung
lay	laid	laid
lie	lay	lain
light	lit (lighted)	lit (lighted)
prove	proved	proven (proved)
ride	rode	ridden
rise	rose	risen
set	set	set
sew	sewed	sewn (sewed)
shine ("glow")	shone	shone
shine ("polish")	shined	shined
show	showed	shown (showed)
shrink	shrank (shrunk)	shrunk (shrunken)
sit	sat	sat
sow	sowed	sown (sowed)
spring	sprang	sprung
swim	swam	swum
swing	swung	swung
wake	woke (waked)	waked
waken	wakened	wakened

Keep Your Moods in Mind

The *indicative mood*, which indicates matters of fact (our usual verb and way of writing), and the *imperative mood*, which commands ("Do this," "Keep your moods in mind"), will give you no trouble. The *subjunctive mood*, which expresses an action or condition not asserted as actual fact, occasionally will. The conditional, provisional, wishful, suppositional ideas expressed by the subjunctive are usually subjoined (*subjunctus*, "yoked under") in subordinate clauses. The form of the verb is often plural, and often in past tense, even though the subject is singular, and the condition present or future.

> She looked as if she *were* confident.
> If I *were* you, Miles, I would ask her myself.
> If this *be* error, and upon me [*be*] proved. . . .
> *Had* she *been* sure, she would have said so.
> I demand that he *make* restitution.
> I move that the nominations *be closed*, and that the secretary
> *cast* a unanimous ballot.

Don't let *would have* (colloquial *would've*) seep into your conditional clause from your main clause:

> FAULTY: If he *would have known*, he never would have said that.

> REVISED: If he *had known*, he never would have said that.

> REVISED: *Had* he *known*, he never would have said that.

Be careful not to write *would of* or *should of* for *would have* (*would've*) or *should have* (*should've*).

Don't Mix Active and Passive Voice

Let's take one parting shot at our friend the passive voice. Avoid misaligning active with passive in the same sentence:

> As she *entered* the room muttering *was heard* [she *heard* mut-   Mixed Voices
> tering].
> After they *laid out* the pattern, electric shears *were used* [they
> *used* electric shears].

You can also think of this as an awkward shift of subject, from *she* to *muttering*, from *they* to *shears*. Here is a slippery sample, where the subject stays the same:

FAULTY: This plan *reduces* taxes and *has been used* successfully in three other cities.

REVISED: This plan *reduces* taxes and *has been* successful in three other cities.

REVISED: This plan *reduces* taxes and *has proved* workable in three other cities.

Agreement: Pronouns

Match Your Pronouns to What They Stand For

Pronouns stand for (*pro*) nouns. They *refer* to nouns already expressed (*antecedents*), or they stand for conceptions (people, things, ideas) already established or implied, as in "*None of them* is perfect." Pronouns must agree with the singular and plural ideas they represent, and stand clearly as subjects or objects.

When a relative pronoun (*who*, *which*, *that*) is the subject of a clause, it takes a singular verb if its antecedent is singular, a plural verb if its antecedent is plural:

> Phil is the only *one* of our swimmers **who** *has* won three gold medals. [The antecedent is *one*, not *swimmers*.]
>
> Phil is one of the best *swimmers* **who** *have* ever been on the team. [The antecedent is *swimmers*, not *one*.]

Pronouns may stand either as subjects or objects of the action, and their form changes accordingly.

Use Nominative Pronouns for Nominative Functions

Those pronouns in the predicate that refer to, or complement, the subject are troublesome; keep them nominative:

Subjective
Complement He discovered that it was *I*.
It was *they* who signed the treaty.
This is *she*.
It is *I*.

Another example is that of the pronoun in *apposition* with the subject (that is, *positioned near*, *applied to*, and meaning the same thing as, the subject):

Apposition
with Subject *We* students would rather talk than sleep.

After *than* and *as*, the pronoun is usually the subject of an implied verb:

> She is taller than *I* [am]. Implied Verb
> You are as bright as *he* [is].
> She loves you as much as *I* [do].

But note: "She loves you as much as [she loves] *me.*" Match your pronouns to what they stand for, subjects for subjects, objects for objects. (But a caution: use an objective pronoun as the subject of an infinitive. See page 228.)

Use a nominative pronoun as subject of a noun clause. This is the trickiest of pronominal problems, because the subject of the clause also looks like the object of the main verb:

> FAULTY: The sergeant asked *whomever* did it to step forward.

> REVISED: The sergeant asked *whoever* did it to step forward.

Similarly, parenthetical remarks like *I think*, *he says*, and *we believe* often make pronouns seem objects when they are actually subjects:

> FAULTY: Ellen is the girl *whom* I think *will succeed.*

> REVISED: Ellen is the girl *who* I think *will succeed.*

Use Objective Pronouns for Objective Functions

Compound objects give most of the trouble:

> They want you and *I* and the working poor to provide them with everything.

Want *I*? No! Want *me*. This is the test to keep you straight. Try the pronoun by itself to hear the disagreement: "invited *I*," "for *I*," "between *I*," "sent *he*." The following examples are all correct:

> They want you and *me* and the working poor. . . . Compound
> The mayor invited my wife and *me* to dinner. [*not* my wife Objects
> and *I*]
> Can you play tennis with Charlie and *me*? [*not* with Charlie
> and *I*]
> Between *her* and *me*, an understanding grew.
> They sent it to Stuart and *him*.
> . . . for you and *me*.

Again, see if the pronoun would stand by itself:

> FAULTY: The credit goes to *he* who tries. ["to he"?]

> REVISED: The credit goes to *him* who tries.

Pronouns in apposition with objects must themselves be objective:

FAULTY: The mayor complimented us both—Bill and *I*.

REVISED: The mayor complimented us both—Bill and *me*.

FAULTY: She gave the advice specifically to us—Helen and *I*.

REVISED: She gave the advice specifically to us—Helen and *me*.

FAULTY: Between us—Elaine and *I*—an understanding grew.

REVISED: Between us—Elaine and *me*—an understanding grew.

FAULTY: He would not think of letting *we* women help him.

REVISED: He would not think of letting *us* women help him.

Notice this one:

FAULTY: Will you please help Leonard and *I* find the manager?

REVISED: Will you please help Leonard and *me* find the manager?

Leonard and me are objective both as objects of the verb *help* and as subjects of the shortened infinitive *to find*. Subjects of infinitives are always in the objective case, as in "She saw *him* go"; "She helped *him* find his keys."

Use a Possessive Pronoun Before a Gerund

Since gerunds are *-ing* words used as nouns, the pronouns attached to them must say what they mean:

FAULTY: She disliked *him* hunting.

REVISED: She disliked *his* hunting.

The object of her dislike is not *him* but *hunting*.

Keep Your Antecedents Clear

If an antecedent is missing, ambiguous, vague, or remote, the pronoun will suffer from "faulty reference" and disagreement.

MISSING: In Alberta *they* produce a lot of oil.

REVISED: Alberta produces a lot of oil.

AMBIGUOUS: Paul smashed into a woman's *car who* was visiting his sister.

REVISED: Paul smashed into the car of a *woman* visiting his sister.

VAGUE: Because Ann had never spoken before an audience, she was afraid of *it*.

REVISED: Because Ann had never spoken before an audience, she was afraid.

REMOTE: The castle was built in 1537. The rooms and furnishings are carefully kept up, but the entrance is now guarded by a coin-fed turnstile. *It* still belongs to the Earl.

REVISED: The castle, which still belongs to the Earl, was built in 1537. The rooms and furnishings are carefully kept up, but the entrance is now guarded by a coin-fed turnstile.

This poses a special problem, especially when heading a sentence ("This is a special problem"). Many good stylists insist that every *this* refer back to a specific noun—*report* in the following example:

> The commission submitted its *report. This* proved windy, evasive, and ineffectual.

"This"

Others occasionally allow (as I do) a more colloquial *this*, referring back more broadly:

> The commission submitted its report. This ended the matter.

Give an Indefinite or General Antecedent a Singular Pronoun

FAULTY: *Each* of the students hoped to follow in *their* teacher's footsteps.

REVISED: *Each* of the students hoped to follow in *his or her* teacher's footsteps.

REVISED: *All* of the students hoped to follow in *their* teacher's footsteps. [Here, we have a single class.]

FAULTY: If the *government* dares to face the new philosophy, *they* should declare *themselves*.

REVISED: If the *government* dares to face the new philosophy, *it* should declare *itself.*

Keep Person and Number in Agreement

Don't slip from person to person (*I* to *they*); don't fall among singulars and plurals—or you will get bad references:

> FAULTY: *They* have reached an age when *you* should know better.
>
> REVISED: *They* have reached an age when *they* should know better.
>
> FAULTY: A motion *picture* can improve upon a book, but *they* usually do not.
>
> REVISED: A motion *picture* can improve upon a book, but *it* usually does not.

Modifiers Misused and Misplaced
Keep Your Adjectives and Adverbs Straight

The adjective sometimes wrongly crowds out the adverb: "He played a *real* conservative game." And the adverb sometimes steals the adjective's place, especially when the linking verb looks transitive but isn't (*feels, looks, tastes, smells*), making the sense wrong: "He feels *badly*" (adverb) means incompetence, not misery. The cure is to modify your nouns with adjectives, and everything else with adverbs:

> He played a *really* conservative game. [adverb]
> He feels *bad*. [adjective]
> This tastes *good*. [adjective]
> I feel *good*. [adjective—spirit]
> I feel *well*. [adjective—health]
> This works *well*. [adverb]

Some words serve both as adjectives and adverbs: *early, late, near, far, hard, only, little, right, wrong, straight, well, better, best, fast*, for example.

> Think *little* of *little* things.

Near is a hard case, serving as an adjective (*the near future*) and as an adverb of place (*near the barn*), and then also trying to serve for *nearly*, the adverb of degree:

> FAULTY: We are nowhere *near* knowledgeable enough.
>
> REVISED: We are not *nearly* knowledgeable enough.

> FAULTY: It was a *near* treasonous statement.
>
> REVISED: It was a *nearly* treasonous statement.

> FAULTY: With Dodge, he has a tie of *near*-filial rapport.
>
> REVISED: With Dodge, he has an *almost* filial rapport.

Slow has a long history as an adverb, but *slowly* keeps the upper hand in print. Notice that adverbs usually go after, and adjectives before:

> The *slow* freight went *slowly*.

Make Your Comparisons Complete

Ask yourself "Than what?"—when you find your sentences ending with a *greener* (adjective) or a *more smoothly* (adverb):

> FAULTY: The western prairies are *flatter*.
>
> REVISED: The western prairies are *flatter than* the northern tundra.

> FAULTY: He plays *more skilfully*.
>
> REVISED: He plays more *skilfully than* most boys his age.

> FAULTY: Jane told her *more than* Ellen.
>
> REVISED: Jane told her *more than she told* Ellen.

> FAULTY: His income is lower than a *dishwasher*.
>
> REVISED: His income is lower than a *dishwasher's*.

Don't Let Your Modifiers Squint

Some modifiers squint in two directions at once. Place them to modify one thing only.

> FAULTY: They agreed *when both sides ceased fire* to open negotiations.
>
> REVISED: They agreed to open negotiations *when both sides ceased fire*.

FAULTY: Several delegations *we know* have failed.

REVISED: *We know* that several delegations have failed.

FAULTY: They hoped to try *thoroughly* to understand.

REVISED: They hoped to try to understand *thoroughly*.

The split infinitive (see page 291) can also make a modifier squint:

FAULTY: He resolved to *dependably* develop plans.

REVISED: He resolved to develop *dependable* plans.

Don't Let Your Modifiers or References Dangle

The *-ing* words (the gerunds and participles) tend to slip loose from the sentence and dangle, referring to nothing or the wrong thing.

FAULTY: Going home, the walk was slippery. [participle]

REVISED: Going home, I found the walk slippery.

FAULTY: When getting out of bed, her toe hit the dresser. [gerund]

REVISED: When getting out of bed, she hit her toe on the dresser.

Infinitive phrases also can dangle badly:

FAULTY: To think clearly, some logic is important.

REVISED: To think clearly, you should learn some logic.

Any phrase or clause may dangle:

FAULTY: When only a freshman [phrase], Jim's history teacher inspired him.

REVISED: When Jim was only a freshman, his history teacher inspired him.

FAULTY: After he had taught thirty years [clause], the average student still seemed average.

REVISED: After he had taught thirty years, he found the average student still average.

Suggested Exercises

Here is an assortment of the usual disagreements. Making them agreeable is probably best done in class orally—to hear the disagreements first.

1. Straighten out these disagreements and misalignments:
   a. These kinds of questions are sheer absurdities.
   b. Conservatism, as well as liberalism, are summonses for change in Canadian life, as we know it.
   c. Neither the make of his car nor the price of his stereo impress us.
   d. Her family were bitter about it.
   e. The grazing ground of both the antelope and the wild horses are west of this range.
   f. The campus, as well as the town, need to wake up.
   g. The extinction of several species of whales are threatened.
   h. None of the group, even Smith and Jones, want to play.
   i. If I would have studied harder, I would have passed.
   j. First she investigated the practical implications, and then the moral implications that were involved were examined.

2. Revise these faulty pronouns, and their sentences where necessary:
   a. None of us are perfect.
   b. Doug is the only one of the boys whom always stand straight.
   c. He took my wife and I to dinner.
   d. She disliked him whistling the same old tune.
   e. He will give the ticket to whomever wants it: he did it for you and I.
   f. My mother insists on me buying my own clothes: everyone likes their independence.

3. Straighten out these adjectives and adverbs:
   a. The demonstration reached near riot proportions.
   b. It smells awfully.
   c. The dress fitted her perfect.
   d. He has a reasonable good chance.
   e. Her car had a special built engine.

4. Complete and adjust these partial thoughts:
   a. She swims more smoothly.
   b. The pack of a paratrooper is lighter than a soldier.
   c. The work of students is more intense than their parents.

5. Unsquint these modifiers:
   a. She planned on the next day to call him.
   b. They asked after ten days to be notified.
   c. The party promised to completely attempt reform.
   d. Several expeditions we know have failed.

6. Mend these danglers:
   a. What we need is a file of engineers broken down by their specialties.
   b. Following the games on television, the batting average of every player was at her fingertips.

c. When entering the room, the lamp fell over.

d. After he arrived at the dorm, his father phoned.

7. Correct the following:

    a. No one likes dancing backward all their lives.

    b. His pass hit the wide receiver real good.

    c. The ball was laying under the bench.

    d. If they would of come earlier, they would of seen everything.

    e. I feel badly about it.

8. Clear up the following:

    a. The professor as well as the students were glad the course was over.

    b. We study hard at university, but you do not have to work all the time.

    c. As he looked up, a light could be seen in the window.

    d. A citizen should support the government, but they should also be free to criticize it.

    e. She hated me leaving so early.

    f. This is one of the best essays that has been submitted.

    g. The responsibility falls upon you and I.

Punctuation, Spelling, Capitalization

Punctuation gives the silent page some of the breath of life. It signals to the reader's eye the pauses and emphases with which speakers point their meanings. It is the writer's way of marking for the reader what the speaker can do with the voice. Loose punctuators forget what every good writer knows: that even silent reading produces an articulate murmur in our heads, that language springs from the breathing human voice, that the beauty and meaning of language depend on what the written word makes us *hear*, on the sentence's tuning of emphasis and pause. Commas, semicolons, colons, periods, and other punctuation transcribe our meaningful pauses to the printed page.

The Period: Marking the Sentence

A period marks a sentence, a subject completed in its verb:

> She walked.

A phrase—which lacks a verb, though it may contain a verb *form (seeing, going)*—subordinates this idea, making it *depend* on some other main clause:

> *While walking,* she thought.

A subordinate clause does the same, making the whole original sentence subordinate:

> *While she walked,* she thought.

Take special care not to break off a phrase or clause with a period, making a fragment that looks like a sentence but isn't (unless you intend a rhetorical fragment—see pages 121–22), and don't use the comma as a period (see page 243).

FAULTY: She dropped the cup. Which had cost twenty dollars.

REVISED: She dropped the cup, which had cost twenty dollars.

FAULTY: He swung furiously, the ball sailed into the lake.

REVISED: He swung furiously. The ball sailed into the lake.

Like a period, and a question mark, an exclamation mark marks a sentence, but much more emphatically: "Plan to revise!" Use it sparingly if you want it to count rhetorically.

The Comma

Here are the four basic commas:

1. The *introducer*—after introductory phrases and clauses
2. The *coordinator*—between "sentences" joined by *and, but, or, nor, yet, so, still, for*
3. The *inserter*—a *pair* around any inserted word or remark
4. The *linker*—when adding words, phrases, or clauses

The Introducer   A comma after every introductory word or phrase makes your writing clearer, more alive with the breath and pause of meaning:

> Indeed, the idea failed.
> After the first letter, she wrote again.
> In the autumn of the same year, he went to Paris.

Without the introductory comma, your reader frequently expects something else:

> After the first letter she wrote, she. . . .
> In the autumn of the same year he went to Paris, he. . . .

Notice how the introducer changes the meaning of *however* in these two sentences:

> However she goes, she goes in style.
> However, she goes when she feels like it.

You can usually avoid the danger of forgetting the comma and spoiling the sense by substituting *but* for your introductory *howevers*: "But she goes when. . . ." Put your *howevers* within the sentence between commas:

> She goes, however, when she feels like it.

But beware! What looks like an introductory phrase or clause may actually be the subject of the sentence *and should take no comma*. A comma can break up a good marriage of subject and verb. The comma in each of these is an interloper, and should be removed:

> That handsome man in the ascot tie, is the groom.
> The idea that you should report every observation, is wrong.
> The realization that we must be slightly dishonest to be truly
> kind, comes to all of us sooner or later.

If your clause-as-subject is unusually long, or confusing, you may relieve the pressure by inserting some qualifying remark after it, between two commas:

> The idea that you should report every observation, *however
> insignificant*, is wrong.
> The realization that we must be slightly dishonest to be truly
> kind, *obviously the higher motive*, comes to all of us sooner
> or later.

The Coordinator   This goes between "sentences" joined by coordinate conjunctions. You will often see the comma omitted when your two clauses are short: "He hunted and she fished." But nothing is wrong with "He hunted, and she fished." The comma, in fact, shows the slight pause you make when you say it.

Think of the "comma-and" (*, and*) as a unit equivalent to the period. The period, the semicolon, and the "comma-and" all designate independent clauses—independent "sentences"—but give different emphases:

He was tired. He went home.	Period
He was tired; he went home.	Semicolon
He was tired, and he went home.	"Comma-and"

A comma tells your reader that another subject and predicate are coming:

> He hunted the hills and dales.
> He hunted the hills, and she fished in the streams.
>
> She was naughty but nice.
> She was naughty, but that is not our business.
>
> Wear your jacket or coat.
> Wear your jacket, or you will catch cold.
>
> It was strong yet sweet.
> It was strong, yet it was not unpleasant.

Of course, you may use a comma in *all* the examples above if your sense demands it. The contrasts set by *but*, *or*, and *yet* often urge a comma, and the even stronger contrasts with *not* and *either–or* demand a comma, whether or not full predication follows:

> It was strong, yet sweet.
> It was a battle, not a game.
> . . . either a bird in the hand, or two in the bush.

Commas signal where you would pause in speaking. The meaningful pause also urges an occasional comma in compound predicates, usually not separated by commas:

> He granted the usual permission and walked away.
> He granted the usual permission, and walked away.

Both are correct. In the first sentence, however, the granting and walking are perfectly routine, and the temper unruffled. In the second, some kind of emotion has forced a pause, and a comma, after *permission*. Similarly, meaning itself may demand a comma between the two verbs:

> He turned and dropped the vase.
> He turned, and dropped the vase.

In the first sentence, he turned the vase; in the second, himself. Your "comma-and" in compound predicates suggests some touch of drama, some meaningful distinction, or afterthought.

You need a comma before *for* and *still* even more urgently. Without the comma, their conjunctive meaning changes; they assume their ordinary roles, *for* as a preposition, *still* as an adjective or adverb:

> She liked him still. . . . [That is, either *yet* or *quiet*!]
> She liked him, still she could not marry him.
> She liked him for his money.
> She liked him, for a good man is hard to find.

An observation: *for* is the weakest of all the coordinators. Almost a subordinator, it is perilously close to *because*. *For* can seem silly if cause and effect are fairly obvious: "She liked him, for he was kind." Either make a point of the cause by full subordination—"She liked him *because* he was kind"—or flatter the reader with a semicolon: "She liked him; he was kind." *For* is effective only when the cause is somewhat hard to find: "Blessed are the meek, for they shall inherit the earth."

To summarize the basic point about the comma as coordinator: put a comma before the coordinator (*and, but, or, nor, yet, so, still, for*) when joining independent clauses, and add others necessary for emphasis or clarity.

The Inserter   Put a *pair* of commas around every inserted word, phrase, or clause—those expressions that seem parenthetical and are called *nonrestrictive*. When you cut a sentence in two to insert something necessary, you need to tie off *both* ends, or your sentence will die on the table:

> St. John's, Newfoundland looks promising. [, Newfoundland,]
> When he packs his bag, however he goes. [, however,]
> The car, an ancient Packard is still running. [, an ancient Packard,]
> April 10, 1999 is agreeable as a date for final payment. [, 1999,]
> John Jones, Jr. is wrong. [, Jr.,]
> I wish, Indira you would do it. [, Indira,]

You do not mean that 1999 is agreeable, nor are you telling John Jones that Junior is wrong. Such parenthetical insertions need a *pair* of commas:

> The case, *nevertheless*, was closed.
> She will see, *if she has any sense at all*, that he is right.
> Sam, *on the other hand*, may be wrong.
> Note, *for example*, the excellent brushwork.
> John Jones, *M.D.*, and Bill Jones, *Ph.D.*, doctored the punch to perfection.
> He stopped at Kingston, *Ontario*, for two hours.

The same rule applies to all nonrestrictive remarks, phrases, and clauses— all elements simply additive, explanatory, and hence parenthetical:

> John, *my friend*, will do what he can.
> Andy, *his project sunk, his hopes shattered*, was speechless.
> The taxes, *which are reasonable*, will be paid.
> That man, *who knows*, is not talking.

Think of *nonrestrictive* as "nonessential" to your meaning, hence set off by commas. Think of *restrictive* as essential and "restricting" your meaning, hence not set off at all (use *which* for nonrestrictives, *that* for restrictives; see pages 130–31).

> The taxes that are reasonable will be paid.   Restrictives
> Southpaws who are superstitious will not pitch on Friday
>   nights.
> The man who knows is not talking.
>
> The taxes, which are reasonable, will be paid.   Nonrestrictives
> Southpaws, who are superstitious, will not pitch on Friday
>   nights.
> The man, who knows, is not talking.

The difference between restrictives and nonrestrictives is one of meaning, and the comma-pair signals that meaning. Our first "Southpaw" sentence says that only the superstitious ones lie low on Fridays; our second one, that *all* of them do. Now, how many grandmothers do I have in the first sentence below (restrictive)? How many in the second (nonrestrictive)?

> My grandmother who smokes pot is ninety.
> My grandmother, who smokes pot, is ninety.

In the first sentence, I still have two grandmothers, since I am distinguishing one from the other by my restrictive phrase (no commas) as the one with the unconventional habit. In the second sentence, I have but one grandmother, about whom I am adding an interesting though nonessential, nonrestrictive detail within a pair of commas. Read the two aloud, and you will hear the difference in meaning, and how the pauses at the commas signal that difference. Commas are often optional, of course. The difference between a restrictive and a nonrestrictive meaning may sometimes be very slight. For example, you may take our recent bridegroom either way (but not halfway):

> That handsome man, in the ascot tie, is the groom. [nonre-
> strictive]
> That handsome man in the ascot tie is the groom. [restrictive]

Your meaning will dictate your choice. But use *pairs* of commas or none at all. Never separate subject and verb, or verb and object, with just one comma.

Some finer points. One comma of a pair enclosing an inserted remark may coincide with, and, in a sense, overlay, a comma "already there":

> In each box, a bottle was broken.
> In each box, however, a bottle was broken.
>
> The team lost, and the school was sick.
> The team lost, in spite of all, and the school was sick.
>
> The program will work, but the cost is high.
> The program will work, of course, but the cost is high.

Between the coordinate clauses, however, a semicolon might have been clearer:

> The team lost, in spite of all; and the school was sick.
> The program will work, of course; but the cost is high.

Beware: *however*, between commas, cannot substitute for *but*, as in the perfectly good sentence: "He wore a hat, *but* it looked terrible." You would be using a comma where a full stop (period or semicolon) should be:

> WRONG: He wore a hat, however, it looked terrible.
> RIGHT: He wore a hat; however, it looked terrible.
> RIGHT: He wore a hat, however; it looked terrible.
> [Notice the two meanings.]

But a simple "comma-but" avoids both the ambiguity of the floating *however* and the ponderosity of anchoring it with a semicolon, fore or aft: "He wore a hat, but it looked terrible."

Another point. *But* may absorb the first comma of a pair enclosing an introductory remark (although it need not do so):

> At any rate, he went.
> But, at any rate, he went.
> But at any rate, he went.
>
> But[,] if we want another party, we had better clean up.
> The party was a success, but[,] if we want another one, we had
>   better clean up.

But avoid a comma *after* "but" in sentences like this:

> I understand your argument, but I feel your opponent has a
> stronger case.

Treat the "he said" and "she said" of dialogue as a regular parenthetical insertion, within commas, and without capitalizing, unless a new sentence begins:

> "I'm going," he said, "whenever I get up enough nerve."
> "I'm going," he said. "Whenever I get up enough nerve, I'm
>   really going."

And Canadian usage puts the comma inside *all* quotation marks:

> "He is a nut," she said.
> She called him a "nut," and walked away.

Finally, the comma goes after a parenthesis, never before:

> On the day of her graduation (June 4, 1989), the weather
>   turned broiling hot.

The Linker   This is the usual one, linking on additional phrases and afterthoughts:

> They went home, having overstayed their welcome.
> The book is too long, overloaded with examples.

It also links items in series. Again, the meaningful pause demands a comma:

> words, phrases, or clauses in a series
> to hunt, to fish, and to hike
> He went home, he went upstairs, and he could remember
>   nothing.
> She liked oysters, soup, roast beef, and song.

Put a linker before the concluding *and*. By carefully separating all elements in a series, you keep alive a final distinction long ago lost in the daily press, the distinction Virginia Woolf makes (see pages 122–23): "urbane, polished, brilliant, imploring and commanding him. . . ." *Imploring and commanding* is syntactically equal to each one of the other modifiers in the series. If Woolf customarily omitted the last comma, as she does not, she could not have reached for that double apposition. The muscle would have been dead. These other examples of double apposition will give you an idea of its effectiveness:

> They cut out his idea, root and branch.
> She lost all her holdings, houses and lands.
> He loved to tramp the woods, to fish and hunt.

A comma makes a great deal of difference, of sense and distinction.

But adjectives in series before a noun change the game a bit. Notice the difference between the following two strings of adjectives:

> a good, unexpected, natural rhyme
> a good old battered hat

With adjectives in series, only your sense can guide you. If each seems to modify the noun directly, as in the first example above, use commas. If each seems to modify the total accumulation of adjectives and noun, as with *good* and *old* in the second phrase, do not use commas. Say your phrases aloud, and put your commas in the pauses that distinguish your meaning.

Finally, a special case. Dramatic intensity sometimes allows you to join clauses with commas instead of conjunctions:

> She sighed, she cried, she almost died.
> I couldn't do it, I tried, I let them all get away.
> It passed, it triumphed, it was a good bill.
> I came, I saw, I conquered.

The rhetorical intensity of this construction—the Greeks called it *asyndeton*—is obvious. The language is breathless, or grandly emphatic. As Aristotle once said, it is a person trying to say many things at once. The subjects repeat themselves, the verbs overlap, the idea accumulates a climax. By some psychological magic, the clauses of this construction usually come in threes. The comma is its sign. But unless you have a stylistic reason for such a flurry of clauses, go back to the normal comma and conjunction, the semicolon, or the period.

Beware of Fragments, Comma Splices, and Run-Ons

Fragments, comma splices, and run-ons are the most persistent problems in using the comma. The rhetorical fragment, as we have seen (pages 121–22), may have great force: "So what." But the grammatical one needs repairing with a comma:

> FAULTY: She dropped the cup. Which had cost twenty dollars.
> REVISED: She dropped the cup, which had cost twenty dollars.

> FAULTY: He does not spell everything out. But rather hints that something is wrong, and leaves the rest up to the reader.
> REVISED: He does not spell everything out, but rather hints . . ., and leaves. . . .

> FAULTY: Finally, the book is obscure. Going into lengthy discussions and failing to remind the reader of the point.
> REVISED: Finally, the book is obscure, going into lengthy discussions. . . .

> FAULTY: Yet here is her husband treating their son to all that she considers evil. Plus the fact that the boy is offered beer.
> REVISED: Yet here is her husband treating their son to all that she considers evil, especially beer.

> FAULTY: She points out that one never knows what the future will bring. Because it is actually a matter of luck.
> REVISED: She points out that one never knows what the future will bring, because it is actually a matter of luck.

> FAULTY: They are off. Not out of their minds exactly, but driven, obsessed.
> REVISED: They are off, not out of their minds exactly, but driven, obsessed.

The comma splice is the beginner's most common error, the opposite of the fragment—putting a comma where we need a period rather than putting a period where we need a comma—splicing two sentences together with a comma:

> The comma splice is a common error, it is the opposite of a fragment.   Comma Splice

Of course, you will frequently see comma splices, particularly in fiction and dialogue, where writers are conveying colloquial speed and the thoughts come tumbling fast. Some nonfiction writers borrow this same speed here and there in their prose. Like the rhetorical fragment, a comma splice between short clauses can be most effective, as we saw above: "If speech and cinema are akin to music, writing is like architecture; *it endures, it has weight.*"[1] But you should learn to recognize these as comma splices and generally avoid them because they may strike your readers as the errors of innocence.

The run-on sentence (fortunately less common) omits even the splicing comma, running one sentence right on to another without noticing:

Run-On   The comma splice is a common error it is the opposite of a fragment.

Here the writer is in deeper trouble, having somehow never got the feel of a sentence as based on subject and verb, and thus needing special help. But most of us can see both the comma splice and run-on as really being two sentences, to be restored as such:

The comma splice is a common error. It is the opposite of a fragment.

Or to be coordinated by adding a conjunction after the comma:

The comma splice is a common error, and it is. . . .

Or to be subordinated by making the second sentence a phrase:

The comma splice is a common error, the opposite. . . .

Here are some typical comma splices:

She cut class, it was boring.
The class was not merely dull, it was useless.
Figures do not lie, they mislead.
He was more than satisfied, he was delighted.

Each of these pulls together a pair of closely sequential sentences. But a comma without its *and* or *but* will not hold the coordination. Either make them the sentences they are:

She cut class. It was boring.
Figures do not lie. They mislead.

or coordinate them with a colon or dash (with a semicolon *only* if they contrast sharply):

The class was not merely dull: it was useless.
He was more than satisfied—he was delighted.

or subordinate in some way:

She cut class because it was boring.
The class was not merely dull but useless.
More than satisfied, he was delighted.

---

[1] Richard Lloyd-Jones, "What We May Become," *College Composition and Communication* 33 (1952): 205. Italics added.

Here are some more typical splices, all from one set of student papers dealing with Shakespeare's *The Tempest*. The highlighted commas should be periods:

> She knows nothing of the evil man is capable of , to her every man is beautiful.
> The question of his sensibility hovers , we wonder if he is just.
> Without a doubt, men discourage oppression , they strive to be free.
> Ariel is civilized society , besides being articulate, he has direction and order.
> Stephano and Trinculo are the comics of the play , never presented as complete characters, they are not taken seriously.

You will accidentally splice with a comma most frequently when adding a thought (a complete short sentence) to a longer sentence:

> The book describes human evolution in wholly believable terms, comparing the social habits of gorillas and chimpanzees to human behaviour, it is very convincing.

But you have confused your readers. Which way is that *comparing* phrase supposed to go? You must help them by repairing your splice with a period, either like this:

> The book describes human evolution in wholly believable terms, comparing the social habits of gorillas and chimpanzees to human behaviour. It is very convincing.

or like this:

> The book describes human behaviour in wholly believable terms. Comparing the social habits of gorillas and chimpanzees to human behaviour, it is very convincing.

In short, be sure to attach all accidental fragments—that *comparing* phrase, by itself, would be a fragment—to your main sentence. But be sure each complete sentence—"It is very convincing"—stands clear and alone with its own capital and period.

Conjunctive adverbs (*however, therefore, nevertheless, moreover, furthermore*, and others) may also cause comma splices and trouble:

> She continued teaching, however her heart was not in it.

Here are three mendings:

> She continued teaching, but her heart was not in it.
> She continued teaching; however, her heart was not in it.
> She continued teaching; her heart, however, was not in it.

Similarly, transitional phrases (*in fact, that is, for example*) may splice your sentences together:

> He disliked discipline, that is, he really was lazy.

You can strengthen the weak joints like this:

> He disliked discipline; that is, he really was lazy.
> He disliked discipline, that is, anything demanding.

Semicolon and Colon

Use the semicolon *only* where you could also use a period, unless desperate. This dogmatic formula, which I shall loosen up in a moment, has saved many a punctuator from both despair and a reckless fling of semicolons. Confusion comes from the belief that the semicolon is either a weak colon or a strong comma. It is most effective as neither. It is best, as we have seen (page 111), in pulling together and contrasting two independent clauses that could stand alone as sentences:

> The novel concentrates on character. The film intensifies the violence.
>
> Semicolon   The novel concentrates on character; the film intensifies the violence.

This compression and contrast by semicolon can go even farther, allowing us to drop a repeated verb in the second element (note also how the comma marks the omission):

> Golf demands the best of time and space; tennis demands the best of personal energy.
> Golf demands the best of time and space; tennis, the best of personal energy.
> Tragedy begins with the apple; comedy, with the banana peel.[2]

Use a semicolon with a transitional word (*moreover, therefore, then, however, nevertheless*) to signal close contrast and connection:

> He was lonely, blue, and solitary; moreover, his jaw ached.

Used sparingly, the semicolon emphasizes your crucial contrasts; used recklessly, it merely clutters your page. *Never* use it as a colon: its effect is exactly opposite. A colon, as in the preceding sentence, signals the meaning to go ahead; a semicolon, as in this sentence, stops it. The colon is a green light; the semicolon is a stop sign.

---

[2] Adapted from Guy Davenport, *Life* 27 March 1970: 12.

Consequently, a wrong semicolon frequently makes a fragment. *Use a semicolon only where you could also use a period*—forget the exceptions—or you will make semicolon-fragments like the italicized phrases following the erroneous semicolons highlighted below:

> The play opens on a dark street in Montreal; *one streetlight giving the only illumination.*
>
> The geese begin their migration in late August or early September; *some groups having started, in small stages, a week or so earlier.*

Each of those semicolons should have been a comma.

Of course, you may occasionally need a semicolon to unscramble a long line of phrases and clauses, especially those in series and containing internal commas:

> Composition is hard because we often must discover our ideas by writing them out, clarifying them on paper; because we must also find a clear and reasonable order for ideas the mind presents simultaneously; and because we must find, by trial and error, exactly the right words to convey our ideas and our feelings about them.

The colon waves the traffic on through the intersection: "Go right ahead," it says, "and you will find what you are looking for." The colon emphatically and precisely introduces a series, the clarifying detail, the illustrative example, and the formal quotation:

> The following players will start: Corelli, Smith, Dupuis, Liu, and Stein.   Colon
>
> Pierpont lived for only one thing: money.
>
> In the end, it was useless: Adams really was too green.
>
> We remember Sherman's words: "War is hell."

Both the semicolon and the colon, unlike the comma and the period, go *outside* quotation marks:

> He called it a "generation gap"; she called it a "gaping generation."
>
> This was no "stitch in time": it was complete reconstruction.

Parentheses and Dash

The dash says aloud what the parentheses whisper. Both enclose interruptions too extravagant for a pair of commas to hold. The dash is the more useful—since whispering tends to annoy—and will remain useful only if not overused. It can serve as a conversational colon. It can set off a concluding phrase—for emphasis. It can bring long introductory matters to focus, concluding a series of parallel phrases: "—all these are crucial." It can insert a full sentence—a clause is really an incorporated sentence—directly next to a key word. The dash allows you to insert—with a kind of shout!—an occasional exclamation. You may even insert—and who would blame you?—an occasional question. The dash affords a structural complexity with all the tone and alacrity of talk.

With care, you can get much the same power from parentheses:

> Many philosophers have despaired (somewhat unphilosophically) of discovering any certainties whatsoever.
>
> Thus did Innocent III (we shall return to him shortly) inaugurate an age of horrors.
>
> But in such circumstances (see page 34), be cautious.
>
> Delay had doubled the costs (a stitch in time!), so the plans were shelved.

But dashes seem more generally useful, and here are some special points. When one of a pair of dashes falls where a comma would be, it absorbs the comma.

> If he wanted to go, he certainly could.
>
> If he wanted to go—whether invited or not—he certainly could.

Not so with the semicolon:

> He wanted to go—whether he was invited or not; she had more sense.

To indicate the dash, type two hyphens (--) flush against the words they separate—not one hyphen between two spaces, nor a hyphen spaced to look exactly like a hyphen.

Put commas and periods *outside* a parenthetical group of words (like this one), even if the parenthetical group could stand alone as a sentence (see the preceding "Innocent III" example). (But if you make an actual full sentence parenthetical, put the period inside.)

Change has had its way with the parentheses around numbers. Formal print and most guides to writing, including this one, still hold to the full parentheses:

Numbered Items

> The sentence really has only two general varieties: (1) the "loose" or strung-along, in Aristotle's phrase, and (2) the periodic.
>
> She decided (1) that she did not like it, (2) that he would not like it, and (3) that they would be better off without it.

Popular print now often omits the first half of the parentheses:

. . . decided 1) that she did not like it, 2) that he. . . .

But for your papers—keep the full parentheses.

Brackets

Brackets indicate your own words inserted or substituted within a quotation from someone else: "Byron had already suggested that [they] had killed John Keats." You have substituted "they" for "the gentlemen of the *Quarterly Review*" to suit your own context. You do the same when you interpolate a word of explanation: "Byron had already suggested that the gentlemen of the *Quarterly Review* [especially Croker] had killed John Keats."

Do not use parentheses: they mark the enclosed words as part of the original quotation. Don't claim innocence because your typewriter lacks brackets. Just leave spaces and draw them in later, or type slant lines and tip them with pencil or with the underscore key: [...]

In the example below, you are pointing out with a *sic* (Latin for "so" or "thus"), which you should not italicize, that you are reproducing an error exactly as it appears in the text you are quoting:

"On no occassion [sic] could we trust them."

Similarly, you may give a correction after reproducing the error:

"On the twenty-fourth [twenty-third], we broke camp."
"In not one instance [actually, Baldwin reports several instances] did our men run under fire."

Use brackets when you need parentheses within parentheses:

(see Roberta Hamilton, *Gendering the Vertical Mosaic* [Toronto: Copp Clark, 1996], 22–24)

Your instructor will probably put brackets around the wordy parts of your sentences, indicating what you should cut:

In fact, [the reason] he liked it [was] because it was different.

Quotation Marks and Italics

Put quotation marks around quotations that "run directly into your text" (like this), but *not* around quotations set off from the text and indented.

You normally inset poetry, as it stands, without quotation marks:

> An aged man is but a paltry thing,
> A tattered coat upon a stick, unless
> Soul clap its hands and sing. . . .
> (Yeats, "Sailing to Byzantium")

But if you run it into your text, use quotation marks, with virgules (slants) showing the line-ends: "An aged man is but a paltry thing, / A tattered coat. . . ." Put periods and commas *inside* quotation marks; put semicolons and colons *outside*:

Period	Now we understand the full meaning of "give me liberty, or give me death."
Comma	"This strange disease of modern life," in Arnold's words, remains uncured.
Semicolon	In Greece, it was "know thyself"; in Canada, it is "know thy neighbour."
Colon	He left after "O Canada": he could do nothing more.

Although logic often seems to demand the period or comma outside the quotation marks, convention has put them inside for the sake of appearance, even when the sentence ends in a single quoted word or letter:

> Clara Bow was said to have "It."
> Mark it with "T."

If you have seen the periods and commas outside, you were probably reading a British book or one of Canada's little magazines.

When you have dialogue, signal each change of speaker with a paragraph's indentation:

> "What magazines in the natural sciences should I read regularly?" inquired the student.
>
> "*Equinox* and *Scientific American* are always worth your time, but you'll want to explore others as well," responded her adviser.

If in a dialogue a single speaker carries on for several paragraphs, place quotation marks before *each* paragraph, but after only the *last* paragraph.

Omit quotation marks entirely in *indirect* quotations:

> She asked me if I would help her.
> The insurance agent told Mr. Jones that his company would pay all valid claims within thirty days.
> In his review of the play, J.K. Beaumont praised the plot as strong and incisive, but faulted the dialogue as listless and contrived in a few scenes. [Here, you are summarizing the reviewer's comments.]

If you are quoting a phrase that already contains quotation marks, reduce the original double marks (") to single ones ('):

> ORIGINAL: Hamlet's "Are you honest?" is easily explained.
> YOUR QUOTATION: He writes that "Hamlet's 'Are you honest?' is easily explained."

Single Quotation Marks

Notice what happens when the quotation within your quotation falls at the end:

> ORIGINAL: A majority of the informants thought *infer* meant "imply."
> YOUR QUOTATION: Kirk reports that "a majority of the informants thought *infer* meant 'imply.'"

And notice that a question mark or exclamation mark falls between the single and the double quotation marks at the end of a quotation containing a quotation:

> "Why do they call it 'the Hippocratic oath'?" she asked.
> "Everything can't be 'cool'!" he said.

But heed the following exception:

> "I heard someone say, 'Is anyone home?'" she declared.

Do not use *single* quotation marks for your own stylistic flourishes; use *double* quotation marks or, preferably, none:

> It was indeed an "affair," but the passion was hardly "grand."
> It was indeed an affair, but the passion was hardly grand.
> Some "cool" pianists use the twelve-tone scale.

Once you have thus established this slang meaning of *cool,* you may repeat the word without quotation marks. In general, of course, you should favour that slang your style can absorb without quotation marks.

Do not use quotation marks for calling attention to words as words. Use italics (an underscore when typing) for the words, quotation marks for their meanings.

> This is taking *tergiversation* too literally.
> The word *struthious* means "like an ostrich."

Italics

Similarly, use italics for numbers as numbers and letters as letters:

> He writes a *5* like an *s.*
> Dot your *i*'s and cross your *t*'s.

But common sayings like "Watch your p's and q's" and "from A to Z" require no italics.

Use quotation marks for titles *within* books and magazines—titles of chapters, articles, short stories, songs, and poems—and for unpublished works, lectures, courses, and television episodes within a series. But use italics for titles or names of books, newspapers, magazines, plays, films, television series, long poems, sculptures, paintings, ships, trains, and airplanes.

Titles and Names

Farley Mowat's style of mixing fact and fiction in his books was attacked in *Saturday Night.*

We saw Michelangelo's *Pietà,* a remarkable statue in white marble.

We took the *Maid of the Mist* across the Niagara River.

She read all of Frye's *The Great Code.*

His great-grandfather went down with the *Titanic.*

She read it in the *Globe and Mail.*

They loved the film *Mission: Impossible.*

Handle titles within titles as follows:

"Tintern Abbey" and Nature in Wordsworth [book about a poem]

"'Tintern Abbey' and Natural Imagery" [article about a poem]

"The Art of *Tom Jones*" [article about a book]

The Art of Tom Jones [book about a book]

In the last example, notice that what is ordinarily italicized, like the title of a book (*Tom Jones*), is set in roman when the larger setting is in italics.

Italicize foreign words and phrases, unless they have been assimilated into English through usage (your dictionary should have a method for noting the distinction; if not, consult one that has):

The paragraph contained two clichés and one *ad hominem* argument.

The author of this naïve exposé suffers from an *idée fixe.*

Foreign expressions not usually italicized include *etc., e.g., et al.,* genre, hubris, laissez-faire, leitmotif, roman à clef, raison d'être, tête-à-tête.

Use neither quotation marks nor italics for the Bible, for its books or parts (Genesis, Old Testament), for other sacred books (Koran, Talmud, Upanishad), for famous documents like the Magna Carta, the Charter of Rights, and the Communist Manifesto, or for instrumental music known by its form, number, and key:

Beethoven's C-minor Quartet

Brahms's Symphony No. 4, Opus 98

When a reference in parentheses is given at the end of a quotation, the quotation marks *precede* the parentheses:

As Ecclesiastes tells us, "there is no new thing under the sun" (1.9).

Ellipsis

1. Use three spaced periods . . . (the ellipsis mark) when you omit something from a quotation. Do *not* use them in your own text in place of a dash, or in mere insouciance.
2. If you omit the end of a sentence, put in a period (with no space before it) and add the three spaced dots. . . .
3. If your omission falls after a completed sentence, just add the three spaced dots to the period already there. . . . It looks the same as case 2.

Here is an uncut passage, followed by a shortened version illustrating the three kinds of ellipsis:

> To learn a language, learn as thoroughly as possible a few everyday sentences. This will educate your ear for all future pronunciations. It will give you a fundamental grasp of structure. And start soon.

> To learn a language, learn . .⁽¹⁾. a few everyday sentences. This will educate your ear. .⁽²⁾. It will give you a fundamental grasp of structure. .⁽³⁾.

The ellipsis mark may fall on either side of any punctuation:

> as many . . ., and several others are
> as many; . . . others are

Do not break an ellipsis at the end of your line:

> "For every accident claiming lives. .
> . . Insurance is mandatory."

Either stretch it two dots more, which is best, or start it on the next line:

> "For every accident claiming lives
> . . . . Insurance is mandatory."

You can omit beginning and ending ellipses when you use a quotation within a sentence:

> Lincoln was determined that the Union, "cemented with the blood of . . . the purest patriots," would not fail.

Use a full line of spaced dots when omitting a line or more of poetry:

> A cloud comes over the sunlit arch,
>
> . . . .
> And you're two months back in the middle of March.
> (Robert Frost, "Two Tramps in Mud Time")

Apostrophe

It's may be overwhelmingly our most frequent misspelling, as in "The dog scratched *it's* ear." No, no! *It's* means *it is. Who's* means *who is. They're* means *they are.* No pronoun spells *its* possessive with an apostrophe: *hers, its, ours, theirs, yours, whose, oneself.*

For nouns, add *'s* to form the singular possessive: *dog's life, hour's work, Marx's ideas.* Add *'s* even to singular words already ending in *s: Yeats's poems, Charles's crown. Sis' plans* and *the boss' daughter* are not what we say. We say *Sissuz* and *bossuz* and *Keatsuz,* and should say the same in our writing: *sis's, boss's, Keats's.* Plurals not ending in *s* also form the possessive by adding *'s: children's hour, women's rights.* But most plurals take the apostrophe after the *s* already there: *witches' sabbath, ten cents' worth, three days' time, the Joneses' possessions.*

I repeat, the rule for making singulars possessive is to add *'s* regardless of length and previous ending. French names ending in silent *s*-sounds also add *s: Camus's works, Marivaux's life, Berlioz's Requiem.* If your page grows too thick with double *s's,* substitute a few pronouns for the proper names, or rephrase: *the death of Themistocles, the Dickens character Pip.*

The apostrophe can help to clarify clusters of nouns. These I have actually seen: *Alistair Jones Renown Combo, the church barbecue chicken sale, the uniform policeman training program, the members charter plane.* And, of course, *teachers meeting* and *workers compensation* are so common as to seem almost normal. But an apostrophe chips one more noun out of the block. It makes your meaning one word clearer, marking *teachers'* as a modifier, and distinguishing *teacher* from *teachers.* Inflections are helpful, and the written word needs all the help it can get: *Jones's Renowned, church's barbecued, uniformed policeman's, members' chartered.* Distinguish your modifiers, and keep your possessions.

Compound words take the *'s* on the last word only: *mother-in-law's hat, the brothers-in-law's attitude* (all the brothers-in-law have the same attitude), *somebody else's problem.* Joint ownership may similarly take the *'s* only on the last word (*Bill and Mary's house*), but *Bill's and Mary's house* is more precise, and preferable.

Again, possessive pronouns have no apostrophe: *hers, its, theirs, yours, whose, oneself.* Remember that *it's* means *it is,* and that *who's* means *who is;* for possession, use *its* and *whose.*

The double possessive uses both an *of* and an *'s: a friend of my mother's, a book of the teacher's, a son of the Joneses', an old hat of Mary's.* Note that the double possessive indicates one possession among several of the same kind: mother has several friends; the teacher, several books.

Use the apostrophe to indicate omissions: *the Spirit of '76, the Class of '02, can't, won't, don't.* Finally, the apostrophe has traditionally been used when adding a grammatical ending to a number, letter, sign, or abbreviation. Some of these are also in italics, or underlined when typed (see page 251):

> 1920's; spelled with two *t*'s; too many *of*'s and *which*'s
> His *3*'s look like *8*'s. She got four A's.
> She X'd each box; K.O.'d in the first round.

Contemporary usage, however, omits the apostrophe in these where an *s* is added to form a plural. Where necessary for pronunciation, an *e* is added before the *s*. The added *(e)s* is *not* in italics, even when the word, letter, or number *is*:

> 1920s; spelled with two *t*s; too many *of*s and *which*es
> His *3*s look like *8*s.

In this usage, the apostrophe is retained in such common expressions as "Mind your p's and q's" where the letters are not italicized.

Hyphen

For clarity, hyphenate groups of words acting as one adjective or one adverb: *eighteenth-century attitude, of-and-which disease.* Distinguish between a *high school* and a *high-school teacher.* Similarly, hyphenate compound nouns when you need to distinguish, for example, *five sentence-exercises* from *five-sentence exercises.*

Hyphenate prefixes to proper names—*ex-Catholic, pro-Napoleon*—and all relatively new combinations like *anti-marriage.* Consult your dictionary.

Hyphenate after those prefixes that demand emphasis or clarity: *ex-husband, re-collect* ("to collect again," as against *recollect,* "to remember"), *re-create, re-emphasize, pre-existent.*

When you must break a word at the end of a line, hyphenate where your dictionary marks the syllables: *dis•cuss,* dis-cuss. If you must break a hyphenated word, break it after the hyphen: *self-/sufficient.* Don't hyphenate an already hyphenated word: *self-suf-/ficient.* It's hard on the eyes. When you write for print, underline those line-end hyphens you mean to keep as hyphens, making a little equals sign: *self=/sufficient.*

Hyphenate suffixes to single capital letters (*T-shirt, I-beam, X-ray*). Hyphenate *ex-champions* and *self-reliances*. Hyphenate to avoid doubling the letter *i* and tripling consonants: *anti-intellectual, bell-like*. Hyphenate two-word numbers: *twenty-one, three-fourths*. Use the "suspensive" hyphen for hyphenated words in series: "We have ten-, twenty-five-, and fifty-pound sizes."

Virgule (Slant, Slash)

Spare this "little rod" (/), and don't spoil your work with the legalistic *and/or*. Don't write "bacon and/or eggs"; write "bacon or eggs, or both." Likewise, don't use it for a hyphen: not "male/female conflict" but "male-female conflict." Use the virgule to mark the end of lines when quoting poetry in your running text: "That time of year thou mayst in me behold / When yellow leaves . . ." (Shakespeare, Sonnet 73).

Spelling

The dictionary is your best friend as you face the inevitable anxieties of spelling, but three underlying principles and some tricks of the trade can help immeasurably.

Principle I   Letters represent sounds: proNUNciation can help you spell. No one proNOUNcing words correctly would make the familiar errors of "similiar" and "enviorment." Simply sound out the letters: *envIRONment* and *goverNment* and *FebRUary* and *intRAmural*. Of course, you will need to be wary of some words not pronounced as spelled: *Wednesday* pronounced "Wenzday," for instance. But sounding the letters can help your spellings. You can even say "convertible" and "indelible" and "plausible" without sounding like a fool, and you can silently stress the *able* in words like "prob*able*" and "immov*able*" to remember the difficult distinction between words ending in *-ible* and *-able*.

Consonants reliably represent their sounds. Remember that *c* and often *g* go soft before *i* and *e*. Consequently, you must add a *k* when extending words like *picnic* and *mimic*—*picnicKing, mimicKing*—to keep them from rhyming with *slicing* or *dicing*. Conversely, you just keep the *e* (where you would normally drop it) when making *peace* into *peacEable* and *change* into *changEable*, to keep the *c* and *g* soft.

Single *s* is pronounced *zh* in words like *vision, occasion, pleasure.* Knowing that *ss* hushes ("sh-h-h") will keep you from errors like *occassion*, which would sound like *passion*.

Vowels sound short and light before single consonants: *hat, pet, kit, hop, cup*. When you add any vowel (including *y*), the first vowel will say its name: *hate, Pete, kite, hoping, cupid*. Notice how the *a* in *-able* keeps the main vowel saying its name in words like *unmistakable, likable*, and *notable*. Therefore, to keep a vowel short, protect it with double consonants: *petting, hopping*. This explains the troublesome *rr* in *occuRRence*: a single *r* would make it say *cure* in the middle. *Putting* a golf ball and *putting* something on paper must both use *tt* to keep from being pronounced *pewting*. Compare *stony* with *sonny* and *bony* with *bonny*. The *y* is replacing the *e* in *stone* and *bone*, and the rule is working perfectly. It works in any accented syllable: compare *forgeTTable* as against *markeTing, begiNNing* as against *buttoNing*. Canadian English, following British usage, makes an exception to this rule when the final consonant is *l*, doubling it even when the final syllable is unaccented, as in *traveLLing*.

When *full* combines and loses its stress, it also loses an *l*. Note the single and double *l* in *fulFILLing*. Similarly, *SOULful, GRATEful, AWful*— even *SPOONful*. Note that Canadian English, again influenced by British, commonly drops the second *l* in *skill* when it is combined with *full* to create *skilful*, and the second *l* in *fill* to create *fulfil*.

Principle II   Here is the old rule of *i* before *e*, and its famous exceptions:

> *I* before *e*
> Except after *c*,
> Or when sounded like *a*
> As in *neighbour* and *weigh*.

It works like a charm:

> "*I* before *e*": *achieve, believe*
> "Except after *c*": *receive, conceive* (Note that *c* needs an *e* to
>   make it sound like *s*.)
> "Or when sounded like *a*": *vein, eight* (Note that *foreign* was
>   once pronounced "forayn," *heifer*, "hayfer," and *leisure*,
>   "laysure.")

Memorize these important exceptions:

> counterfeit, forfeit
> either, neither
> protein, seize, sheik, weird
> height, sleight, seismograph, kaleidoscope

Deity sounds both vowels. Another small group has *i* before *e* after a *c*: *ancient, conscience, efficient, science. Financier,* another exception, follows its French origin.

Words ending in *-eed* and *-ede* are thorny—especially *proceed* and *precede*—but their numbers are few:

> The only word ending *-sede*: supersede
> The only words ending *-eed*: exceed, proceed, succeed
> The *-cede* group: accede, concede, intercede, precede, recede, secede

Principle III   Most big words, following the Latin or French from which they came, spell their sounds letter for letter. Look up the derivations of the words you misspell (note that double *s,* and explain it). You will never again have trouble with *desperate* and *separate* once you discover that the first comes from *de-spero,* "without hope," and that *sePARate* divides equals, the PAR values in stocks or golf. Nor with *definite* or *definitive,* once you see the kinship of both with *finite* and *finish.* Derivations can also help you a little with the devilment of *-able* and *-ible,* since, except for a few ringers, the *i* remains from Latin and the *-able*s are either from the French (*ami-able*) or Anglo-Saxon copies (*workable*). Knowing origins can help at crucial points: *resemblAnce* comes from Latin *simulAre,* "to copy"; *existEnce* comes from Latin *existEre,* "to stand forth."

The biggest help comes from learning the common Latin prefixes, which, by a process of assimilation (*ad-similis,* "like to like"), account for the double consonants at the first syLLabic joint of so many of our words:

> AD- (toward, to): *abbreviate* (shorten down), *accept* (grasp to)
> CON- (with): *collapse* (fall with), *commit* (send with)
> DIS- (apart): *dissect* (cut apart), *dissolve* (loosen apart)
> IN- (into): *illuminate* (shine into), *illusion* (playing into)
> IN- (not): *illegal* (not lawful), *immature* (not ripe)
> INTER- (between): *interrupt* (break between), *interrogate* (ask between)
> OB- (toward, to): *occupy* (take in), *oppose* (put to), *offer* (carry to)
> SUB- (under): *suffer* (bear under), *suppose* (put down)
> SYN- (together [this one is Greek]): *symmetry* (measuring together), *syllogism* (logic together)

Spelling takes a will, an eye, and an ear. And a dictionary. Keep a list of your favourite enemies. Memorize one or two a day. Write them in the air in longhand. Visualize them. Imagine a blinking neon sign, with the wicked letters red and tall—*definIte*—*definIte.* Then print them once, write them twice, and blink them a few times more as you go to sleep. But best of all, make up whatever devices you can—the crazier the better—to remember their tricky parts:

DANCE attenDANCE.

ExisTENce is TENse.

There's IRON in this envIRONment.

The resISTANCE took its STANCE.

There's an ANT on the defendANT.

LOOSE as a gOOSE.

LOSE loses an o.

ALLOT isn't A LOT.

ALready isn't ALL RIGHT.

I for gaIety.

The LL in paraLLel gives me *el.*

PURr in PURsuit.

When an unaccented syllable leads to misspelling, you can also get some help by trying to remember a version of the word that accents the troublesome syllable:

academy — academic

definitely — definition

irritable — irritate

mandatory — mandate

preparation — prepare

Many foreign words, though established in English, retain their native diacritical marks, which aid in pronunciation; *naïveté, résumé, séance, tête-à-tête, façade, Fräulein, mañana, vicuña.* Many names are similarly treated: *Müller, Gödel, Göttingen, Poincaré, Brontë, Noël Coward, García Lorca, Havlíček.* As always, your dictionary is your best guide, as it is, indeed, to all words transliterated to English from different alphabets and systems of writing (Russian, Arabic, Chinese, Japanese, and so on).

Here are more of the perpetual headaches. Asterisked items are in the Glossary of Usage in Chapter 14.

accept — except

accommodate

acknowledgment — judg-
  ment

advice — advise*

affect — effect*

all right* — a lot*

allusion — illusion —
  disillusion*

analysis — analysing

argue — argument

arrangement

career

censor — censure*

committee

complement — compli-
  ment*

continual — continuous*

controversy

council — counsel —
  consul*

criticize — criticism

curriculum*

decide — divide —
  devices

desert — dessert

dilemma — condemn

disastrous

discreet — discrete*

embarrassment — harass-
  ment

eminent — imminent —
  immanent*

exaggerate

explain — explanation

familiar — similar

forward — foreword

genius — ingenious* —
  ingenuous

height — eighth
hypocrisy — democracy
irritable
its — it's*
lonely — loneliness
marriage — marital — martial
misspell — misspelling
obstacle
occurrence
possession
potatoes — heroes — tomatoes
precede — proceed — procedure

primitive
principle — principal*
questionnaire
rhythm
stationary — stationery
succeed — successful
suppressed
their — they're
truly
unnoticed
until — till
weather — whether
who's — whose*

Canadian spelling developed as a mixture between British and American spelling. Over the years, trends have changed, sometimes favouring traditional Canadian spelling, sometimes leaning toward American spelling. In fact, Canadian dictionaries often offer options—*colour/color, traveller/traveler, analyse/analyze*—the first representing the preferred Canadian spelling (often a British form), and the second usually American usage. In recent years, American spelling has become more common in Canada, and some of our newspapers, magazine and book publishers, and visual media have adopted it. This text, however, uses Canadian spelling, following the *Gage Canadian Dictionary*, which is recommended as a basic tool.

In some circumstances, either Canadian or American spelling is acceptable. Check whether your instructor (or your employer, or the newspaper to which you want to submit an article) has a preference. Whichever you choose, *be consistent.* Do not mix *neighbour* and *favor, centre* and *theater.* If you are using software with a spell-check program, check whether it is Canadian or American; if necessary, you can customize the program's dictionaries to accept your Canadian spelling.

Capitalization

You know about sentences and names, certainly; but the following points are troublesome. Capitalize:

1. Names of races, nationalities and languages, and religions—Asian, Black, Caucasian; Cree, English, French; Christian, Jewish, Muslim,

Protestant. It is also becoming more common to see *White* with a capital, following the pattern of *Black*: "The representation of Blacks and Whites on the town council reflects the population of the town."

2. North, South, East, and West *only* when they are regions— "Europeans have always been fascinated by the mysterious East"; "The West is wary of Quebec's influence in federal politics"—or parts of proper nouns—the Eastern Townships, North Battleford.

3. The *complete* names of churches, rivers, hotels, and the like—the First Baptist Church, the Empress Hotel, the Ottawa River (not First Baptist church, Empress hotel, Ottawa river).

4. All words in titles, except prepositions, articles, conjunctions, and the "to" of infinitives. But capitalize even these if they come first or last, or if they are longer than four letters—*Life Before Man, Gone with the Wind,* "I'll Stand By," *How to Gain Friends and Influence People, Who Do You Think You Are?, From the Fifteenth District.* Capitalize nouns, adjectives, and prefixes in hyphenated compounds—*The Eighteenth-Century Background, The Anti-Idealist* (but *The Antislavery Movement*). But hyphenated single words and the names of numbered streets are *not* capitalized after the hyphen: *Self-fulfilment, Re-examination, Forty-second Street.*

   When referring to magazines, newspapers, and reference works in sentences, footnotes, and bibliographies, you may drop the *The* as part of the title; the *Atlantic Monthly,* the *Winnipeg Free Press,* the *Encyclopaedia Britannica.* (Euphony and sense preserve *The* for a few: *The New Yorker, The Spectator.*)

5. References to a specific section of a work—the Index, the Preface, Chapter 1, Volume IV, Act II, but "scene iii" is usually not capitalized because its numerals are also in lower case.

6. Abstract nouns, when you want emphasis, serious or humorous—"the truths contradict, so what is Truth?"; Very Important Person; the Ideal.

Do not capitalize the seasons—spring, winter, midsummer.

Do not capitalize after a colon, unless what follows is normally capitalized:

> Again we may say with Churchill: "Never have so many owed so much to so few."
>
> *Culture, People, Nature: An Introduction to General Anthropology* [title of book]
>
> Many lost everything in the earthquake: their homes had vanished along with their supplies, their crops, their livestock.

Do not capitalize proper nouns serving as common nouns: *china, cognac, napoleon* (a pastry), *chauvinist, watt* (electricity). Usage divides on some proper adjectives: *French [french] pastry, Cheddar [cheddar] cheese, German [german] measles, Venetian [venetian] blinds.* Also somewhat uncertain are names with lower-case articles or prepositions like [Charles] de Gaulle, [John] von Neumann; in such cases, follow the lower-case form within sentences—*de Gaulle, von Neumann*—but always capitalize in full at the beginning of a sentence: *De Gaulle, Von Neumann.* (Many names, however, drop the article or preposition when the surname appears alone: *[Ludwig van] Beethoven, [Guy de] Maupassant.*) Breeds of animals, as in *Welsh terrier,* and products of a definite origin, as in *Scotch whisky,* are less uncertain.

When in doubt, your best guides are your dictionary and, for proper names, a biographical dictionary or an encyclopedia.

Suggested Exercises

1. Correct these omissions of the comma, and, in your margin, label the ones you insert as *introducer, coordinator, inserter,* or *linker*:
   a. We find however that the greatest expense in renovation will be for labour not for materials.
   b. They took chemistry fine arts history and English.
   c. We met June 1 1996 to discuss the problem which continued to plague us.
   d. A faithful sincere friend he remained loyal to his roommate even after the unexpected turn of events.
   e. Though she was a part-time instructor teaching advanced calculus given at night during the winter did not intimidate her.
   f. C. Wright Mills's *The Power Elite* which even after almost three decades is still one of the finest examples of sociological analysis available ought to be required reading in any elementary sociology course.
   g. My father, who is a good gardener keeps things well trimmed.

2. Correct these fragments, comma splices, and run-ons, adding commas and other punctuation marks as necessary:
   a. His lectures are not only hard to follow they are boring.
   b. Stephano and Trinculo are the comics of the play. Never presented as complete characters they are not taken seriously.
   c. The book deals with the folly of war its stupidity, its cruelty, however. In doing this the author brings in too many characters repeats episodes over and over and spoils his comedy by pressing too hard.
   d. He left his second novel unfinished. Perhaps because of his basic uncertainty, which he never overcame.
   e. She seems to play a careless game, But actually knows exactly what she is doing, and intends to put her opponent off guard.
   f. His idea of democracy was incomplete; he himself had slaves.
   g. She knows her cards that is she never overbids.
   h. The problem facing modern architects is tremendous; it involves saving energy on a grand scale with untested devices and still achieving beautiful buildings.
   i. The solution was elegant; besides being inexpensive, it was a wholly new approach.
   j. Don't underestimate the future, it is always there.

3. Add or delete commas and semicolons as necessary in these sentences:
   a. Their travels are tireless, their budget however needs a rest.
   b. They abhor economizing, that is, they are really spendthrifts.
   c. Muller wants efficiency, Nakamura beauty.
   d. Minoza won the first set with a consistent backhand; some beautiful forehand volleys also helping at crucial moments.
   e. The downtown parking problem remains unsolved; the new structures, the new meters, and the new traffic patterns having come into play about three years too late.

4. Adjust the following sentences concerning the colon:
   a. Many things seem unimportant, even distasteful, money, clothes, popularity, even security and friends.
   b. People faced with inflation, of which we have growing reminders daily, seem to take one of two courses; either economizing severely in hopes of receding prices, or buying far beyond their immediate needs in fear of still higher prices.
   c. Depressed, refusing to face the reality of his situation, he killed himself, it was as simple as that.
   d. To let him go was unthinkable: to punish him was unbearable.

5. Add quotation marks and italics to these:
   a. Like the farmer in Frost's poem Mending Wall, some people believe that Good fences make good neighbors.
   b. Here see means understand, and audience stands for all current readers.
   c. For him, the most important letter between A and Z is I.
   d. Why does the raven keep crying Nevermore? he asked.
   e. In Canada, said the Chinese lecturer, people sing Home, Sweet Home; in China, they stay there.
   f. Her favourite books were Fugitive Pieces, Beautiful Losers, and the Bible, especially the Song of Songs.
   g. Germaine Greer's The Female Eunuch is memorable for phrases like I'm sick of peering at the world through false eyelashes and I'm a woman, not a castrate.

6. Make a list of your ten most frequent misspellings. Then keep it handy and active, removing your conquests and adding your new troubles.

7. Capitalize the following, where necessary:
   a. go west, young man.
   b. the niagara river
   c. the west might leave confederation if quebec does.
   d. the east side of town
   e. the edmonton public library
   f. the introduction to *re-establishing liberalism in ontario*
   g. east side, west side
   h. *the neo-positivistic approach* [book]
   i. the tall black spoke french.
   j. the montreal gazette [add italics]
   k. she loved the spring.
   l. *health within seconds* [book]
   m. *clear through life in time* [book]
   n. 33 thirty-third street
   o. a doberman pinscher
   p. the tundra occupies a large portion of northern canada.
   q. the united church

CHAPTER 14

A Glossary of Usage

Speech keeps a daily pressure on writing, and writing returns the compliment, exacting sense from new twists in the spoken language and keeping old senses straight. Usage, generally, is "the way they say it." Usage is the current in the living stream of language; it keeps us afloat, it keeps us fresh—as it sweeps us along. But to distinguish yourself as a writer, you must always swim upstream. You may say, *hoojaeatwith?*; but you will write: *With whom did you eat?* Usage is, primarily, talk; and talk year by year gives words differing social approval, and differing meanings. Words move from the gutter to the penthouse, and back down the elevator shaft. *Bull*, a four-letter Anglo-Saxon word, was unmentionable in Victorian circles. One had to say *he-cow*, if at all. Phrases and syntactical patterns also have their fashions, mostly bad. *Like unto me* changes to *like me* to *like I do*; *this type of thing* becomes *this type thing*; *wise*, after centuries of dormancy in only a few words (*likewise, clockwise, otherwise*), suddenly sprouts out the end of everything: *budgetwise, personalitywise, beautywise, prestigewise. Persuade them to vote* becomes *convince them to vote*. Suddenly, everyone is saying *hopefully*, and *near-perfect* shoves old *nearly* off the page. As usual, the marketplace changes more than your money.

But the written language has always refined the language of the marketplace, and writers have dreamed they have done so:

> I have laboured to refine our language to grammatical purity, and to clear it from colloquial barbarisms, licentious idioms, and irregular combinations. Something, perhaps, I have added to the elegance of its construction, and something to the harmony of its cadence.

—wrote Samuel Johnson in 1752 as he closed his *Rambler* papers. And he had almost done what he hoped. He was to shape English writing and speech for the next hundred and fifty years, until it was ready for another dip in the stream and another purification. His work, moreover, lasts. We would not imitate it now; but we can read it with pleasure, and imitate its enduring drive for excellence and meaning—making words mean what they say.

Johnson goes on to say that he has "rarely admitted any word not authorized by former writers." But even such a practice requires principle. If we accept "what the best writers use," we still cannot tell whether it is valid: we may be aping their bad habits. Usage is only a court of first appeal, where we can say little more than "He said it." Beyond that helpless litigation, we can test our writing by asking what the words mean, and by simple principles: clarity is good, economy is good, ease is good, gracefulness is good, fullness is good, forcefulness is good. As with all predicaments on earth, we judge by appeal to meanings and principles, and we often find both in conflict. Do *near* and *nearly* mean the same thing? Do *convince* and *persuade*? *Lie* and *lay*? Is our writing economical but unclear? Is it full but cumbersome? Is it clear but too colloquial for grace? Careful judgment will give the ruling.

The Glossary

A, an. *A* goes before consonants and *an* before vowels. Use *a* before *h* sounded in a first syllable: *a hospital, a hamburger.* But use *an* before a silent *h*: *an honour, an heir, an hour.* With *h*-words accented on the second syllable, most ears prefer *an*: *an hypothesis, an historical feat.* But *a hypothesis* is fully acceptable. Use *a* before vowels pronounced as consonants: *a usage, a euphemism.*

Abbreviations. Use only those conventional abbreviations your reader can easily recognize: *Dr., Mr., Mrs., Ms., Jr., St.* All traditionally take periods. College degrees are usually recognizable: *B.A., M.A., Ph.D., D.Litt., M.D., LL.D.* Similarly, dates and times: A.D., B.C., *a.m., p.m.* (See A.D., B.C.) A number of familiar abbreviations go without periods: *TV, CBC, USA, YMCA.* Certain scientific phrases also go without periods, especially when combined with figures: *55 km/h, 300 rpm, 4000 kWh.* But *U.N.* and *U.S. delegation* are customary. Note that in formal usage *U.S.* serves only as an adjective; write out *the United States* serving as a noun.

Abbreviations conventional in running prose, unitalicized, are "e.g." (*exempli gratia,* "for example"), "i.e." (*id est,* "that is"), "etc." (*et cetera,* better written out "and so forth"), and "viz." (*videlicet,* pronounced "vi-DEL-uh-sit," meaning "that is," "namely"). These are followed by either commas or colons after the period:

The commission discovered three frequent errors in management, i.e., failure to take appropriate inventories, erroneous accounting, and inattention to costs.

The semester included some outstanding extracurricular programs, e.g.: a series of lectures on civil rights, three concerts, and a superb performance of *Oedipus Rex.*

The abbreviation *vs.*, usually italicized, is best spelled out, unitalicized, in your text: "The antagonism of Capulet versus Montague runs throughout the play." The abbreviation c. or ca., standing for *circa* ("around") and used with approximate dates in parentheses, is not italicized: "Higden wrote *Polychronicon* (c. 1350)." See also pages 174–75.

Above. For naturalness and effectiveness, avoid such references as "The above statistics are . . .," and "The above speaks for itself." Simply use "These" or "This."

Action. A horribly overused catchall. Be specific: *invasion, rape, murder, boycott, lawsuit.*

A.D., B.C., a.m., p.m. A.D. (*anno Domini,* "the year of the Lord") goes *before* its year: *A.D. 1990.* B.C. ("before Christ") goes after: *320 B.C.* Some scholars prefer C.E. ("of the common era") and B.C.E. ("before the common era"). Though these are conventionally printed as small capitals, regular capitals in your classroom papers are perfectly acceptable. The times, *a.m.* and *p.m.,* go after their numbers, and usually in small letters, though capitals are all right. Do not use either as a noun: "At seven in the p.m."; "Late in the a.m." Do not use with "o'clock" to distinguish seven in the morning from seven at night ("seven o'clock p.m."). Just write "seven p.m."

Adapt, adopt. To *adapt* is to adjust something to a new purpose. To *adopt* is to take it over as it is.

Adverse, averse. Both from the Latin for "turn away." But *adverse* means "bad luck," and *averse* means "opposed": "They ran into *adverse* winds, but were *averse* to changing course."

Advice, advise. Frequently confused. *Advice* (noun) is what you get when advisers *advise* (verb) you.

Aesthetic. An adjective: an *aesthetic* judgment, his *aesthetic* viewpoint. *Aesthetics* is a singular noun for the science of beauty: "Santayana's *aesthetics* agrees with his metaphysics."

Affect, effect. *Affect,* a verb, means "to influence, to have an *effect* on." *Affective* is a technical term for *emotional* or *emotive,* which are clearer terms.

Aggravate. Means to add gravity to something already bad enough. Avoid using it to mean "irritate."

> WRONG: He aggravated his mother.
> RIGHT: The rum aggravated his mother's fever.

All, all of. Use *all* without the *of* wherever you can to economize: *all this, all that, all those, all the people, all her lunch.* But some constructions need *of*: *all of them, all of Faulkner.*

All ready, already. Two different meanings. *All ready* means that everything is ready; *already* means "by this time."

All right, alright. *Alright* is not *all right*; you are confusing it with the spelling of *already.* Never use *alright.*

Allusion, illusion, disillusion. The first two are frequently confused, and *disillusion* is frequently misspelled *disallusion.* An *allusion* is a reference to something; an *illusion* is a mistaken conception. You *disillusion* someone by bringing him back to hard reality from his illusions.

Alot. You mean *a lot,* not *allot.*

Also. Do not use for *and,* especially to start a sentence: not "*Also,* it failed" but simply "And it failed." Not "They had three cats, *also* a dog" but "They had three cats and a dog."

Among. See **Between.**

Amount of, number of. Use *amount* with general heaps of things; use *number* with amounts that might be counted: *a small amount of interest, a large number of votes.* Use *number* with living creatures: *a number of applicants, a number of squirrels.*

And/or. An ungainly thought-stopper. See "Virgule," page 256.

Ante-, anti-. *Ante-* means "before": *antecedent* (something that comes before); *antedate* (to date before). *Anti-* means "against": *antifeminist, antiseptic.* Hyphenate before capitals, and before *i* and other vowels that confuse the reading: *anti-American, anti-intellectual, anti-aircraft.*

Anxious. Use to indicate angst, agony, and anxiety. Does not mean cheerful expectation: "He was *anxious* to get started." Use *eager* instead.

Any. Do not overuse as a modifier.

> POOR: She was the best of any violinist in the class.
> GOOD: She was the best violinist in the class.

> POOR: If any people know the answer, they aren't talking.
> GOOD: If anyone knows the answer, that person is not talking.

Add *other* when comparing likes: "She was better than *any other* violinist in the class." But "This third-year student was better than any fourth-year student."

Anybody, nobody, somebody. Don't write as two words—*any body, no body, some body*—unless you mean it: "No body of water daunted him."

Any more. Written as two words, except when an adverb in negatives and questions:

> She never wins *anymore.*
> Does she play *anymore?*

Anyone. Don't write as two words—*any one*—unless you mean "any one thing."

Anyplace, someplace. Use *anywhere* and *somewhere* (adverbs), unless you mean "any *place*" and "some *place.*"

Appear. Badly overworked for *seem.*

Appearing. Don't write "an expensive-appearing house." "An expensive-looking house" is not much better. Write "an expensive house" or "the house looked expensive."

Appreciate. Means "recognize the worth of." Do not use to mean simply "understand."

> LOOSE: I *appreciate* your position.
> CAREFUL: I *understand* your position.

> LOOSE: I *appreciate* that your position is difficult.
> CAREFUL: I *realize* that your position is difficult.

Apt to, likely to, liable to. *Apt* is the more colloquial choice, but fully acceptable for known physical tendencies: "He is *apt to* overshoot his volleys." *Likely to* is for general probabilities:

> It is *likely to* rain.
> She is *likely to* succeed.

Liable to implies vulnerability:

> He is *liable to* lose on powder snow.
> Overconfidence is *liable to* end in disappointment.

Don't use *liable* or *apt* for mere probability: "She is liable [apt] to come tomorrow" for "She may come tomorrow."

Area. Drop it. *In the area of finance* means "in finance," and *conclusive in all areas* means simply "conclusive," or "conclusive in all departments (subjects, topics)." Be specific.

Around. Do not use for *about*: it will seem to mean "surrounding."

> POOR: *Around* thirty people came.
> GOOD: *About* thirty people came.

> POOR: He sang at *around* ten o'clock.
> GOOD: He sang at *about* ten o'clock.

As. This is the right one: not "Nobody loves you *like* I do" but "Nobody loves you *as* I do." (See also **Like.**) Do not use *as* for *such as*: "Many things, *as* nails, hats, toothpicks. . . ." Write instead "Many things, *such as* nails. . . ." Do not use *as* for *because* or *since*; it is ambiguous:

> AMBIGUOUS: *As* I was walking, I had time to think.
> PRECISE: *Because* I was walking, I had time to think.

Do not use *as* to mean "that" or "whether" (as in "I don't know *as* he would like her").

As . . . as. Use positively, not forgetting the second *as*:

> WRONG: *as* long if not longer than the other
> RIGHT: *as* long *as* the other, if not longer

Negatively, use *not so . . . as.* It is clearer (but more formal) than *as . . . as*:

> It is *not so* long *as* the other.
> His argument is *not so* clear *as* hers.

As far as. A wordy windup.

> WORDY: *As far as* winter clothes are concerned, we are well supplied.
> IMPROVED: We have a good supply of winter clothes.

As if. Takes the subjunctive: ". . . as if he *were* cold."

As of, as of now. Avoid. Use *at*, or *now*, or delete entirely.

> POOR: He left, *as of* ten o'clock.
> IMPROVED: He left *at* ten o'clock.

> POOR: *As of* now, I've sworn off.
> IMPROVED: I've just sworn off.

As to. Use only at the beginning of a sentence: "As to his first allegation, I can only say. . . ." Change it to *about*, or omit it, within a sentence: "He knows nothing *about* the details"; "He is not sure [whether] they are right."

As well as. You may mean only *and.* Check it out. Avoid such ambiguities as "She worked as well as her husband."

Aspect. Overused. Try *side, part, portion.* See **Jargon.**

At. Do not use after *where.* "Where is it at?" means "Where is it?"

Authored. Terrible. Write "She has *written* three plays."

Awhile, a while. You usually want the adverb: *linger awhile, the custom endured awhile longer.* If you want the noun, emphasizing a period of time, make it clear: "The custom lasted for a while."

Back of, in back of. *Behind* says it more smoothly.

Bad, badly. *Bad* is an adjective: *a bad trip. Badly* is an adverb: *he wrote badly.* Linking verbs take *bad: he smells bad; I feel bad; it looks bad.*

Balance, bulk. Make them mean business, as in "He deposited the balance of his allowance" and "The bulk of the crop was ruined." Do not use them for people:

> POOR: The *balance* of the class went home.
> IMPROVED: The *rest* of the class went home.
>
> POOR: The *bulk* of the crowd was indifferent.
> IMPROVED: *Most* of the crowd was indifferent.

Basis. Drop it: *on a daily basis* means "daily."

Be sure and. Write *be sure to.*

Because of, due to. See **Due to.**

Besides. Means "in addition to," not "other than."

> POOR: Something *besides* smog was the cause [unless smog was also a cause].
> IMPROVED: Something *other than* smog was the cause.

Better than. Unless you really mean *better than,* use *more than.*

> POOR: The lake was *better than* two kilometres across.
> IMPROVED: The lake was *more than* two kilometres across.

Between, among. *Between* ("by twain") has *two* in mind; *among* has more than two. *Between,* a preposition, takes an object; *between us, between you and me.* ("Between you and I" is sheer embarrassment; see **Me.**) *Between* also indicates geographical placing: "It is midway between Toronto,

Ottawa, and Montreal." "The grenade fell between Jones and me and the gatepost"; but "The grenade fell among the fruit stands." "Between every building was a plot of petunias" (or "In between each building. . . .") conveys the idea, however nonsensical "between a building" is. "Between all the buildings were plots of petunias" would be better, though still a compromise.

Bimonthly, biweekly. Careless usage has damaged these almost beyond recognition, confusing them with *semimonthly* and *semiweekly.* For clarity, better say "every two months" and "every two weeks."

But, cannot but. "He can but fail" is old but usable. After a negative, however, the natural turn in *but* causes confusion:

> POOR: He *cannot but* fail.
> IMPROVED: He can only fail.

> POOR: He *could not* doubt *but* that it. . . .
> IMPROVED: He could not doubt that it. . . .

> POOR: He *could not* help *but* take. . . .
> IMPROVED: He could not help taking. . . .

When *but* means "except," it is a preposition. "Everybody laughed but me." Too frequent *but*s keep your readers off balance:

> POOR: The campaign was successful *but* costly. *But* the victory
>   was sweet.
> IMPROVED: The campaign was costly, *but* victory was sweet.

But that, but what. Colloquial redundancies.

> POOR: There is no doubt *but that* John's is the best steer.
> IMPROVED: There is no doubt *that* John's is the best steer.
> IMPROVED: John's is *clearly* the best steer.

> POOR: There is no one *but what* would enjoy it.
> IMPROVED: *Anyone* would enjoy it.

Can, may (could, might). *Can* means ability; *may* asks permission, and expresses possibility. *Can I go?* means, strictly, "Have I the physical capability to go?" In speech, *can* usually serves for both ability and permission, though the clerk will probably say, properly, "May I help you?" In assertions, the distinction is clear: "He can do it." "He may do it." "If he can, he may." Keep these distinctions clear in your writing.

Could and *might* are the past tenses, but when used in the present time they are subjunctive, with shades of possibility, and hence politeness: "*Could* you come next Tuesday?" "*Might* I inquire about your plans?" *Could* may mean ability almost as strongly as *can*: "I'm sure he could do it." But *could* and *might* are usually subjunctives, expressing doubt:

> Perhaps he *could* make it, if he tries.
> I *might* be able to go, but I doubt it.

Cannot, can not. Use either, depending on the rhythm and emphasis you want. *Can not* emphasizes the *not* slightly.

Can't hardly, couldn't hardly. Use *can hardly, could hardly,* since *hardly* carries the negative sense.

Can't help but. A marginal mixture in speech of two clearer and more formal ideas, *I can but regret* and *I can't help regretting.* Avoid it in writing.

Case. Chop out this deadwood:

> POOR: *In many cases,* ants survive. . . .
> IMPROVED: Ants *often.* . . .
>
> POOR: *In such a case,* surgery is recommended.
> IMPROVED: *Then* surgery is recommended.
>
> POOR: *In case* he goes. . . .
> IMPROVED: *If* he goes. . . .
>
> POOR: Everyone had a great time, *except in a few scattered cases.*
> IMPROVED: *Almost* everyone had a great time.

Cause, result. Since *all* events are both causes and results, suspect yourself of wordiness if you write either word.

> WORDY: The invasions *caused depopulation of* the country.
> ECONOMICAL: The invasions *depopulated* the country.
>
> WORDY: She lost *as a result of* poor campaigning.
> ECONOMICAL: She lost *because* her campaign was poor.

Cause-and-effect relationship. Verbal adhesive tape. Recast the sentence, with some verb other than the wordy *cause*:

> POOR: Othello's jealousy rises in a *cause-and-effect relationship* when he sees the handkerchief.
> IMPROVED: Seeing the handkerchief *arouses* Othello's jealousy.

Censor, censure. Frequently confused. A *censor* cuts out objectionable passages. To *censor* is to cut or prohibit. To *censure* is to condemn: "The *censor censored* some parts of the play, and *censured* the author as an irresponsible drunkard."

Centre around. A physical impossibility. Make it *centres on,* or *revolves around,* or *concerns,* or *is about.*

Circumstances. *In these circumstances* makes more sense than *under these* *circumstances*, since the stances are standing around (*circum*), not standing under. Often jargon: "The economy is in difficult circumstances" means, simply, "The economy is in trouble."

Clichés. Don't use unwittingly. But they can be effective. There are two kinds: (1) the rhetorical—*tried and true, the not too distant future, sadder but wiser, in the style to which she had become accustomed,* and (2) the proverbial—*apple of his eye, skin of your teeth, sharp as a tack, quick as a flash, twinkling of an eye.* The rhetorical ones are clinched by sound alone; the proverbial are metaphors caught in the popular fancy. Proverbial clichés can lighten a dull passage. You may even revitalize them, since they are frequently dead metaphors (see page 147). Avoid the rhetorical clichés unless you turn them to your advantage: *tried and untrue, gladder and wiser, a future not too distant.*

Come and, be sure and, go and, try and. Colloquial ways of saying *come to, be sure to, go to, try to.* "Come and see us" means "Come to see us," and so forth.

Compare to, compare with. To compare *to* is to show similarities (and differences) between different kinds; to compare *with* is to show differences (and similarities) between like kinds.

> Composition has been compared *to* architecture.
> He compares favourably *with* Mavis Gallant.
> Compare Trudeau *with* Mulroney.

Complement, compliment. Frequently confused. *Complement* is a completion; *compliment* is a flattery: "When the regiment reached its full *complement* of recruits, the general gave it a flowery *compliment.*"

Concept. Often jargonish and wordy.

> POOR: The concept of multiprogramming allows. . . .
> IMPROVED: Multiprogramming allows. . . .

Connotation. See pages 142–44.

Considerable. Jargon. Say *terrible, grim, excessive, worrysome, big.*

Contact. Don't *contact* anyone: *call, write, find, tell.*

Continual, continuous. You can improve your writing by *continual* practice, but the effort cannot be *continuous.* The first means "frequently repeated"; the second, "without interruption."

> It requires *continual* practice.
> There was a *continuous* line of clouds.

Contractions. We use them constantly in conversation: *don't, won't, can't, shouldn't, isn't.* Avoid them in writing, or your prose will seem too chummy. But use one now and then when you want some colloquial emphasis: "You can't go home again."

Convince, persuade. *Convince . . . that* and *persuade . . . to* are the standard idioms. *Convince . . . of* is also standard. Nevertheless, *convince* is frequently creeping in before infinitives with *to.*

> POOR: They *convinced* him *to* run.
> RIGHT: They *persuaded* him *to* run.
> RIGHT: They *convinced* him *that* he should run.
> RIGHT: They *convinced* him *of* their support.

Could, might. See **Can, may.**

Could care less. You mean *couldn't care less.* Speech has worn off the *n't,* making the words say the opposite of what you mean. A person who cares a great deal could care a great deal less; one who does not care "*couldn't* care less": he's already at rock bottom.

Could of, would of. Phonetic misspellings of *could've* ("could have"), and *would've* ("would have"). In writing, spell them out completely: *could have* and *would have.*

Couldn't hardly. Use *could hardly.*

Council, counsel, consul. *Council* is probably the noun you mean: a group of deliberators. *Counsel* is usually the verb "to advise." But *counsel* is also a noun: an adviser, an attorney, and their advice. Check your dictionary to see that you are writing what you mean. A *counsellor* gives you *counsel* about your courses, which may be submitted to an academic *council.* A *consul* is an official representing your government in a foreign country.

Criteria. Plural: *These criteria are.* The singular is *criterion.*

Curriculum. The plural is *curricula,* though *curriculums* will get by in informal prose. The adjective is *curricular.*

Data. A plural like *criteria, strata, phenomena:* "The data are inconclusive."

Definitely. A high-school favourite, badly overused.

Denotation. See pages 142–44.

Different from, different than. Avoid *different than,* which confuses the idea of differing. Things *differ from* each other. Only in comparing several differences does *than* make clear sense: "All three of his copies differ from the original, but his last one is *more* different *than* the others." But here *than* is controlled by *more*, not by *different*.

> WRONG: It is different *than* I expected.
> RIGHT: It is different *from* what I expected.
> RIGHT: It is not what I expected.

> WRONG: He is different *than* the others.
> RIGHT: He is different *from* the others.

Discreet, discrete. Frequently confused. *Discreet* means someone tactful and judicious; *discrete* means something separate and distinct: "She was *discreet* in examining each *discrete* part of the evidence."

Disinterested. Does not mean "uninterested" nor "indifferent." *Disinterested* means impartial, without private interests in the issue.

> WRONG: You seem disinterested in the case.
> RIGHT: You seem uninterested in the case.
> RIGHT: The judge was disinterested and perfectly fair.

> WRONG: She was disinterested in it.
> RIGHT: She was indifferent to it.

Double negative. A negation that cancels another negation, making it accidentally positive: "He couldn't hardly" indicates that "He could easily," the opposite of its intended meaning. "They can't win nothing" really says that they *must* win something.

But some doubled negations carry an indirect emphasis—a mild irony, really—in such tentative assertions as "One cannot be certain that she will not prove to be the century's greatest poet," or "a not unattractive offer."

Drastic. A catchall for *severe, harsh, murderous, bold.*

Due to. Never begin a sentence with "*Due* to circumstances beyond his control, he. . . ." *Due* is an adjective and must always relate to a noun or pronoun: "The catastrophe *due* to circumstances beyond his control was unavoidable," or "The catastrophe was *due* to circumstances beyond his control" (predicate adjective). But you are still better off with *because of, through, by,* or *owing to. Due to* is usually a symptom of wordiness, especially when it leads to *due to the fact that,* a venerable piece of plumbing meaning *because.*

> WRONG: He resigned *due to* sickness.
> RIGHT: He resigned *because of* sickness.

> WRONG: She succeeded *due to* hard work.
> RIGHT: She succeeded *through* hard work.

WRONG: He lost his shirt *due to* leaving it in the locker room.
RIGHT: He lost his shirt *by* leaving it in the locker room.

WRONG: The Far East will continue to worry the West, *due to* a general social upheaval.
RIGHT: The Far East will continue to worry the West, *owing to* a general social upheaval.

WRONG: The program failed *due to the fact that* a recession had set in.
RIGHT: The program failed *because* a recession had set in.

Effect. See **Affect.**

Either, neither. One of two, taking a singular verb: *Either is a good candidate, but neither speaks well. Either . . . or* (*neither . . . nor*) are parallelling conjunctions. See page 118.

Eminent, imminent, immanent. Often confused. *Eminent* is something that stands out; *imminent* is something about to happen. *Immanent,* much less common, is a philosophical term for something spiritual "remaining within, indwelling." You usually mean *eminent.*

Enormity. Means "atrociousness"; does not mean "enormousness."

the *enormity* of the crime
the *enormousness* of the mountain

Enthuse. Don't use it; it coos and gushes.

WRONG: She *enthused* over her new job.
RIGHT: She gushed on and on about her new job.

WRONG: He was *enthused.*
RIGHT: He was *enthusiastic.*

Environment. Frequently misspelled. It is business jargon, unless you mean the world around us.

WORDY: in a DOS environment
IMPROVED: in DOS; with DOS

WORDY: They work in an environment of cost analysis.
IMPROVED: They analyse cost.

Equally as good. A redundant mixture of two choices, *as good as* and *equally good.* Use only one of these at a time.

Etc. Substitute something specific for it, or drop it, or write "and so forth."

Everyday, every day. You wear your *everyday* clothes *every day.*

Everyone, everybody. Avoid the common mismatching *their*: "Everyone does *his* [or *her* but not *their*] own thing."

Exists. Another symptom of wordiness.

> POOR: a system like that which *exists* at the university
> IMPROVED: a system like that at the university

Facet. Usually jargon. It means "little face," one of the many small *surfaces* of a diamond. Use it metaphorically or not at all.

> POOR: This problem has several *facets.*
> IMPROVED: This problem has five *parts.*
> IMPROVED: Each *facet* of the problem sparkles with implications.

The fact that. Deadly with *due to,* and usually wordy by itself.

> POOR: *The fact that* Rome fell *due to* moral decay is clear.
> IMPROVED: *That* Rome fell *through* moral decay is clear.

> POOR: This disparity is in part *a result of the fact that* some of the best indicators make their best showings in an expanding market.
> IMPROVED: This disparity arises in part *because* some of the best indicators. . . .

> POOR: *In view of the fact that* more core is used. . . .
> IMPROVED: *Because* more core. . . .

Factor. Avoid it. We've used it to death. Try *element* when you mean "element." Look for an accurate verb when you mean "cause."

> POOR: The increase in drug use *is a factor in* juvenile delinquency.
> IMPROVED: The increase in drug use *has contributed to* juvenile delinquency.

> POOR: Puritan self-sufficiency *was an important factor in* the rise of capitalism.
> IMPROVED: Puritan self-sufficiency *favoured* the rise of capitalism.

Farther, further. The first means distance, actual or figurative; the second means more in time or degree. You look *farther* and consider *further,* before you go *farther* into debt.

Feasible. See **Viable.**

Fewer, less. See **Less.**

The field of. Try to omit it—you usually can—or bring the metaphor to life. It is trite and wordy.

> POOR: He is studying *in the field of* geology.
> IMPROVED: He is studying geology.

Firstly. Archaic. Trim all such terms to *first, second,* and so on.

Flaunt, flout. *Flaunt* means to parade, to wave impudently; *flout* means to scoff at. The first is metaphorical; the second, not: "She *flaunted* her wickedness and *flouted* the police."

Flounder, founder. Frequently confused. *Flounder* means to wobble clumsily, to flop around; *founder*, to sink ("The ship foundered"), or, figuratively, to collapse or go lame (said of horses).

For. See page 238.

Former, latter. Passable, but they often make the readers look back. Repeating the antecedents is clearer:

> POOR: The Athenians and Spartans were always in conflict. *The former* had a better culture; *the latter* had a better army.
> IMPROVED: The Athenians and Spartans were always in conflict. Athens had the better culture; Sparta, the better army.

Fun. A noun. Avoid it as an adjective: *a fun party* ("The party was fun").

Further. See **Farther.**

Good, well. *Good* is the adjective: *good time. Well* is the adverb: *well done.* In verbs of feeling, we are caught in the ambiguities of health. *I feel good* is more accurate than *I feel well,* because *well* may mean that your feelers are in working order. But *I feel well* is also an honest statement: "I feel that I am well." Ask yourself what your readers might misunderstand from your statements, and you will use these two confused terms clearly.

Got, gotten. Both acceptable. Your rhythm and emphasis will decide. British usage favours *got;* American prefers *gotten.*

Hanged, hung. *Hanged* is the past of *hang* only for the death penalty: "They hung the rope and hanged the man."

Hardly. Watch the negative here. "I *can't hardly*" means "I *can* easily." Write: "One *can hardly* conceive the vastness."

Healthy, healthful. Swimming is *healthful;* swimmers are *healthy.*

His/her, his (her). Shift to the neutral plural ("*Students* should sign *their* papers on the first page"), employ an *occasional* "his or her," or otherwise rephrase: *s/he* is cumbersome; *she/he,* not much better. See page 143.

Historically. A favourite windy throat-clearer. Badly overused.

History. The *narrative,* written or oral, of events, not the events themselves. Therefore, avoid the redundancy "*recorded* history," likewise "*annals* of history," "*chronicles* of history." *History* alone can suffice or even itself disappear. "Archeologists have uncovered evidence of events previously unknown to history" would be better without the misleading *to history.*

Hopefully. An inaccurate dangler, a cliché. "Hopefully, they are at work" does not mean that they are working hopefully. Simply use *I hope* or *one hopes* (but *not* "it is hoped").

> POOR: They are a symbol of idealism, and, *hopefully,* are representative.
> IMPROVED: They are a symbol of idealism and are, *one hopes,* representative.

However. Only use *however* at the beginning of a sentence as adverb: "However long the task takes, it will be done." For the "floating" *however,* and *however* versus *but,* see pages 236 and 240–41.

Hung. See **Hanged.**

The idea that. Like *the fact that*—and the cure is the same. Cut it.

If, whether. *If* is for uncertainties; *whether,* for alternatives. Usually the distinction is unimportant: "I don't know *if* it will rain"; "I don't know *whether* it will rain [or not]."

If not. Usually ambiguous for *and indeed.* "They made good, *if not* excellent, profits" usually intends to say that the profits were really a bit better than good, but it actually says negatively that they were OK but not outstanding. Say "They made good, *and indeed* excellent, profits."

Imminent, immanent. See **Eminent.**

Imply, infer. The author *implies*; you *infer* ("carry in") what you think he means.

> He *implied* that all women are hypocrites.
> From the ending, we *infer* that tragedy ennobles as it kills.

Remember this rhyme by G. Sterling Leiby, called "Perfect Communication": "Confusion would / More surely fly / If you'd infer / What I imply."

Importantly. Often an inaccurate (and popular) adverb, like *hopefully*.

> INACCURATE: *More importantly*, he walked home.
> IMPROVED: *More important*, he walked home.

In connection with. Always wordy. Say *about*.

> POOR: They liked everything *in connection with* the university.
> IMPROVED: They liked everything *about* the university.

Includes. Jargonish, as a general verb for specific actions.

> POOR: The report *includes* rural and urban marketing.
> IMPROVED: The report *analyses* rural and urban marketing.

Individual. Write *person* unless you really mean someone separate and unique.

Infer. See **Imply.**

Ingenious, ingenuous. Sometimes confused. *Ingenious* means "clever"; *ingenuous*, "naïve." *Ingenius* is a common misspelling for both.

Inside of, outside of. "They painted the *outside of* the house" means what it says, but these idioms can be redundant and inaccurate.

> POOR: *inside of* half an hour
> IMPROVED: *within* half an hour

> POOR: He had nothing for dinner *outside of* a few potato chips.
> IMPROVED: He had nothing for dinner *but* a few potato chips.

Instances. Redundant. *In many instances* means *often, frequently*.

Interesting. Make what you say interesting, but never tell the readers *it is interesting*: they may not believe you. *It is interesting* is merely a lazy preamble.

> POOR: *It is interesting* to note that nicotine is named for Jean Nicot, who introduced tobacco into France in 1560.
> IMPROVED: Nicotine is named for Jean Nicot, who introduced tobacco into France in 1560.

Irregardless. A faulty word. The *ir-* (meaning *not*) is doing what the *less* already does. You are thinking of *irrespective*, and trying to say *regardless*.

Is when, is where. Avoid these loose attempts:

> LOOSE: Combustion *is when* [*where*] oxidation bursts into flame.
> SPECIFIC: Combustion *is* oxidation bursting into flame.

It. Give it a specific reference, as a pronoun. See pages 129–30 and 228–29.

Its, it's. Don't confuse *its*, the possessive pronoun, with *it's*, the contraction of *it is*.

-ize. A handy way to make verbs from nouns and adjectives (*patron-ize*, *civil-ize*). But handle with care; do not fall into jargon. Manufacture new *-izes* only with a sense of humour and daring.

Jargon. A technical, wordy phraseology that becomes characteristic of any particular trade or branch of learning, frequently with nouns modifying nouns, and in the passive voice. Break out of it by making words mean what they say.

> JARGON: The *plot structure* of the play provides no *objective correlative.*
> CLEAR MEANING: The play fails to act out and exhibit the hero's inner conflicts.
> CLEAR MEANING: The plot is incoherent.
> CLEAR MEANING: The structure is lopsided.
>
> JARGON: The *character development* of the heroine is excellent.
> CLEAR MEANING: The author sketches and deepens the heroine's personality skilfully.
> CLEAR MEANING: The heroine matures convincingly.
>
> JARGON: Three *motivation profile studies* were developed *in the area of production management.*
> CLEAR MEANING: The company studied its production managers, and discovered three kinds of motivation.
>
> JARGON: He *structured* the meeting.
> CLEAR MEANING: He organized (planned, arranged) the meeting.

Kind of, sort of. Colloquialisms for *somewhat, rather, something,* and the like. Usable, but don't overuse.

Lay, lie. Don't use *lay* to mean *lie.* To *lay* means "to put" and needs an object; to *lie* means "to recline." Memorize both their present and past tenses, frequently confused:

> I *lie* down when I can; I *lay* down yesterday; I have *lain* down often. [intransitive, no object]
> The hen *lays* an egg; she *laid* one yesterday; she has *laid* four this week. [transitive, *lays* an object]
> Now I *lay* the book on the table; I *laid* it there yesterday; I have *laid* it there many times.

Lead, led. Because *lead* (being in front) is spelled like the *lead* in *lead pencil,* people frequently misspell the past tense, which is *led.*

Lend, loan. Don't use *loan* for *lend*. *Lend* is the verb; *loan*, the noun: "Please *lend* me a five; I need a *loan* badly." Remember the line: "I'll *send* you to a *friend* who'll be willing to *lend*."

Less, few. Don't use one for the other. *Less* answers "How much?" *Few* answers "How many?"

> WRONG: We had *less* people than last time.
> RIGHT: We had *fewer* people this time than last.

Level. Usually redundant jargon. *High-level management* is *top management* and *college-level courses* are *college courses*.

Lie, lay. See **Lay**.

Lighted, lit. Equally good past tenses for *light* (both "to ignite" and "to descend upon"), with *lit* perhaps more frequent. Rhythm usually determines the choice. *Lighted* seems preferred for adverbs and combinations: *a clean well-lighted place*; *it could have been lighted better*.

Like, as, as if. Usage blurs them, but the writer should distinguish them before he decides to go colloquial. Otherwise, he may throw his readers off.

> He looks *like* me.
> He dresses *as* [the way] I do.
> He acts *as if* he were high.

Note that *like* takes the objective case, and that *as*, being a conjunction, is followed by the nominative:

> She looks like *her*.
> She is as tall as *I* [am].
> She is tall, like *me*.

Like sometimes replaces *as* where no verb follows in phrases other than comparisons (*as . . . as*):

> It works *like* a charm. (. . . *as* a charm *works*.)
> It went over *like* a lead balloon. (. . . *as* a lead balloon *does*.)
> They worked *like* beavers. (. . . *as* beavers *do*.)

Literally. Often misused, and overused, as a general emphasizer: "We *literally* wiped them off the field." Say "We wiped them off the field."

Loan. See **Lend**.

Loose, lose. You will *lose* the game if your defence is *loose*.

Lots, lots of, a lot of. Conversational for *many, much, great, considerable*. Try something else. See **Alot**.

Majority. Misused for *most*: "*The majority* of the play is comic" [wrong].

May. See **Can, may.**

Maybe. Conversational for *perhaps*. Sometimes misused for *may be*. Unless you want an unmistakable colloquial touch, avoid it altogether.

Manner. A sign of amateur standing. Use *way*, or *like this*, not *in this manner*.

Me. Use *me* boldly. It is the proper object of verbs and prepositions. Nothing is sadder than faulty propriety: "between you and *I*," or "They gave it to John and *I*," or "They invited my wife and *I*." Test yourself by dropping the first member "between I" (*no*), "gave it to I" (*no*), "invited I" (*no*). And do *not* substitute *myself*. See pages 227–28.

Medium, media. The singular and the plural. Avoid *medias*, and you will distinguish yourself from the masses.

Might. See **Can, may.**

Most. Does not mean *almost*.

> WRONG: *Most* everyone knows.
> RIGHT: *Almost* everyone knows.

Must, a must. A *must* is popular jargon. Try something else:

> JARGON: *The English Patient* is really a *must* for every viewer.
> IMPROVED: Everyone interested in film should see *The English Patient*.
>
> JARGON: This is a *must* course.
> IMPROVED: Everyone should take this course.

Myself. Use it only reflexively ("I hurt *myself*"), or intensively ("I *myself* often have trouble"). Fear of *me* leads to the incorrect "They gave it to John and *myself*." Do not use *myself, himself, herself, themselves* for *me, him, her, them*.

Nature. Avoid this padding. Do not write *moderate in nature, moderate by nature, of a moderate nature*; simply write *moderate*.

Near. Avoid this wordy and popular atrocity: "*near* perfect"; "a *near* ecstatic applause"; "the *near* extermination of a species." Say *almost, nearly, virtually*, or nothing: "an ecstatic applause"; "almost exterminating the species."

Neither. See **Either.**

No one. Two words in Canada, not *noone*, or *no-one*.

None. This pronoun means "no one" and takes a singular verb, as do *each*, *every*, *everyone*, *nobody*, and other distributives. See page 221.

Nowhere near. Use *not nearly*, or *far from*. See **Near.**

Nowheres. You mean *nowhere.*

Number of. Usually correct. See **Amount of.**

Numbers. Spell out those that take no more than two words (*twelve, twelfth, twenty-four, two hundred*); use numerals for the rest (*101, 203, 4,510*). Spell out *all* numbers beginning a sentence. But use numerals to make contrasts and statistics clearer: "20 as compared to 49"; "only 1 out of 40"; "200 or 300 times as great." Change a two-word number to numerals when it matches a numeral: "with 400 [not *four hundred*] students and 527 parents." Numbers are customary with streets—*42nd Street, 5th Avenue*—which may also be spelled out for aesthetic reasons: *Fifth Avenue*. Use numbers also with dates, times, measurements, and money: *1 April 1996; 6:30 a.m.* (but *half past six*); *240 by 100 metres; 6 '3 "* (but *six feet tall*); *$4.99; $2 a ticket* (but *16 cents a bunch*).

You may use Roman numerals (see your dictionary) with Arabic to designate parts of plays and books: "Romeo's mistake (II.iii.69)"; "in *Tom Jones* (XII.iv.483)." But the new style is all Arabic: (2.3.69), (12.4.483). See page 175. Also see **Per cent.**

Off of. Write *from*: "He jumped *from* his horse."

On the part of. Wordy.

> POOR: There was a great deal of discontent *on the part of* those students who could not enrol.
> IMPROVED: The students who could not enrol were deeply discontented.

One. As a pronoun—"*One* usually flunks the first time"—see pages 23–24. Avoid the redundant numeral:

> POOR: *One* of the most effective ways of writing is rewriting.
> IMPROVED: The best writing is rewriting.

> POOR: *Fifth Business* is *one* of the most interesting of Davies's books.
> IMPROVED: *Fifth Business* is Davies at his best.

> POOR: The meeting was obviously a poor *one*.
> IMPROVED: The meeting was obviously poor.

In constructions such as "one of the best that . . ." and "one of the worst who . . .," the relative pronouns often are mistakenly considered singular. The plural noun of the prepositional phrase (*the best, worst*), not the *one*, is the antecedent, and the verb must be plural too:

> WRONG: one of the best [*players*] who *has* ever swung a bat
> RIGHT: one of the best [*players*] who *have* ever swung a bat

Only. Don't put it in too soon; you will say what you do not mean.

> WRONG: He *only liked* mystery stories.
> RIGHT: He liked *only mystery stories.*

Overall. Jargonish. Use *general,* or rephrase.

> DULL: The *overall* quality was good.
> IMPROVED: The lectures were *generally* good.

Oversight. An unintentional omission: "Leaving you off the list was an *oversight.*" Unfortunately, officialdom uses it for *overview* or *supervisory.* The Canadian government now has more than one "oversight committee"—which sounds like a committee set up to catch omissions. Avoid this ambiguity. Keep your *oversights* meaning *oversights.*

Parent. One of those nouns aping a verb: *to rear, bring up, supervise, raise, love.*

Per. Use *a*: "He worked ten hours *a* day." *Per* is jargonish, except in conventional Latin phrases: *per diem, per capita* (not italicized in your running prose).

> POOR: This will cost us a manhour *per* machine *per* month a
>   year from now.
> IMPROVED: A year from now, this will cost us a manhour *a*
>   machine *a* month.

> POOR: As *per* your instructions, ...
> IMPROVED: *According to* your instructions, ...

Per cent, percent, percentage. *Percent* (one word) seems preferred, though *percentage*, without numbers, still carries polish: "A large *percentage* of nonvoters attended." Use both the % sign and numerals only when comparing percentages as in technical reports; elsewhere, use numerals with *percent* when your figures cannot be spelled out in one or two words (*2 1/2 percent, 150 percent, 48.5 percent*). Otherwise, spell out the numbers as well: *twenty-three percent, ten percent, a hundred percent.* See **Numbers.**

Perfect. Not "more perfect," but "more nearly perfect."

Personally. Almost always superfluous.

POOR: I want to welcome them *personally.*
IMPROVED: I want to welcome them [*myself*].

POOR: *Personally,* I like it.
IMPROVED: I like it.

Phase. Do not use when *part* is wanted; "a *phase* of the organization" is better put as "a *part* of the organization." A phase is a stage in a cycle, as of the moon, of business, of the financial markets.

Phenomena. Frequently misused for the singular *phenomenon*: "This is a striking *phenomenon*" (not *phenomena*).

Phenomenal. Misused for a general intensive: "His popularity was *phenomenal.*" A phenomenon is a fact of nature, in the ordinary nature of things. Find another word for the extraordinary: "His success was *extraordinary*" (*unusual, astounding, stupendous*).

Plan on. Use *plan to.* "He planned on going" should be "He planned to go."

Plus. Say *and* unless you mean "two *plus* two": "The dinner was great, *and* it cost us nothing."

Prejudice. When you write "He was *prejudice,*" your readers may be *puzzle.* Give it a *d*: "He was *prejudiced*"; then they won't be *puzzled.*

Presently. Drop it. Or use *now.* Many readers will take it to mean *soon*: "He will go *presently.*" It is characteristic of official jargon:

POOR: The committee is meeting *presently.*
IMPROVED: The committee is meeting.
IMPROVED: The committee is meeting *soon.*

POOR: He is *presently* studying Greek.
IMPROVED: He is studying Greek.

Principle, principal. Often confused. *Principle* is a noun only, meaning an essential truth, or rule: "It works on the *principle* that hot air rises." *Principal* is the adjective. The high-school *principal* acts as a noun because usage has dropped the *person* the adjective once modified. Likewise, *principal* is the principal amount of your money, which draws interest.

Process. Often verbal fat. For example, the following can reduce more often than not: *production process* to *production; legislative* (or *legislation*) *process* to *legislation; educational* (or *education*) *process* to *education; societal process* to *social forces.*

Proof, evidence. *Proof* results from enough *evidence* to establish a point beyond doubt. Be modest about claiming proof:

> POOR: This *proves* that Fielding was in Bath at the time.
> IMPROVED: Evidently, Fielding was in Bath at the time.

Provide. If you *absolutely* cannot use the meaningful verb directly, you may say *provide*, provided you absolutely cannot *give, furnish, allow, supply, enable, authorize, permit, facilitate, force, do, make, effect, help, be, direct, encourage.* . . .

Providing that. Use *provided*, and drop the *that*. *Providing*, with or without *that*, tends to make a misleading modification.

> POOR: I will drop, *providing that* I get an incomplete.
> IMPROVED: I will drop, *provided* I get an incomplete.

In "I will drop, *providing that* I get an incomplete," *you* seem to be providing, contrary to what you mean.

Put across. Try something else: *convinced, persuaded, explained, made clear. Put across* is badly overused.

Quality. Keep it as a noun. Too many *professional quality writers* are already producing *poor quality prose*, and *poor in quality* means *poor*.

Quite. An acceptable but overused emphatic: *quite good, quite expressive, quite a while, quite a person.* Try rephrasing it now and then: *good, very good, for some time, an able person.*

Quote, quotation. Quote your quotations, and put them in quotation marks. Distinguish the verb from the noun. The best solution is to use *quote* only as a verb and to find synonyms for the noun: *passage, remark, assertion.*

> WRONG: As the following *quote* from Milton shows, ...
> RIGHT: As the following *passage* [or *quotation*] from Milton shows, ...

Raise. See **Rise, raise.**

Rarely ever. Drop the ever: "Shakespeare *rarely* misses a chance for comedy."

Real. Do not use for *very. Real* is an adjective meaning "actual."

> POOR: It was *real* good.
> IMPROVED: It was *very* good.
> IMPROVED: It was *really* good.

Reason . . . is because. Knock out *the reason . . . is*, and *the reason why . . . is*, and you will have a good sentence: "[The reason] they have difficulty with languages [is] because they have no interest in them."

Regarding, in regard to. Redundant or inaccurate.

> POOR: *Regarding* the banknote, Jones was perplexed. [Was he *looking* at it?]
> IMPROVED: Jones was perplexed *by* the banknote.
>
> POOR: He knew nothing *regarding* money.
> IMPROVED: He knew nothing *about* money.
>
> POOR: She was careful *in regard to* the facts.
> IMPROVED: She respected the facts.

Regardless. This is correct. See **Irregardless** for the confusion.

Relevant. Something like *significant* will do, but *relevant* asks for specifics: relevant to abortion, the monetary crisis, working mothers.

Respective, respectively. Usually redundant.

> POOR: The armies retreated to their *respective* trenches.
> IMPROVED: The armies retreated to their trenches.
>
> POOR: Ranadive and Leung won the first and second prize *respectively.*
> IMPROVED: Ranadive won the first prize; Leung, the second.

Reverend, Honourable. Titles of the clergy and cabinet ministers (among others); the prime minister is given the title "Right Honourable." The fully proper forms, as in the heading of a letter, are *The Reverend Mr. Claude C. Smith*; *The Honourable Adam A. Jones* (*the* would not be capitalized in your running prose). In running prose, *Rev. Claude Smith* and *Hon. Adam Jones* will get by, but the best procedure is to give the title and name its full form for first mention, then continue with *Mr. Smith* and *Mr. Jones*. Do not use "Reverend" or "Honourable" with the last name alone.

Rise, raise. Frequently confused. *Rise, rose, risen* means to get up. *Raise, raised, raised* means to lift up. "He *rose* early and *raised* a commotion."

Sanction. Beatifically ambiguous, now meaning both "to approve" and "to penalize." Stick to the root; use it only "to bless," "to sanctify," "to approve," "to permit." Use *penalize* or *prohibit* when you mean just that. Instead of "They exacted *sanctions*," say "They exacted *penalties*" or "enacted *restrictions*."

Sarcasm. A cutting remark. Wrongly used for any irony.

Seldom ever. Redundant. Cut the *ever*. (But *seldom if ever* has its uses.)

Set, sit. Frequently confused. You *set* something down; you yourself *sit* down. Confine *sitting* mostly to people (*sit, sat, sat*), and keep it intransitive, taking no object. *Set* is the same in all tenses (*set, set, set*).

> POOR: The house *sets* too near the street.
> IMPROVED: The house *stands [sits]* too near the street.

> POOR: The package *set* where he left it.
> IMPROVED: The package *lay [sat]* where he left it.

> POOR: She *has set* there all day.
> IMPROVED: She *has sat* there all day.

Shall, will; should, would. The older distinctions—*shall* and *should* reserved for I and we—have faded; *will* and *would* are usual: "I will go"; "I would if I could"; "he will try"; "they all would." But *shall* remains in first-person questions: "Shall I call you tomorrow?" *Shall* in the third person expresses determination: "They shall not pass." *Should*, in formal usage, is actually ambiguous: "We should be happy to comply," intended to mean "would be happy," seems to say "ought to be happy."

Should of. See **Could of.**

Similar to. Use *like*:

> POOR: This is *similar* to that.
> IMPROVED: This is *like* that.

Sit. See **Set, sit.**

Situate. Usually wordy and inaccurate. Avoid it unless you mean, literally or figuratively, the act of determining a site, or placing a building: "Do not *situate* heavy buildings on loose soil."

> FAULTY: He is well *situated.*
> IMPROVED: He is rich.

> FAULTY: Ottawa is a city *situated* on the Ottawa River.
> IMPROVED: Ottawa is a city on the Ottawa River.

> FAULTY: The control panel is *situated* on the right.
> IMPROVED: The control panel is on the right.

> FAULTY: The company is well *situated* to meet the competition.
> IMPROVED: The company is well prepared to meet the competition.

Situation. Usually jargon. Avoid it. Say what you mean: *state, market, mess, quandary, conflict, predicament.*

Size. Often redundant. A *small-sized country* is a *small country. Large in size* is *large.*

Slow. Go SLOW is what the street signs and the people on the street all say, but write "Go slowly."

So. Should be followed by *that* in describing extent: "It was *so* foggy *that* traffic almost stopped." Avoid its incomplete form, the gushy intensive— *so nice, so wonderful, so pretty*—though occasionally this is effective.

Someplace, somewhere. See **Anyplace.**

Somewheres. You mean *somewhere.*

Sort of. See **Kind of.**

Split infinitives. Improve them. You see them every day, of course. About 52 percent of magazine and newspaper editors now accept "to instantly trace," which 90 percent found unprintable less than a decade ago. Nevertheless, adolescents and beginners love them. They are cliché traps: *to really know, to really like, to better understand, to further improve.* They indicate a wordy writer, and usually produce redundancies: *to really understand* is *to understand. They* are misleading: *to better . . ., to further . . ., to well . . ., to even.* . . . All look like and sound like infinitives: *to further investigate* starts out like *to further our investigation,* throwing the readers off track. *To better know* is "to make know better," *to even like* is "to make like even"—which is not what you mean.

The quickest cure is to drop the splitting adverb, giving *know* and *like* their full weight. Or you can spell out the adverbial thought: "To understand completely for the first time"; "to improve even more."

Or you can change the adverb to an adjective:

> POOR: *to adequately think* out solutions
> IMPROVED: *to think* out *adequate* solutions
>
> POOR: to enable us *to effectively plan* our advertising
> IMPROVED: to enable us *to plan effective* advertising

That, which, who. *That* defines and restricts; *which* is explanatory and nonrestrictive; *who* stands for people, and may be restrictive or nonrestrictive. See **Who**, and pages 114, 130–31, and 239–40.

There is, there are, it is. However natural and convenient, it is wordy. Notice that *it* in the previous sentence refers to something specific, differing distinctly from the *it* in "It is easy to write badly." (Better: "Writing badly is easy.") This indefinite subject, like *there is* and *there are,* gives the trouble. Of course, you will occasionally need an *it* or a *there* to assert existences:

> There are ants in the cupboard.
> There is only one Kenneth.
> There are craters on the moon.
> It is too bad.

They. Often a loose indefinite pronoun; tighten it. See page 228.

Till, until. Both are respectable. Note the spelling. Do not use *'til*.

Too. Awful as a conjunctive adverb: "Too, it was unjust." Also poor as an intensive: "They did not do too well" (note the difference in Shakespeare's "not wisely but too well"—he really means it). Use *very*, or (better) nothing: "They did not do well" (notice the nice understated irony).

Tool. Overused for "means." Try *instrument, means*.

Toward, towards. *Toward* is more common in Canadian usage (*towards* in British), though both are acceptable.

Trite. From Latin *tritus*: "worn out." Many words get temporarily worn out and unusable: *factor, viable, situation*, to name a few. And many phrases are permanently frayed; see **Clichés**.

Try and. You mean *try to*.

Type. Banish it, abolish it. If you must use it, insert *of*: not *that type person* but *that type of person*, though even this is really jargon for *that kind of person, a person like that*. See page 133.

Unique. Something unique has nothing in the world like it.

> WRONG: The *more* unique the organization. . . .
> RIGHT: The *more nearly unique*. . . .
>
> WRONG: the *most unique* man I know
> RIGHT: the *most unusual* man I know
>
> WRONG: a very *unique* personality
> RIGHT: a *unique* personality

Upon. Stuffy. Make it *on*.

Use, use of. A dangerously wordy word. See page 131.

Use to. A mistake for *used to*.

Utilize, utilization. Like *use*, wordy. See page 131.

> POOR: He *utilizes* frequent dialogue to enliven his stories.
> IMPROVED: Frequent dialogue enlivens his stories.

POOR: The *utilization* of a scapegoat eases their guilt.

IMPROVED: A scapegoat eases their guilt.

Very. Spare the *very* and the *quite, rather, pretty,* and *little.* I would hate to admit (and don't care to know) how many of these qualifiers I have cut from this text. You can do without them entirely, but they do ease a phrase now and then.

Viable. With *feasible,* overworked. Try *practicable, workable, possible.*

Ways. Avoid it for distance. Means *way*: "He went a short *way* into the woods."

Well. See **Good.**

Whether. See **If.**

Which. See **Who.**

While. Reserve for time only, as in "*While* I was talking, she smoked constantly." Do not use for although.

WRONG: *While* I like her, I don't admire her.

RIGHT: *Although* I like her, I don't admire her.

Who, which, that. *Who* may be either restrictive or nonrestrictive: "The ones *who win* are lucky"; "The players, *who are all outstanding,* win often." *Who* refers only to people. Use *that* for all other restrictives, *which* for all other nonrestrictives. Cut every *who, that,* and *which* not needed. See page 126, "the of-and-which disease" (pages 130–31), and, on restrictives and nonrestrictives, pages 239–40.

Avoid *which* in loose references to the whole idea preceding, rather than to a specific word, since you may be unclear:

FAULTY: He never wore the hat, *which* his wife hated.

IMPROVED: His wife hated his going bareheaded.

IMPROVED: He never wore the hat [*that*] his wife hated.

Whom, whomever. The objective forms, after verbs and prepositions; but each is often wrongly put as the subject of a clause (see page 227).

WRONG: Give the ticket to *whomever* wants it.

RIGHT: Give the ticket to *whoever wants it.* [The whole clause is the object of *to; whoever* is the subject of *wants.*]

WRONG: The president, *whom* he said would be late. . . .

RIGHT: The president, *who* he said *would be late.* . . . [Commas around *he said* would clear the confusion.]

WRONG: *Whom* shall I say called?

RIGHT: *Who* shall I say called?

BUT:

> They did not know *whom* to elect. [The infinitive takes the objective case.]

Who's, whose. Sometimes confused in writing. *Who's* means "who is" in conversational questions: "Who's going?" Never use it in writing (except in dialogue), and you can't miss. *Whose* is the regular possessive of *who*: "The committee, *whose* work was finished, adjourned."

Will. See **Shall.**

-wise. Avoid all confections like *marketwise, customerwise, pricewise, grade-wise, confectionwise*—except for humour.

Would. For habitual acts, the simple past is more economical:

> POOR: The parliament *would* meet only when called by the king.
> IMPROVED: The parliament *met* only when called by the king.

> POOR: Every hour, the sentry *would make* his round.
> IMPROVED: Every hour, the sentry *made* his round.

Would sometimes seeps into the premise of a supposition. Rule: Don't use *would* in an *if* clause.

> WRONG: If she *would have* gone, she would have succeeded.
> RIGHT: If she *had* gone, she would have succeeded.
> RIGHT: *Had* she gone, she would have succeeded. [more economical]

Would of. See **Could of.**

You (I, we, one). See pages 23–24.

Index

deduction, 100
definitions
    function of, 75, 87–88
    pitfalls in writing, 90
    steps in writing, 90
    types of, 89
    in wordy sentences, 134–35
denotation, 142–45
derivatives
    Greek, 53, 139, 145
    Latin, 138–39, 149–50, 258
description, 70–73
diacritical marks, 259
dialectic order, 45, 95
dialogue, 167, 250
diction, 148–50
Dictionary of Canadian Biography, 157,
    216
dictionaries, 140, 157, 216, 256, 260
discourse, 5. **See also** argumentation;
    exposition
distinctions, 134–35
documents, 99, 172, 252
double possessives, 254–55
drafting an essay, 11–13, 25–27, 54,
    164–68

e.g., 252
ed. (edited by, edition, editor), 175
editing, 13, 17
editions, 171
effect. **See** cause and effect
either–or, 118, 221–22. **See also** fallacies
ellipsis, 253
emphasis, 9, 10, 44
empirical verification, 94–95, 99
Encarta, 157
Encyclopaedia Britannica, 154, 157
encyclopedias, 157–58, 216, 261
end notes. **See** footnotes
end paragraphs, 43, 63–64
English, Standard, 17, 138–40
Essay and General Literature Index, 159
essay exams, 41
essays. **See also** structure
    drafting, 11–14, 164–68
    failure of, 33
    funnel approach, 9–12, 55–56,
        63–65

keyhole pattern, 65–67
    parts of, 9, 10, 12
    pro–con technique, 9, 10
essential clauses, 239–40
et al. (*et alii*), 174, 252
etc., 252
euphemisms, 144
evidence
    assessing, 97–99
    common fallacies in, 102–105
    degrees of, 93–96
    documentary, 99
    inductive traps, 100–105
example, definition by, 89
exclamation marks, 236, 251
exposition, 5, 14, 50
    as argumentative tactic, 56, 75–76
    cause and effect, 75, 80–83
    classification, 75, 83–90
    comparison and contrast, 75–79
    defined, 24–25
    neutral, 35
    sample research paper, 198–216

facts, 93–94, 95, 99, 100
fallacies
    argumentum ad hominem, 104
    argumentum ad ignorantum, 105
    argumentum ad misericordum, 104
    argumentum ad populum, 104–105
    and authorities, 97–98
    bandwagon, 105
    begging the question, 103
    common, 102–105
    complex question, 105
    defined, 8
    and documents, 99
    either–or, 103
    guilt by association, 105
    ignoring the question, 103
    inductive traps, 100–102
    logical, 97
    non sequitur, 103
    oversimplification, 103–104
    post hoc, ergo propter hoc, 80, 104
    in thesis, 37–38
figurative language, 13, 77, 101, 145–47,
    150
films, 172

plain metaphor, 146
plays, 175
plurals, 220–22, 230, 254
poetry, 175, 250, 253, 256
point-by-point comparisons, 49–50
Poole's Index to Periodical Literature, 159
possessives, 133, 228, 254–55
predicates. **See** verbs
preferences, 96
prefixes, 139, 255, 258
present perfect tense, 223
present tense, 222
prewriting, 3
probability, 102
process analysis, 7–8, 50, 73
pronouns
    agreement of, 226–30
    antecedents for, 226, 228–29
    in apposition, 226, 228
    indefinite, 221
    nominative, 226–27
    objective, 227–28
    as objects, 227–28
    plural, 230
    possessive, 228, 254–55
    relative, 112, 226
    singular, 229
    as subjects, 227
proof, evidence, 97
proofreading, 14, 220
proper nouns, 262
pros and cons, 9, 10, 43–48, 65, 95,
    164–65
punctuation. **See also** colons; commas;
    etc.
    in compound sentences, 110–11
    with ellipses, 253
    purpose of, 235
    in quotations, 167–68
    in titles, 38

question marks, 251
questions, 7–9, 31, 103
quotation marks
    colons with, 247
    commas with, 241, 250
    dialogue with, 250
    double, 249–51
    exclamation marks with, 251

    and insets, 168, 250
    parentheses with, 252
    periods with, 250
    question marks with, 251
    semicolons with, 247
    single, 251
    for titles, 251
quotations
    brackets in, 249
    direct, 167–68
    ellipses in, 253
    indirect, 167–68, 250–51
    punctuation in, 167–68
    in quotations, 251
    in research papers, 167–68

Reader's Digest Atlas of Canada, 157
Reader's Guide to Periodical Literature, 158,
    159, 160
readers. **See** audience
recordings, 172
reference books, 154–59. **See also** "Works
    Cited"
    Canadian, 216–18
references, 166–67
relative clauses, 130
relative pronouns, 112, 226
relatives understood, 114
repetition, 62
research papers
    bibliographical cards for, 160
    and computers, 154, 157–60,
        162–64, 166, 173
    drafts for, 164–68
    and the Internet, 3, 155, 157,
        163–64, 173, 216
    library use for, 154, 157–59
    note cards for, 159–61
    outlines for, 165–66
    persuasion in, 156
    and plagiarism, 161–62
    purpose of, 154
    quotations in, 162, 167–68, 170
    samples, 177–215
    thesis in, 155–56
    topics for, 155–56
    works cited in, 158–62, 166–73
restrictives, 130–31, 239–40
rev. (revised), 175

thesaurus, 140

thesis. **See also** argumentation; pros and
    cons
    in argumentation, 32–33, 34–35,
      43–49
    in beginning paragraphs, 55
    development of, 6–9, 30–33
    in end paragraphs, 63
    and essay exams, 41
    failures of, 33–34
    fallacies in, 37–38
    and opposition, 36–37, 39, 45–49
    and reading, 41
    for research paper, 155–56
    sample expansion of, 39–40
    sharpening, 35–37
    and title, 38
    and topics, 6, 30–33

thesis sentences, 41, 55–56

third person, 220

this, 229

Times Atlas of the World, 157

title search, 158

titles
    capitalization in, 38, 261
    italics for, 252
    punctuation in, 38
    quotation marks for, 251–52
    and thesis, 38
    within titles, 252

to be, 129–30

topic sentences, 54, 55, 58, 60, 61

topics. **See also** thesis; topic sentences
    attitude toward, 18
    for research paper, 155–56
    selecting, 30–32
    and thesis, 32–33

tr., trans. (translated by), 175

transitions, 10, 61–64, 245–46

unity, 9–10

usage, 1, 265–66. **See also entries for
    specific problems; "Glossary of
    Usage"** (266–94)

verbs
    agreement of, with subjects, 220–22
    aligning, 222–26

implied, 227
    infinitive, 227, 228
    intransitive, transitive, 223
    irregular, 223–24
    mood of, 225
    from nouns, 131–34
    in simple sentences, 109
    tense of, 222–24
    voice of, 225–26

videotapes, 173

viewpoint, 22–24, 34

virgules, 250, 256

vocabulary, 138–40

voice. **See also** viewpoint
    active, 128–29, 225–26
    mixed, 225–26
    passive, 127–29, 130, 225–26
    writer's, 21–22

vol., vols. (volume, volumes), 175

vowels, 257

we, 23–24

Webster's Biographical Dictionary, 157

Webster's New Geographical Dictionary, 157

which, 131. **See also** *that, which*

who, which, that, 130–31, 239–40, 293

whom, 130, 227

wordiness. **See** wordy sentences

words
    abstract, 140–42
    and allusions, 147–48
    Anglo-Saxon, 138–39, 149–50, 258
    breaking, 255
    compound, 254
    concrete, 140–42
    connotations of, 142–44
    counting, 126–27, 135
    denotations of, 142–44
    and diction, 148–49
    and euphemisms, 144
    foreign, 252, 259
    Greek derivatives, 53, 139, 145
    increasing vocabulary of, 138–40
    Latin derivatives, 138–39, 149–50
    and metaphors, 145–47
    with *s* endings, 254
    short versus long, 138–39
    as words, 251